GAMBLING ON GOALS

GAMBLING ON GOALS

A Century of Football Betting

GRAHAM SHARPE

MAINSTREAM
PUBLISHING

EDINBURGH AND LONDON

Dedication
To all the goals I've known before . . .

First published in Great Britain in 1997 by
MAINSTREAM PUBLISHING COMPANY (EDINBURGH) LTD
7 Albany Street
Edinburgh EH1 3UG

ISBN 1 85158 903 1

A catalogue record for this book is available from the British Library

Typeset in 11 on 13pt Plantin Light
Printed and bound in Great Britain by Butler and Tanner Ltd, Frome

CONTENTS

ACKNOWLEDGEMENTS

In no particular order of priority, thanks to Tom Kelly at the Betting Office Licensees Association for giving me access to certain relevant documents; and to former William Hill director Charles Layfield for sharing memories of his time with that company and of working for his father, who established the family firm of Layfield Bros Bookmakers.

Thanks to Mihir Bose for words of support and for sharing a Japanese meal, and for permission to use sections of his *False Messiah* (André Deutsch, 1996).

Thanks to George Turner, who has written for *BOS* magazine on the subject and who helpfully pointed me towards other useful contacts.

Thanks to the two Dereks – well, more accurately, Derrick Shaw and Derek McGovern of the *Life* and *Post* – for proving the theory that fellow journalists can still be persuaded to perform for a free lunch!

Thanks to Joe Fagan at Coral for assistance and 'good luck' wishes.

John MacFarlane gave me his first-hand account of the birth of individual-odds betting, including several anecdotes which cannot yet see the light of day – thanks, indeed.

Thanks also to Lou Macari for speaking frankly; Dave Bennett for searching through his files to help out; David Barber at the FA Library; staff at Colindale's British Newspaper Library. And to Robert Sangster and Edward Grayson, who were both hugely helpful.

Thanks to everyone else who helped in any way.

FOREWORD/PROLOGUE

This book is principally a history of 125 years of football betting. It is also a highly critical look at football's - and in particular the FA's – attitude towards gambling on the game.

As the book was being completed in October 1997, the FA were awaiting the deliberations of Sir John Smith's investigation into football betting and review of their existing Rules on betting and forecasting for those within the sport, following the outcome of the 'match fixing' trials of Bruce Grobbelaar, Hans Segers, John Fashanu and Hang Seung Lim – all of whom in August 1997 at Winchester Crown Court were acquitted of all the charges brought. They were also in the process of charging Grobbelaar and Segers with contravening FA Rules on betting, by forecasting results for money – a controversial move which looked difficult to justify as the Rules stood, and which had prompted West Ham manager Harry Redknapp to comment: 'How is their alleged offence any different to what I do for this newspaper (betting daily, the *Racing Post*)? I'm asked to give my opinion on football matches and I'm paid for doing so. There's nothing sinister in it. It's just a bit of fun.' Some were calling for players to be banned from betting on matches, apparently unaware that FA Rules which already prohibited just that had almost never been implemented for over 30 years.

Surely the FA's actions could not have been designed to throw up a short-term smokescreen to cloud over the all too obvious fact that it had signally failed to approach and deal with the question of betting on the game with any urgency, understanding or consistency for many years?

Others demanded that the FA should ban bookmakers from taking bets on single, usually televised, matches – although it is hard to see what purpose this would serve as there have been no proven cases of match rigging for betting purposes in this country since the early '60s, and it would be impossible to implement such a policy against foreign – based bookmakers in any case. They are not currently subject to the same fixture copyright restrictions which could be initiated against domestic bookies. Illegal betting on matches would also soon become a problem if such a policy was introduced.

One also wonders whether the FA will be sharp enough to notice that the insurance industry is beginning to cash in on promotion and relegation policies – effectively gambling, in my opinion, which could easily be extended to individual game risk policies . . .

CHAPTER ONE

Football's Hypocritical Attitude to Betting

I accuse the football authorities of Britain, Europe and the world (well, there's no point in being parochial) of hypocrisy. I accuse them of effectively tarnishing the reputation of one of the country's longest established and most respectable industries with implications of dishonesty and lack of integrity, whilst profiting directly from its continuing existence and relationship with the sport. For over one hundred years, football has tried to distance itself from the idea that people should enjoy a harmless flutter, or even a serious wager, on the outcome of football matches and the various competitions of which they are a part. The justification for this has always been that such activities lead to pressures being exerted on those involved in the game to resort to underhand or even criminal activities in order to influence the results of matches. In a century and more of the organised history of football there have been a tiny number of occasions when such skulduggery has been proved conclusively to have taken place. This, the football authorities will doubtless assert, is because they have taken such stringent action to ensure that it does not happen.

However, they have been singularly unable to prevent a far greater number of scandals and match-influencing incidents which have had nothing whatsoever to do with betting. These involve attempting to 'buy' success for clubs – either by trying to bribe referees and linesmen (sorry, referees' assistants), or opposing clubs' officials. They, in turn, have used their best offices to ensure that the 'right' results have been forthcoming. Other financial irregularities, popularly known as 'bungs', are slowly but surely being revealed.

I do not propose to include these well-documented affairs and their wider implications and recognise that the vast majority of such cases are of foreign origin. Instead, in this book, I concentrate on the relationship between football and betting during the whole of the twentieth century and the latter stages of the nineteenth. British punters today gamble, at a conservative estimate, up to one billion pounds per annum on football, including pools, individual match betting, spread betting *et al.*

I am not a historian. I am not an academic. I am not a sociologist. I am, though, a journalist who has worked for a major bookmaking company for the best part of a quarter of a century, and who has a great interest in, and love for, football. I am a season-ticket holder at Luton Town, chairman of Sunday league club, Hatch End, and a director of Wealdstone Football Club, amongst whose 'old boys' are numbered two international captains – Stuart Pearce of England, and Vinnie Jones of Wales. Through my company, William Hill, I have sponsored the Isthmian League's Manager of the Month and Season awards, without any complaint of which I am aware. I have also sponsored a section of the Umbro Veterans' Trophy competition. But, according to long-standing Football Association rules, I have been risking permanent suspension from the game by doing any of these things.

FA Rule 26 (a) (vi) states that it

> . . . shall be misconduct if any Association, League, Combination, Club, Director, Official, Referee, Assistant Referee or Player (in this Rule for ease of reference called the 'Member') is proved to the satisfaction of the Council or a Commission thereof to have done or permitted or assisted in doing or permitting any of the following: appointed or continued in Office as a Director, Official, Referee, Assistant Referee or Player, a person who acts as Bookmaker or Assistant to a Bookmaker or any other person directly connected with the organisation of Betting Lotteries, Coupon Football Betting, or the like without the written consent of the Association.

This means, of course, that I should not be a director of Wealdstone. It also means that I should not have been permitted to play for any team for the past 25 years, during which time I have worked for a bookmaker, without the written consent of the FA so to do.

Why not, for God's – or Graham Kelly's – sake? Why should I be regarded as any less desirable or worthy a person to be involved with football than a bank manager, a pawn broker, a porn broker, a murderer, an estate agent, or an insurance agent, none of whom appear to be regarded as unsuitable characters according to the rules?

How could this rule ever sit alongside the fact that so many football grounds have, for a considerable number of years, boasted on-site betting shops, including the home of the national team, Wembley Stadium?

How can it be acceptable for Ladbrokes to be appointed as one of the sponsors of Euro '96 (at considerable cost, no doubt), yet not be acceptable for anyone connected with that company to be associated with the game?

The game has made money from the pools for many years. It charges bookmakers for use of its fixtures on individual-odds coupons. But it evidently regards bookmakers as the lowest of the low, for reasons best known to itself.

Perhaps the FA's other rule covering gambling could be regarded as somewhat less contentious. Rule 26 (a) (iv) forbids any Association, League, Combination, Club, Director, Official, Referee, Assistant Referee or Player 'to bet on any Football match other than on authorised and registered Football Pools.' The potential punishment is permanent suspension.

You might conclude that this is a reasonable prohibition. It has certainly appeared in the rules for as long as any living person can recall. But it is a rule which has been consistently flouted, often in public, by people at all levels of the game, as I will demonstrate later in this chapter.

In an effort to come up with some rational answers to such issues, I decided I had better go to the very top; so I wrote to FIFA to ask them about their attitude to bookmakers and betting. Director of Communications for the Federation Internationale de Football Association, Keith Cooper, did not mince his words, or mess about. He replied:

> In general, FIFA does not actively encourage betting on football matches, and obviously active participants are not allowed to do so. Although there are no specific rules to prevent players betting on other matches, this too is discouraged. While acknowledging that a wide section of the public in certain countries regularly bet on the outcome of

11

matches, the occasional cases of illegal betting and the unfortunately constant threat of corruption have reinforced FIFA's disaffection with this activity.

Each national association is entitled to decide whether or not to permit betting facilities at stadiums. Certainly FIFA does not permit this at any stadiums where FIFA competition matches are being played.

FIFA would not accept a bookmaker as a sponsor of the World Cup, as we do not feel this would reflect well on the image of the game which we try to project.

Well, he didn't beat about the bush, anyway. I wondered what UEFA's attitude would be. Martin Kallen, Section Manager, Marketing Affairs for the Union des Associations Européennes de Football replied to my correspondence on the subject.

We do not have anything against betting on the outcome of football matches, if there is no bad influence on the outcome of football matches. Unfortunately there has been some bad examples in the past. What is clear to us is that football should be able to make a profit out of such betting systems.

We do not permit bookmaking facilities to be operated at grounds staging matches under our auspices. We care about football and not about betting. We think also that such betting at grounds could have some influence on the matches.

I asked whether UEFA were happy that Ladbrokes was the official bookmaker to Euro '96: 'We have sold all marketing rights for the Euro '96 to ISL, including the rights for bookmakers companies. We haven't heard any negative comment about Ladbrokes.'

Are players or officials permitted to wager on the outcome of matches taking place under UEFA auspices? 'No, we do not permit such wagers, it could have some influence on the outcome of the matches. Once again we care first of all about football and as the governing body of European football, we cannot allow officials/players to wager.'

The next answer, to my enquiry about betting facilities at grounds in Britain, produced something of a bombshell: 'We weren't aware that many clubs were using such facilities. We will study this matter and would then give you our comment. In a general way, we think that those betting facilities could represent a danger to the outcome of the game.'

Just re-read that answer and the one about Ladbrokes as Euro '96 sponsor – surely some illogical thought going on. My parting question to Mr Kallen was: 'Are you aware of any incidents in which betting-facility-related offences have affected the outcome of any match(es) played under UEFA auspices?'

'No, we are not aware of such incidents and we are quite sure that no incident has ever happened.'

So, now we know the views of Daddy and Big Brother. Let's find out what the FA has to say for itself. A letter addressed to Graham Kelly produced a polite reply promising a detailed answer, which duly arrived, under the signature of Graham Noakes (for Chief Executive):

> Your letter to Graham Kelly has been passed to me for a detailed response.
>
> Your enquiry relates to FA Rule 26 (a) (iv) which states that it shall be misconduct for any Association, League or Combination, Club, Director, Official, Referee, Assistant Referee or Player . . . to bet on any Football Match other than on authorised and registered Football Pools; and 26 (a) (iv) [sic] which states that it shall be misconduct to have appointed or continued in Office as a Director, Official, Referee, Assistant Referee or Player a person who acts as Bookmaker or Assistant to a Bookmaker or any other person directly connected with the organisation of Betting Lotteries, Coupon Football Betting or the like without the written consent of the Association.
>
> The Football Association's rules relating to betting are based on the principle that a Club and its players must play to win. The Association has been anxious to ensure that there should not be any perception that an outside interest, such as betting and other gambling considerations, should cast any suspicion on the fact, that Clubs are playing to win.
>
> The need for the 'play to win' principle to be upheld is the bedrock of Football Association regulations concerning gambling.
>
> The Football Association continues to draw to the attention of Clubs the problems which arise when the play-to-win principle is threatened. However, I can confirm that no further action has been taken under this Rule in recent years.
>
> With regard to Betting Shops featuring at FA Premier League grounds, this practice is not covered by any FA Rules

and is a commercial undertaking by each Club. Although the proximity of a Betting Shop to a major ground may influence whether those involved in football make use of the facility, I believe that those intent on betting on matches in which they are involved would do so whether or not the Betting Shop is part of the Club's ground.

The Football Association would not claim that bookmakers and/or their 'assistants' are less honourable people or any less fit to occupy a position within a football club. However, historically there has, as I have indicated earlier, been a need to ensure that nothing erodes the play-to-win precept. Permission for bookmakers or 'assistant bookmakers' to become involved in Clubs would not be unreasonably withheld. Requests for permission, as with similar restrictions on remunerations to Directors, should be directed to the Chief Executive of The Football Association.

Bookmakers are free to sponsor football clubs, just as bookmakers are free to occupy positions within Clubs with permission of The Football Association. Bookmakers would not be considered suitable as sponsors of youth football teams. Football Association regulations do not permit advertising or sponsorship for youth teams from companies whose products, services or activities might be considered detrimental to players of this age. In particular the regulations would prevent tobacco, alcohol or gambling being associated with youth teams.

Finally, The Football Association is conducting a comprehensive rules revision exercise which is designed to remove any anachronistic provisions and improve the wording of the regulations governing the administration of the game. As you can imagine, this is a considerable task which will take some time.

I hope that this helps with your history of football betting and wish you every success with the publication. Have you approached The Football League for its views?

Indeed I did, but according to their spokesman, Chris Hull, they didn't actually have any, or none that they were prepared to share with me, and, therefore, with you. They said that they abided by FA regulations concerning gambling. At least the FA were open and comprehensive in facing up to the issues I put to them, even if I could not go along with all of their logic.

An approach to the Scottish Football Association also produced a comprehensive round-up of their views, courtesy of Chief Executive, J. Farry, who responded:

> Perhaps the simplest answer to the points which you raise is to refer you to the terms of the Association's Articles covering betting, which state: 'A club, official, player, referee or other person under the jurisdiction of the Association shall not bet in any way on a football match. Any such club or person found guilty of betting of any description on football, authorised and registered football pools excepted, shall be deemed guilty of misconduct and shall be liable to fine, suspension, expulsion or any other penalties or conditions which the Council may think proper.'
>
> In addition, you are quite correct that the Association does not encourage bookmakers to offer odds on incidents occurring on the field of play, such as whether a player will be yellow carded or red carded in a match. It is contrary to the spirit of the game.
>
> With regard to the matter of clubs entering into partnerships with betting companies to provide facilities at football grounds, this is entirely different, providing that the betting facilities offered are purely on specifics relative to the match and the match result rather than the speculative type wagers on the actions or incidents which might arise during the course of the game.

The latter section sounds very much as though it is aimed principally towards the increasingly popular spread-betting activities, covered fully elsewhere, which are tending to move towards off-beat betting markets on matches. There are also one or two interesting areas in which the Scottish approach seems to differ from the FA's, who have not, as far as I am aware, expressed an opinion about the desirability or otherwise of betting on matters such as the awarding of yellow and red cards.

Having ascertained the opinions and views of the ruling bodies, I decided to ask the players what *they* felt about the question of gambling and the game, via their own organisation, the Professional Footballers Association, whose Chief Executive Gordon Taylor responded:

> Bearing in mind the latest court case involving Bruce Grobbelaar, Hans Segers and John Fashanu, I feel it would be

GAMBLING ON GOALS

most appropriate for the football bodies to agree that there should be no shades of grey in this matter with regard to players or anybody connected to a football club betting on football games in any manner whatsoever and neither should such a person be involved in the forecasting of matches.

You may consider this a Draconian response but in the light of this recent court case and various problems with corruption over the years I think it is the only attitude to take if we had to try and keep public confidence in the integrity of the game.

After the final verdicts were announced, Taylor maintained his stance: 'I will support any motion to outlaw betting in football of any description by players and anybody else connected with the game.'

Another unequivocal response with which I may not wholeheartedly agree but which I accept would eliminate the 'grey', although I suspect it would merely succeed in pushing such activity into the netherworld of illegality.

And not everyone supported Taylor's views. West Ham boss, Harry Redknapp, writing in the *Racing Post*, fumed: 'I can't believe they're considering stopping players and mangers from betting as a result of the match-fixing trial. Where's the harm in it? It's not as if I'm betting against my own side, which is definitely not on.'

Redknapp surely had a point. The defendants were found *not* guilty, so in a period of 30-plus years no cases at all of betting-related match rigging have been proved within the domestic game.

I also contacted the Liverpool-based Football Supporters' Association to canvass their opinion, which was that footballers should be forbidden to bet on any individual matches at all, and for any amount of money. The FSA spokesman believed that this is essential so that supporters can be confident in the honesty and integrity of the games they are watching. However, he seemed quite relaxed about permitting players to bet on the pools, which he considered 'harmless'.

This attitude received backing from a slightly unexpected source when Tom Kelly of the Betting Office Licensees Association made a general statement about sportsmen and sportswomen gambling:

While not willing to comment on any specific allegation, governing bodies should prohibit sportsmen from betting on games in which they are participating. The integrity of activities on which betting takes place must be beyond reproach and this must be totally apparent to the public.

16

Kelly was speaking in early 1997 after allegations had been made that some snooker players were being advised to bet on their opponent if they reached a major final, as a kind of insurance against defeat.

During the course of my research for this book, I have come up with numerous examples of officials and players quite openly discussing bets they have placed on football matches in which they or their teams were involved, or on competitions involving their clubs.

It is unclear whether the FA rule covers placing a bet on a side to win promotion, avoid relegation, win a divisional championship or Cup. However, each of these types of bet, regardless of when they are placed, can easily end up depending on the result of a single game. Take, for example, bets struck by Gillingham Chairman P.D. Scally, who told me on 21 March 1997: 'Last season we were involved in two separate bets, the first which cost us £7,500 was that we would be promoted, and for that we received a return of £125,000, which was useful to help pay the promotion bonuses to the players and management.

'The second was a private one with the managing director of a company by the name of Sarkpoint Reprographics Limited, who put up a wager of £20,000 on the basis that I play at least ten minutes in a football league game for Gillingham FC before the season ended. To achieve this I needed to register as a player before the transfer deadline date on the last Thursday of March and then convince my manager to select me for the final game here at Priestfield Stadium, at home to Scarborough.

'Unfortunately, due to political problems, it was difficult for me to take the place of a player who had played all season, or been involved in the squad, but nonetheless the decision was left to me on the day. I was unable to justify going on and of course it would have been a huge stigma for a player to have been replaced by the 40-year-old chairman of his football club and therefore I didn't achieve the bet.

'I ought to say it was close, and had I come on for the last ten minutes it would have been a fine end to a fine season, but there is always this year.'

Now, I am fairly sure that no one could object to a 'fun' bet such as the second wager described by Mr Scally. What the official attitude towards the first bet he described may be, I know not.

Another chairman who cashed in with a significant win was Victor Green who staked £1,000 on his Stevenage Borough to win the

Vauxhall Conference title in season 1995–96 – when they did so, his wager at odds of 25/1 produced a £25,000 profit.

Slightly lower down the pyramid, Beau Reynolds, chairman of Isthmian League-side Worthing, landed a £7,000 win from William Hill when his side won a divisional championship in 1992, when the League was sponsored by Diadora.

On page 157 I tell the story of how Owen Oyston, then chairman of Blackpool, took me on to the pitch to accept publicly a £30,000 wager from him on his team.

In the *Racing Post* of 12 February 1997, Joe Royle, then manager of Everton, was quoted as saying: 'I bet quite often on football, but I'm not a big gambler. Certainly no bookie would win a fortune off me.'

In February 1997, shortly after he had left the post of manager of Blackburn Rovers to join West Bromwich Albion, Ray Harford confessed in print that he fancied Rovers to win the FA Cup: 'In fact, I even had a bet on them at 25/1,' he told the *Sport*.

During the 1996–97 season bizarre stories of Manchester United boss Alex Ferguson betting £30 on Manchester City to be promoted at odds of 1000/1 did the rounds. Well-respected writer Jeff Powell of the *Daily Mail* reported the story in his paper on 8 March 1997. I wrote to Mr Ferguson requesting the name of this mega-generous bookie with whom he was supposed to have placed the wager on his neighbours. No reply was forthcoming, but a source from within the club later told me that Ferguson was extremely irate about the story. Presumably not quite as irate as City when they didn't go up.

However, despite Mr Ferguson's decision not to respond to my enquiries he was 'outed' as a punter by fellow Premiership boss and unashamed gambler, West Ham's Harry Redknapp, who in May 1997 told a story of how he rang his bookmaker, Surrey Racing, to place a bet on his telephone credit betting account, only to discover that the clerk taking his bet thought he was Ferguson.

'Alex's account is one number different from mine. I phoned to put a bet on and they thought I was him. This fella is saying, "Mr Ferguson" this and "Mr Ferguson" that and I thought, "Hold on Harry, you could have a result here if you keep quiet. If it loses it goes on his account; if it wins you phone up and claim there has been a mistake." But I didn't.' Perhaps it was Harry who bet on City!

Reflecting on this story, Derek McGovern of the *Racing Post* asked Surrey Racing's supremo Mervyn Wilson, 'Who's the biggest punter – Harry or Fergie?' and was told, 'I can't discuss a client's business.' He carried on, 'Did either bet on the Premiership or relegation battles?' receiving the identical answer. But when McGovern asked Wilson, 'Why Surrey Racing?' he answered, 'Because they are top managers and so obviously want to bet with the top firm,' thereby confirming, by implication, that the pair have accounts with his company.

Spurs boss Gerry Francis gave *Racing Post* readers advance notice of a bet he intended to stake on his side winning the 1997–98 Premiership championship when, on 25 February 1997, he was quoted as saying, after Spurs were offered at 40/1 by Hill's for the coming season's title: 'I'm not a betting man but will have a go next season because if we have everyone fit we can surprise a few people. I don't know how much I will put on.' FA rules specify no minimum amount of wager which is deemed acceptable, or otherwise.

When Peterborough were relegated from division three at the end of the 1996–97 season, manager Barry Fry revealed that he had bet on them winning the divisional championship.

'I put my money where my mouth is – £12,000,' he told the *Sport*. 'I had £5,000 each-way and then after we had lost our first game I went out and had another couple of grand on it.' That confession certainly qualified him for the description 'mug punter', but should it also render him liable to suspension from the game? I think not.

Whilst I was writing this chapter, the then Leicester City striker Steve Claridge was appearing on a Channel 4 programme called *Under the Moon*, promoting his recently published life story, *Tales from the Boot Camps*. In the first chapter, entitled 'A Gambling Man', he confesses to having lost £300,000 by gambling. On the programme, interviewed by host Danny Kelly, Claridge cheerfully admitted that, 'I backed us to stay up – I did Manchester United a couple of weeks ago at 1/2 to win the League which I thought was a good thing.' He also confessed to backing himself to score the first goal in matches.

In the *Daily Sport* newspaper, two days before Leicester's Coca-Cola Cup Final game against Middlesbrough, Claridge was reported by Hugh Southon as saying: 'I grabbed a bit of the 7/2 available on City before the semi-final against Wimbledon. I'm not going to tell you how much I've had on, but it will be a very nice little pick-up if I win.'

When Leicester went on to win the Coca-Cola Cup following a replay with Middlesbrough, Claridge's gambling really did hit the headlines. He scored the winning goal in extra-time which excited several soccer writers who displayed their startling ignorance of football betting rules by asking him whether he had backed himself to score the first goal of the game – obviously unaware that all 'first scorer' betting is on a 90 minute play basis. Claridge himself, possibly carried away by the emotion of the moment, also seemed a little confused, commenting, 'If I'd had a bet I would have missed it.'

But what did bring the betting issue to the boil was Claridge's admission that he had had a bet, one of whose components was Manchester United to win the Premiership title – and Leicester still had a fixture to come against the Old Trafford side. On 18 April 1997 the *Mirror* carried a banner headline: 'FA's Bet Ban On Cup Hero'. The story reported that a member of the public, said in another paper to be a Liverpool fan (and they were also in contention for the title), had complained to the FA about Claridge's bet.

FA spokesman Steve Double said, 'The Premier League received a complaint about Claridge from a member of the public. They passed it on to us, and Claridge was immediately informed that he had to call off the bet.'

Declared the *Mirror*: 'Clearly the FA are concerned that suggestions of match-fixing could have been raised.' Even though it was not clear whether Claridge was asked to call off only the bet he'd placed on United for the title, or every bet he'd had, he told the media: 'I accept what the FA tell me. It wasn't a massive wager. I stood to pocket hundreds of pounds rather than thousands.'

He also said that it had been a private wager with no money having thus far changed hands: 'I made three separate bets,' he told the *Express*, 'Leicester staying in the Premiership, us winning the Coca-Cola Cup and United winning the League at 3/1. The FA wrote to me pointing out the conflict of interest. I was happy to cancel it.'

Is it not somewhat peculiar that the FA did not take any action of its own volition but, rather like an incompetent referee prompted by a vigilant linesman (assistant referee, if you will), only creaked into action when alerted from outside? Presumably they would have been aware of the situation already, but only deemed it to be of importance when it threatened to become the focal point of a controversy.

Express chief football writer Paul McCarthy saw no problem with the potential Claridge betting coup: 'Good work all round if it comes off,' he wrote.

His view was backed by the *People*'s 'Voice of Sport', Roy Collins, who blasted that the FA's action was 'a piece of mind-boggling idiocy, even by their standards' and went on to compare the FA fear that Claridge might be tempted not to 'give of his best' against

United with the increasing examples of clubs putting out less than full strength sides in fixtures which might not be of the highest priority to them, but whose outcome could affect the fate of other teams – 'Isn't that match fixing?' demanded the thought-provoking Collins.

The business of Claridge cancelling the bet just like that was interesting, though. Who says a bookmaker would be automatically willing to void a bet which was already running? Did the FA demand any written proof that it actually was called off? Did this FA action herald a new, crusading attitude towards participants betting on football? Time will tell.

Chesterfield were the giant-killing sensations of the 1996–97 FA Cup season and their striker, Andy Morris, made a confession to the *Sunday Mirror*'s Ian Hyland on the day of their semi-final against Middlesbrough: 'I've backed us to lose in every round this season, so if I stop now the lads won't be very happy.' Morris had clearly been placing the bets as a kind of good-luck charm, but FA rules forbid it nonetheless.

In March 1997, Italian star Fabrizio Ravanelli revealed to the media that he had 'already taken money off the people who said Italy wouldn't beat England at Wembley, and I am ready to collect again. So if anyone wants a bet on us [Middlesbrough] staying up, then I'll take it.' Not that good a forecaster then!

Blackburn's Scottish international, Colin Hendry, was quoted in the 1997–98 *News of the World Football Annual:* 'My only vice? Ten pounds on me to score the first goal – every game.' In September 1997, the *Daily Record* reported that Arbroath full-back John Gallagher regularly 'helps his office pals to fill in their fixed odds coupons'.

Southampton goalkeeper Dave Beasant appeared on 6 March 1997 on the *Do I Not Like That* discussion programme on Carlton TV, hosted that night by Gary Newbon, who had asked, 'Do you have a bet on football matches?'

'Yeah, we do,' answered Beasant. 'A bet you don't like to do is one on your own game. I wouldn't bet on our own game or against ourselves.'

On the same programme, betting pundit John McCririck was asked: 'Should players be allowed to bet?'

'The best guarantee the fans have got is the bookmakers themselves,' replied Big Mac. 'They've got a pyramid system – if people start going around the various betting shops putting on whatever they want to put on, the bookmakers are the first to be alerted. They'll alert the FA. If there is any fiddle going on, the most acute antennae – far greater than the MI5 and MI6 – belong to the bookmakers' intelligence service. That's the best safeguard we've got. They're not going to be taken for a ride by footballers or anyone else.'

Calling Mac back to the subject in hand, Newbon again asked, 'Do you think players should be allowed to bet on football matches?'

'You can't stop it, so yes,' was the pointed reply.

Support for the McCririck opinion was supplied by TV football pundit Jimmy Hill, who told me, 'It can easily be done through a friend, so a ban cannot be effective.' On the question of betting shops at grounds, Jimmy, formerly leader of the PFA, commented: 'As long as it is legal they will remain.'

David Garbacz, football market-maker for Sporting Index, a spread- betting company, takes a relaxed but far from complacent view of the potential for betting skulduggery by those involved in the game: 'I would estimate that at least 50 per cent of footballers enjoy a bet. However, the rewards of the game are so high these days that it is difficult to see how it would be worthwhile to risk everything for the sake of relatively modest winnings from a bookmaker.'

He did accept, though, that particularly in some volatile spread-betting markets, quite substantial winnings would be possible in theory, but felt that any attempted manipulation of the markets would inevitably reveal itself and risk high-profile exposure.

Sporting Index director, Lindsay McNeile, added his thoughts about the attitude of some of those involved in the administration of the game to betting on it: 'It will often be condemned by people who see no hypocrisy in then going off to play golf with their friends for side-bets.'

Bets by players taking part in matches on who will score the opening or final goal in that game are commonplace and over the years have generally been reported virtually without comment, but on Friday, 23 September 1994, the *Sun* quoted FA spokesman David Davies as saying, 'We will be writing to Liverpool to ask for their observations', as part of a story revealing the scandalous fact that Neil Ruddock, Steve McManaman and Jamie Redknapp 'are in trouble after betting that new team-mate John Scales would score the first goal in the Coca-Cola Cup against Burnley'.

Scales was 33/1 and he did score the first goal. The players apparently each had a tenner on him to do so. Whatever 'observations' were submitted, Scales was clearly an old hand at such matters. In January 1994, the *Sunday Express* had reported that

Scales had won himself £800, Vinnie Jones £2,000 and the rest of the Wimbledon team a further £2,000, when he scored the first goal of a 2–1 win over Sunderland in the third minute of the game. He told Ian Stafford, 'The odds [40/1] were too good to ignore and I encouraged some of the others to have a flutter. I fancied myself to score from a set-piece and luckily the chance came early on.'

Scales and five of his Wimbledon team-mates had a bet on the four clubs to win each English division.

'If we got it right,' he said, 'it would have pocketed us £150,000. Unfortunately Manchester United let us down.'

So what concerned the FA about the Scales first-goal flutter? Surely, having backed one of their own to score the first goal there was no likelihood that such a bet would make the side play any the less enthusiastically?

I could understand there being a certain amount of concern if the players had backed someone from the opposing side to score the first goal. But even if they had, as David Garbacz said, how likely is it that a Premiership footballer, on the kind of wages they earn these days, would risk that for a few hundred quid?

Maybe the club's management might object if a player danced through the opposition defence, rounded the keeper and then stopped the ball on the line and waved for his team's keeper to come up and knock it in because they'd all backed him at 250/1, but other than the fact that it transgressed the FA rule, I can't see the problem. They had made no secret of the fact that they'd had the bet, after all.

Bookies may have to face the occasional players' coup, for example when a side changes their penalty taker or dead-ball specialist, but the player punters are still taking a chance that the right situation will come along for them to cash in. Perhaps it has once or twice.

Colchester United defender Martin Granger was offered at odds of 20/1 to score the first goal in their home game with Northampton Town in December 1992. Bookie Vic Horton, who had just opened up a betting shop in the club's ground, was surprised to take £200 worth of cash for Granger to grab that opening score. He realised why he'd taken it when Colchester were awarded a penalty and instead of normal spot-kick man Roy McDonough stepping forward, Granger strode up and duly hammered the ball home – scoring a £4,000 win for his team-mates, who had clubbed together to place the £200 bet.

'We just took advantage of inside knowledge,' said one player at the time.

Chelsea captain Dennis Wise scored a penalty and lost potential betting winnings of over £1,000 during a game against Wimbledon in April 1993. Wise and his colleague, Tony Cascarino, had both placed bets of £20 at odds of 28/1 on midfielder Damian Matthew scoring the first goal of the game. So when Chelsea were awarded the spot-kick with the score still at 0–0, Wise initially handed the ball to Matthew to take the penalty but then thought better of it.

'I just tapped him on the shoulder and said, "I'll take it." Cas was not happy, but he knew I couldn't really let him take it.'

Personally, I can see little wrong in such bets. The likelihood of a match being rigged to allow a particular player to score first is so unlikely as to be virtually irrelevant. It would not be possible, either, to stake sufficiently large bets to make it worthwhile for such chicanery to be contrived. Nonetheless, it has, without a shadow of a doubt, for long been definitely against FA rules.

What action have the FA ever taken? Well, a season or so ago they drew the attention of clubs and players to their rules regarding such behaviour but, as far as I can make out, took no specific action against anyone or any club. Possibly that was why, when the Steve Claridge affair came along, there seemed initially to be a general lack of awareness both in and out of the game that such bets were contrary to the rules. By implication the FA had been forgiving, if not actually condoning, any such bets already placed and not exactly forbidding any future ones.

The difficulty in all of this, though, is how could you ever guarantee to prevent it happening? If you endeavour to enforce the rule, a player could just get someone else to place the bet for him. It is not practical to put the burden on to the bookmakers by making them check the bona fides of any anonymous visitor to one of their branches. You could hardly expect them to turn away business from a legitimate telephone betting client, either, even if they knew him to be a footballer taking part in the match on which they were betting. By doing that they would be breaking no bookmakers' rules, only the FA's, who have already shown themselves to be less than hugely concerned.

Interestingly, too, this rule permits players and others concerned in the game to bet on the pools. So, one presumes, the FA fears the possible rigging of a few matches but not enough to influence a pools payout – rather an inexact and, if you accept the implied suggestion in the rule that a certain amount of match rigging is not impossible, surely rather a dangerous assumption.

In my opinion, any player or official likely to succumb to the temptation of becoming involved in match fixing is likely to do so regardless of the FA rules on the subject. This is not to argue that we should not have laws against murder as they would not deter someone bent on committing such an offence; after all, having the law enables a punishment to be levied against the perpetrator. Match fixing is not murder – well, not in any instance I have come across in this country, anyway – and anyone found guilty of exerting an untoward influence on the outcome of matches for betting purposes could be dealt with under other Association rules relating to misconduct or bringing the game into disrepute. A blanket ban on all betting for those involved in the game would be ineffective, impractical, imperfect, impossible to police and an unnecessarily Draconian over-reaction.

'It is outrageous to suggest that I, or any of the others would refuse to give a scoring pass just because it might wreck a bet' – this was an England international footballer speaking in March 1995 – an England international rugby union footballer. It was one Victor Ubogu, who had fallen foul of that game's authorities by trying (unsuccessfully as it transpired) to place a £100 bet on himself at 18/1 to score the first try of a Five Nations match against Wales. England manager Jack Rowell later told his players, 'There'll be no gambling,' to which Ubogu responded, 'It's a bit rich to stop us from betting a few quid when gate receipts for a game from which we won't earn a single penny are going to top one million pounds.' This was, of course, before rugby union went openly professional. The row produced a comment from *Racing Post* sports editor, Derek McGovern, who wrote: 'English football chiefs turn a blind eye to players betting so long as they don't back against themselves. But in Scotland footballers are banned for life if they are found betting on matches.'

Bookmakers are quite possibly the best 'policemen' for such wagers. They are the obvious targets, who stand to lose money as a result of match fixing, unless you happen to believe that bookmakers could be behind such activity in the first place. That, I submit, is as likely or unlikely as a bank manager or member of any other profession you care to name, doing the same.

Bookmakers, particularly the larger ones, can detect suspicious betting patterns with great accuracy – they would not survive in business if they couldn't. They also all belong to the previously mentioned Betting Office Licensees Association, an umbrella organisation which is capable of collating information from a large number of bookmaking sources and taking the kind of united action for the industry which an individual bookie or company would find impractical. Bookmakers protecting their own interests might not be able to guarantee 100 per cent the integrity of the game of football – but football itself has had a hundred years or so to do just that. It is for others to decide whether they believe it has been entirely successful in that aim.

Bookmakers do have a vested interest in their own financial well-being and, with football betting, taking into account all of its different aspects, accounting for such a massive turnover, can be relied upon to shout very loudly should they ever suspect all is not well. If you doubt this just consider that bookies have been around for over 200 years, taking bets on horse racing, without ever looking likely to go out of business as a profession. Horse racing thrives on gossip, rumour and suggestion that strokes are being pulled left, right and centre. But look closely and you will discover very few examples of skulduggery proved beyond reasonable doubt. Jockeys are not permitted to bet by the Jockey Club – officially – but there is no such restriction on owners and trainers who would be more than capable of 'putting on' for any rider requiring a flutter. But the sport of Kings – and Queens – is, by and large, as straight as is humanly possible. Can the same be said for football? At the moment I think it can, but by trying to get needlessly tough with betting as some kind of knee-jerk reaction I think the sport would only drive a great deal of it underground, thus making it completely impossible to regulate.

In a nutshell, I believe the FA has been hypocritical by ignoring its own rules about betting, but that those rules are an anachronism and really represent an unjustified attack on those who provide the betting facility rather than those who seek to use such facilities. The sooner those rules are done away with or drastically streamlined, the better for all concerned.

Hypocritical and inconsistent though I may accuse the FA rules of being, there can be little doubt that they would be upheld by the legal system if anyone ever chose to challenge them through the courts. I consulted eminent barrister, and founder President of the British Association for Sport and Law, Edward Grayson, also the author of *Sport and the Law* and co-author of *The Royal Baccarat Scandal*. He told me: '1997 provides a global showcase when every multi-media mechanism brings the world game into sight and reach of every predator's sticky fingers. Thus, the United Kingdom's second soccer conspiracy corruption trial, with its Far Eastern connection, should not divert attention from the international dimension.'

Grayson referred to reports of alleged corruption in football in

Singapore and Brazil; the latter had resulted in Pelé, now Sports Minister, saying in a televised interview that 'the guilty would have to be jailed'. While there was no evidence that these incidents were connected to gambling, Mr Grayson commented, 'Such a high-level, high-profile activity reflects the gravity of the problem and the seriously responsible approach from such a renowned footballing nation.' He addressed the question of FA Rule 26 (a) (iv) and its definition of 'misconduct' as 'to bet on any Football match other than on authorised and registered Football Pools.'

'How far and to what extent such an offence could ever be proved must always depend upon evidence, consistent with modern rules of fair play and justice – two co-existing concepts.'

Pointing out that as long ago as 1908 an FA consultative committee unanimously passed a resolution which described gambling upon football matches as 'evil', Mr Grayson declared: 'That attitude down the years towards gambling as "evil", however debatable and arguable, will always be an issue if any attempt is ever made to challenge the FA's current prohibition in its Rule 26 (a) (iv) as being in Restraint of Trade.

'For the criteria contained in Article 3 (2) of the objects for which the Association is established under its company law Memorandum of Association include "to promote the game of Association Football in every way in which the Association or the Council of the Association shall think proper, and to take all such steps as shall be deemed necessary or advisable for preventing infringements of the Rules of the Association and Laws of the Game, or other improper methods or practices in such game, and for protecting it from abuses". A United Kingdom court of law would uphold any such alleged restraint of trade to be within the standard defensive argument of being reasonable in the public interest.

'Furthermore, if any dispute or challenge surrounds that position, the current trends from as far and wide as Singapore and Brazil, with even Pelé, perhaps, as a potential witness, could be relied upon to support it.

'Gambling and human nature have always been renowned for double standards. When they come together in the football world no one should really be surprised.'

It also surprises me that the FA seem to have demonstrated absolutely no hostility to the use of popular, high-profile footballers and footballing characters, like Ian Wright and Alan Hansen, to promote betting on the game via the pools in, for example, TV advertising by Littlewoods. Surely this contravenes at the very least the spirit of FA Rules on betting, and suggests double standards at work?

There is another aspect of betting on football by those involved within the game itself which also deserves some attention. The FA regulations make no mention at all of club sponsors being permitted to wager on the team they support. I have seen correspondence from the high-profile sponsor of a very senior club to a bookmaker, which discloses that under the deal they had at the time of writing the sponsors were obliged to pay certain bonuses to the club, dependent on them winning various competitions. The letter asked the bookmaker to supply odds for the sponsor to place bets on the team winning the relevant competitions. The bets would have involved potential winnings of a little under £500,000.

I am also unaware of any FA regulation prohibiting clubs from taking out insurance to cover themselves in the event of having to pay players' bonuses for a successful season. Again, I am aware of correspondence between a bookmaker and another high-profile club in which the club secretary wrote on behalf of the chairman 'to investigate the possibilities of placing a bet with you rather than the choice of insurance'. The club was taking this action, said the letter intriguingly, because 'you will, no doubt, be aware that last year a number of football clubs had a bad experience by insuring in the event of promotion'. The letter asked for odds to cover the club finishing in the top three of its division, to cover a payout of £250,000. You have to ask yourself is there, in principle, any difference between 'insurance cover for bonus payment' and 'a bet on myself scoring the first goal'. I don't think so – do you?

And another slant on this angle emerged recently. In September 1997 *The European* newspaper revealed that Spanish First Division team Deportivo La Coruna had effectively bet on themselves being relegated! In fact, they had taken out an insurance policy against relegation. Club president, Augusto Cesar Lendoiro commented: 'All that we have done is take a position based on our financial obligations.' Lendoiro would not reveal the sum covered in the deal with a Swiss insurance company.

A bet of this nature would be against FA Rules for a British club but, although *The European* declared that the 'Spanish club is the first to take out cover against being relegated', the paper quoted Jonathan Ticehurst of London-based brokers Windsor Insurance as confirming that his company was 'beginning to receive enquiries about relegation insurance from other clubs'. Where those enquiries came from was unclear. One un-named broker was quoted as saying of such sporting insurance policies, 'It's not the sort of thing we want to talk about, because people say it's a bit like gambling.' Personally, I would have said it is *exactly* like gambling – and should be covered by the same FA Rules which relate to betting.

CHAPTER TWO

Century of Soccer Betting

Betting on football matches could not begin in any organised manner until the game had formed itself into a structured system of league and Cup competitions. In doing this, the game made itself attractive to those who enjoyed speculating on the outcome of competitive sporting fixtures, which until then had meant almost exclusively horse racing.

The earliest reference I have discovered to betting on the outcome of football matches reveals that the Royal Engineers were installed as 4/7 favourites to win the very first FA Cup final, played at the Kennington Oval on 16 March 1872. The Royals – presumably to the despair of backers – became probably the first beaten odds-on favourites in football (although very far from the last!) as they went down to a 1–0 defeat by the Wanderers.

By 1877, betting on football had already become an accepted practice, if not a universally welcomed one, for the *Manchester Guardian* was already hoping to see the back of it, commenting in November of that year that betting was noticeable at local matches where this 'objectionable practice' was indulged in by players and 'umpires' alike.

The next month the *Athletic News* was confirming that betting on the outcome of games was happening, although it seemed to look down on such an activity which, it said, 'cannot possibly assume the character of gambling. There being only two sides or parties to the contest, long odds cannot possibly be obtained unless people are foolish enough to back a hopelessly inferior team. The betting cannot consequently assume any more objectionable form than the members of a club or team backing this club or team to win; and this, we submit, is perfectly legitimate betting.'

The idea of betting on several matches must have entered a number of minds at around the same time – some of those minds residing within the heads of bookmakers of the day, others more normally exercised with assembling the pages of sporting publications. Circulation-boosting competitions offering fixed cash prizes, which according to history lecturer Mark Clapson in his book *A Bit of a Flutter* soon became known as 'fixed-odds', and which required entrants to predict a number of correct results of football matches, began to appear during the 1880s in Lancashire-based sporting papers such as *The Football Field* (Bolton) and *The Lantern* (St Helens). Up to twenty-two shillings and sixpence (£1.12½p) was to be won.

According to his book *Association Football and English Society*, social historian Tony Mason believes that:

> In so far as one is able to collect evidence on such betting on football matches as there was in the 1880s, it seems to have been mostly confined to the grounds before and during the games.

Writing in the bookmaking trade magazine, *Bookmakers Office Supplies*, George Turner confirmed how quickly betting linked itself with the growth of the fledgling sport of football:

> The FA was formed on the 26 October 1863, with the object of standardising the game. Once standardised, the game became the ideal betting medium, a fact not lost on the bookmakers of the day, who soon produced a local primitive coupon on an ad hoc basis. The turn of the century saw fixed-odds football coupons developed and promoted to such an extent that they represented a major part of the off-course bookmakers' turnover during the winter months.

Coupons would be collected by an agent, handed to a street-corner runner, or posted on to the bookie via the cheap and reliable postal system of the day, with stakes being paid by postal order, the frankage on which was minimal.

In 1882, the Birmingham Football Association AGM was informed that the greatest evil which it faced was the 'betting nuisance'. In April 1887, the *Birmingham Guardian* put forward anecdotal evidence that the 'nuisance' was still present when it reported of the Aston Villa v West Bromwich Albion FA Cup final that 'many working men staked whole week's wages' on the game.

Bookmaking historian Carl Chinn, writing in his 1991 book *Better Betting with a Decent Feller*, recorded that 'the quietness of the winter months was the inducement which, from the 1890s, had led some bookmakers to adopt fixed-odds betting on football matches.' Chinn also records how such a form of betting was potentially costly to small operators in particular, and he tells the tale of Plymouth bookie James 'Ginger' Duke, who served as a teenager in the Boer War, and later in the First World War. After being demobbed, Duke worked at the docks before beginning to take bets on a regular basis. He went on to become one of the first car owners in the city – chauffeur driven, of course. But one 'Black Saturday' of football results cleaned him out – 'Every penny we had was pay-out' – and his son told Chinn that this disaster 'killed him in the end at 56 years'.

David Dixon, writing in *From Prohibition to Regulation*, places the origins of football betting in 1888 when the Football League, founded that year, 'attracted the interest of bookmakers and football betting became a considerable part of their business, providing a useful substitute outside the flat-racing season. This was mainly fixed-odds combination betting.' Acknowledged soccer betting expert E. Johnstone picked up on this point when in 1960 he wrote an article for the authoritative book, *Association Football*. Johnstone, whose *nom-de-plume* in the *Sunday Dispatch* was Jack Boulder, said:

> It is impossible to say when some enterprising bookmaker decided that by asking for the results of a number of different matches as a single wager the odds could be made more attractive. It is certain that at the turn of the century the practice, known later as fixed-odds betting, was in operation.
>
> Early fixed odds consisted of slips on which betters wrote names of teams they wished to combine as winners. The bookmaker offered certain odds against their success. Later, a variety of different combination bets was made possible by the issue of printed coupons, allowing for the forecasting of various numbers of homes, aways or draws.
>
> Combination football betting arose from an idea of J. Jervis Benard, who adapted the *pari-mutuel* and totalisator principles to betting on football. From a one-roomed office in Birmingham he began to issue coupons which did not offer a stated price for success, but made an offer that after deducting 10 per cent the

balance would be distributed among winners in proportion to the amounts of their stakes.

The fixed-odds better knew what he had to receive if he won. The pool investor received an amount equal to the division of what money was left after the promoter had taken his commission and expenses.

It is clear that a method of betting which enabled a stake holder to deduct his own expenses and commission before declaring a dividend was open to serious abuse. Competition between hundreds of operators made it necessary for them to keep expenses to a minimum.

1889 It should be noted that Major Seton Churchill, Vice-President of the National Anti-Gambling League, was, to say the very least, not the greatest advocate of a little flutter to add to the enjoyment of watching a football match. In fact, he was downright hostile to the concept. However, with the salt cellar by our side, we can read in his 1894 work, *Betting and Gambling* that:

> To such an extent has gambling and betting injured sport that the committee of the Yorkshire Football Club in 1889, called upon its constituent societies to see if they could not do something to stop gambling and betting at matches, and to keep professional bookmakers off the ground.

Churchill also described betting on Football as 'repulsive' and those who did so as 'parasites of our national pleasures'.

In 1889, 18 February to be precise, *Athletic News* carried one of the earliest advertisements for bookmaker football betting. It was placed by a man called Brook whose address was Rose Cottage, Dewsbury: 'English Cup – £2 2s given for having four winners in Third Round' he enticed. 'Send list [of selections, presumably] and six penny stamps by March 2nd.'

By December of the same year, a rather more sophisticated coupon was being touted by a Blackburn bookmaker named Astley. This seemed to be a forerunner of the pools, offering a guaranteed amount of prize money – £12 initially – to be shared between winners. It was called the Universal Football Programme and Prize Coupon and was available both wholesale and retail, presumably to encourage the enlistment of agents to spread distribution and therefore increase the prize-money pool. A Manchester bookmaker was reportedly offering £25 for punters predicting the correct half-time and full-time score of the FA Cup Final – presumably he got off lightly, as the result was Blackburn 6 Sheffield Wednesday 1!

c1890 Sheffield magistrate Edwin Richmond, of the Social Questions League, pushed through a Council resolution instructing the Chief Librarian to delete all betting news contained in papers kept by the local libraries.

1891 Bookmakers, then often described as 'pencillers', were reported to have 'copt it hot' after taking a large number of 'thick' bets from 'punters' at a Sheffield Wednesday v Sheffield United derby game.

1892 There seems to be little doubt that betting on football matches was banned for officials and players in 1892. Researchers disagree, though, on who took the first step – the FA (founded in 1863), says Maurice Golesworthy, author of the 1965 edition of *The Encyclopaedia of Association Football*; the Football League (founded 1888), declares Simon Inglis in 1985's *Soccer in the Dock*.

The Inglis version seems the more likely, as he backs it up by reporting that the FA's ban – which included spectators – did not come into force until 'a decade later', adding a humorous postscript about FA Council member Dr Edward Morley of Blackburn who was concerned lest his annual side-bet with a friend on the likelihood of Blackburn Rovers winning the FA Cup – the stake was a top-hat – should be declared to contravene the rules. Such a wager was, indeed, forbidden, confirmed Chairman, Charles Clegg.

In his *Association Football and English Society*, Tony Mason gave another vote to 1892 when, he says, 'The FA Council was trying to outlaw all betting on football.'

Sheffield was in the football betting news again when it was alleged by an official of Blackburn Rovers during an FA Council meeting that the city was the only place in which 'open and noisy betting on the field was practised'.

Geoffrey Green's 1953 volume, *The History of the FA*, confirms that on 9 May 1892, the FA ruled that 'Neither officials nor players shall make bets on any football match, and clubs are required to take all reasonable measures to prevent gambling by spectators. Clubs and players failing to observe or enforce this rule will be guilty of serious misconduct.'

1895 A Blackburn Rovers official poured scorn on Anti-Gambling League claims of excessive betting on football, telling his local *Weekly Standard and Express* newspaper that more money changed hands in one London club in one week than in an entire season's football matches.

The National Anti-Gambling League endeavoured unsuccessfully to prosecute publishing company Stoddarts for accepting stake money on newspaper football coupons.

1896 The FA took further action to discourage all possibility of players or officials being tempted to rig matches: 'It shall be considered misconduct under the Rules of the Association for any Association or Club, or any player, official or member of any Association or Club to offer . . . any consideration whatever to another Club, player or players of any other Clubs with a view to influence the result of a match.'

1899 'There were many thousands present at Shrewsbury on Easter Monday, and the concomitants of betting, drinking and bad language were fearful to contemplate.' An early example of men behaving badly at a football match, recorded in the contemporary *Bye-Gones relating to Wales and Border Counties*. Discussing the same period, Morris Marples, in his 1954 *History of Football* declared:

> Not much is said about betting, but it must have been general among a population already prone to gambling in other forms. One must confess that a bad example had been set in this respect by the 'gentlemen' pioneers of the sixties and seventies who were accustomed to place bets on football matches, as they did on all other kinds of sporting contests, including the Oxford v Cambridge boat race.

Bad example? What could he have meant? Sounds thoroughly admirable to me!

Betting was not widespread in football, declared the *Athletic News*, claiming that 'nowadays' bookmakers were nowhere to be seen at Cup finals, suggesting of course that they had been in earlier years. *Athletic News* could never have dreamed that an official betting shop would be a part of the facilities at the Cup Final venue in years to come.

1900 London sporting newspaper *Pearson's Weekly* was successfully prosecuted for running a football prize game, as were Manchester publishers Stoddarts. This would herald the gradual demise of such newspaper-run football coupon betting operations, although some operators moved abroad to get around the problem, continuing to accept stake money by post.

1902 The FA extended their ban on betting, which already applied to players and officials, to everyone attending football grounds, impossible though that would be to impose.

At the turn of the century, the House of Lords had appointed a select committee to report on the situation in respect of betting, particularly illegal cash betting. It began its report:

> The Committee are of the opinion that Betting is generally prevalent in the UK, that the practice of Betting has increased considerably of late years, especially amongst the working classes, whilst, on the other hand, the habit of making large bets, which used at one time to be the fashion amongst owners and breeders of horses has greatly diminished. Betting is not confined to horse racing, but is also prevalent at athletic meetings and football matches . . . Betting is undoubtedly more widespread and general than it used to be.

Robert Spittal, an apprentice cooper aged 20, set up a pools-coupon business operating out of his home in Edinburgh, where he printed the coupons and sold them for 2d (just under 1p) each, offering an initial prize of two guineas (£2.10p) per week, which soon shot up to £70 as he distributed over 5,000 coupons each week. The business survived until 1923.

A Liverpool football coupon carried an unusual request to investors as part of the continuing skirmish between the Anti-Gambling League, who were pledged to do away with football betting, and the National Sporting League, who were equally determined to preserve it: 'Gentlemen whose names are on the Parliamentary or Municipal Voting Registers are requested to sign the appended form for the purpose of having their names placed on the register of the NSL for Electioneering purposes.'

1905 'Recently, a very insidious form of gambling has made its presence known in the North of England, and unless some means can be found for stopping this undoubted evil we are afraid the future of football will be as bad as horse racing has become.' The *Manchester Evening News*, owned, purely coincidentally, by anti-gambler Russell Allen, was railing against newspaper football prize competitions (for which it would not run or accept advertisements) and also against bookmaker football coupons.

1906 The National Anti-Gambling League (founded 1890) was increasingly promoting football gambling as a major problem, supporting this case by pointing out that FA President (1890–1923) Lord Kinnaird was one of their vice-presidents, while Aston Villa director William McGregor was also an influential supporter. The League's *Bulletin* forfeited much public sympathy, though, by hysterically alleging that football's 'once untainted contests' had become 'merely the money struggles of sporting hooliganism'.

The Chief Constable of Leeds, in his annual report, described the existence of 'an organised system of gambling in many of the factories and workshops of the city, conducted in the form of betting on the results of football matches. There is reason to believe that this practice has obtained enormous proportions.'

This year also saw the imposition of the Street Betting Act. Because penalties were imposed for keeping a house, office, room or other place for betting purposes (Betting Act 1853), bookmakers began to conduct their business in the streets and other places. The Street Betting Act was introduced to prevent this practice, and prohibited 'bookmaking, betting, wagering or agreeing to bet or wager, or paying or receiving or settling bets by any person frequenting or loitering for that purpose in streets or public places', according to Solicitor of the Supreme Court, J.T. Chenery in his 1961 guide, *Betting and Bookmaking*. Offenders under the Act could be arrested.

In 1909, a court case established that loitering for the purpose of distributing handbills, advertising a betting business, or football coupons, was tantamount to loitering for the purpose of betting.

The statutes did not, however, affect credit betting (registered credit clients could still receive investment forms or fixed-odds coupons through the post). The use of the telephone to conduct betting transactions on credit became the principal means of getting round the law, whilst letters containing bets and cash were sent to offices in Scotland in flagrant disregard of the law. The Betting Act of 1853 had prohibited cash betting by post but there was a delay in applying it to Scotland, which was one of the reasons for the use by bookmakers of offices there for the purpose of receiving postal ready-money bets. Even when the Act was belatedly applied, the authorities were hampered in enforcing the law by a ruling of the courts that they were not entitled to open letters seized unopened during a raid on a betting house. No effective steps were taken by the Scottish authorities to stamp out the practice even when their powers were identical to those of the police in England. Bookmakers were quick to exploit this situation.

A number of southern-based companies, amongst them Layfield Brothers, Toppin & Spindler, and White Fisher resorted to the Continent to run their football betting businesses. Coupons were distributed throughout England in envelopes printed with a return address in Flushing, Holland. George Turner recalled: 'Bookmakers travelled on the Saturday night packet boat from Harwich and collected their mail containing football coupons from the post office in Flushing on Sunday morning. The envelopes contained not only the completed football coupon, but the postal order to cover the stake, providing a neat little way to circumvent an unpopular law.'

After a few years the Dutch authorities were 'persuaded' to stop this practice, so the majority of bookmakers moved to Geneva, from where the service was maintained until the outbreak of war in 1914.

1907 A survey carried out in Liverpool claimed that up to 250,000 football fixed-odds betting coupons were collected in a single week as the obsession with football wagering took hold. Even allowing for possible exaggeration by statistican Ainslie J. Robertson to impress his employer, the National Anti-Gambling League, this is an astounding figure.

'Betting on the results of individual matches had gone on from the beginning,' reported Richard Holt in *Sport and the British* in 1989. 'But once a system of betting on the results of a whole series of games was introduced the element of skill was lost . . . It was the provincial newspapers that first promoted this form of betting, though specialised companies soon moved in.'

Historian Mark Clapson declares: 'The role of bookmakers in football betting was the transitional link between football betting in the press and the growth of the pools firms from the 1920s.'

Football coupons were reportedly being hawked at football matches in Leicester.

1908 In February a consultative committee of the FA recorded: 'There are a number of persons throughout the country who are preying on the public by various schemes for gambling upon football matches. The FA have on numerous occasions called the attention of the Home Office, the authorities at Scotland Yard, and the Chief Constables of a number of towns to these practices, apparently without any satisfactory result.' The committee also revealed that 'in Bury, action was taken which resulted in one man being sentenced to six months, and another to two'.

1909 Three men who had been distributing football betting coupons outside Villa Park were prosecuted. They were employed by a bookmaker, and one of them was fined £1, or 14 days inside. Liverpool police prosecuted a man doing the same thing for a bookmaker with offices in London and Holland. One of the unexpected results of this case was that bookmakers throughout the land became acquainted with the idea, and promptly copied it.

Secretary of the FA, F.J. Wall, reported that he had been in communication with the Postmaster General, 'with the view to action being taken to prevent the distribution of betting circulars through the post.' F.J. was not best pleased when the PG replied that he was powerless to take action as they were not permitted to intercept and open letters.

1910 The FA Council ruled that any player or official proven to have taken part in football coupon betting would be suspended permanently both from football and from its management. Senior FA figure, J.C. Clegg – a former international player himself – declared that 'if ever betting got a firm foothold, the game as we know it would be done forever.' He was concerned that the problems brought into athletics in the 1890s by betting should not infiltrate football.

At a meeting in September 'the attention of the FA Council was drawn to instances of programmes being used for advertising purposes by betting firms – the secretary was instructed to draw the attention of clubs to the necessity of excluding such advertisements.'

1910 The *East London Advertiser* of 3 December 1910 carried a fascinating article headed 'Raid On East London Betting House'. Bear in mind that this was over 50 years before betting shops were legalised:

> James Pattman, a well-known East End bookmaker; Edith Pattman, his wife; George Shipp, F.W. Taylor, Hy. Richardson, J. Owers and F.A. Hardy were brought up in custody and charged before Mr Dickinson at Thames Police Court on Friday with being found at a house in Dunkeld Street, Poplar, for the purpose of betting.
>
> The defendants, prior to the opening of the case, elected to be tried by a jury.
>
> Mr Knight, who prosecuted on behalf of the Commissioner of Police, said that all the defendants were arrested on a warrant under the Betting House Act. The premises were in the occupation of James Pattman, and it was alleged that they were used for the purpose of betting.
>
> There would be a further charge under the same Act against the defendants for using the premises for the purpose of receiving ready-money bets. The place had been watched for some time, and on many occasions persons had been seen to take betting slips there. When Divisional Inspector A. Hexamer, K Division, executed the warrant he found Edith Pattman, Shipp, Taylor and Richardson, in the house. The last-named defendants acted as clerks to James Pattman in his betting business.
>
> Hardy and Owers, who acted as 'runners' for Pattman, afterwards came to the house, and one of them had betting slips in an envelope in his possession. At six o'clock James Pattman appeared, and he was also arrested. That defendant said 'I thought it was legal. Only the runners come here.'
>
> An enormous betting business, continued Mr Knight,

appeared to be carried on, for no fewer than 8,500 betting slips were found, and of these 1,600 related to races being run that day. In addition there were 1,000 betting coupons relating to matches to be played on Saturday. There were also 2,800 bill-heads relating to betting accounts, 277 books of racing rules, 24 paying-out books, and 5,719 blank coupons relating to football matches to be played on Saturday. In the safe was a sum of £6 15s in coppers, £126 in gold and 149 postal orders for 1 shilling and upwards. During the time the police were in possession of the place, a number of telegraph and special messengers arrived with messages relating to betting; and telephone calls with regard to the same business also occurred.

C.J. Lloyd, of the Tower Hamlets Local History Library and Archives, holds that report as well as an original football coupon from Pattman for matches played on Good Friday in March 1910. The coupon features six matches from the First League, amongst them Liverpool v Sheffield Utd, Manchester Utd v Bristol City and Blackburn v Notts C. There were six more from the Second League, amongst them Gainsborough v Leicester Fosse and Lincoln C v Wolves. A further nine matches in the Southern League featured Watford v New Brompton and Luton v Coventry C. Punters were invited to bet on a minimum of four homes, the odds for which were 3/1, one draw at 7/2, four aways at 10/1 or one home and three aways at 7/1.

We often hear that 'odds ain't what they used to be' and that 7/2 about one draw sounds decent value – you'll certainly struggle to find that sort of offer nowadays.

However, Pattman quoted 8/1 about any six homes – William Hill's Weekend Coupon for 7, 8, 9 February 1997 guaranteed minimum odds of 17/2 for six homes; Pattman went 100/1 about four draws – William Hill, 86 years later, offered minimum 103/1 for four draws. Perhaps they weren't entirely Good Old Days!

Also in this year, investigations showed that football betting was rife in the Army, while many pub landlords were running football-based lotteries.

1911 With the National Anti-Gambling League co-ordinating objections to gambling transactions being carried on via the postal services (in 1909 they claimed that the Post Office had become 'the great receptacle of betting deposits') many bookmakers had resorted to running their postal businesses, for both racing and football, from abroad. The Post Office had remained keen to conduct business with the bookmakers, from whom they made a considerable amount of money.

But in 1911, at Britain's request, British bookmakers were expelled from Holland, from where many had been running their postal businesses. Many now relocated to Switzerland, from where, by 1914, 70 firms were said to be operating in an effort to evade Britain's betting laws.

Once the War got underway, the bookmakers reverted to using the British postal system (the authorities – particularly in Scotland – were inclined to turn a blind eye to what they regarded as innocent entertainment for war-weary workers), only to resume their overseas businesses after the conflict.

1912 In recent years the National Anti-Gambling League had stepped up its attacks on football, accusing the football authorities of displaying 'timidity and procrastination' by failing to tackle the problems it claimed to have identified.

Confirming the spreading influence of fixed-odds coupon betting, the *Swindon Advertiser* reported in September: 'The firms have their agents everywhere, who are willing to buy any number of addresses from clerks in shops and offices.' These addresses would be used to build up a network of punters.

Written much later – in 1938 – but referring back to 1911–12, *The Story of the Football League*, an officially commissioned book, commented:

> At this time the game began to be the object of increased activity
> amongst betting agents who did not hesitate to get into contact
> with players and give rise to suspicions regarding the bona-fides
> of certain games, and this brought a declaration from the
> Commission that any participation in betting on the games by
> any official or player would be dealt with as misconduct and be
> severely visited.

1913 In March, the *Spectator* magazine took a look at what it called *Coupon Betting: The Football Fungus*, in an article by Charles E.B. Russell:

> Some years ago among junior teams in the north there sprang up
> with great rapidity a system which was called 'making a book'. A
> boy would head a page of a grubby little book, say, 'Liverpool v
> Sunderland' with the date, and below would list lines for entries,
> providing for wins for either side up to possibly six goals, and a
> draw. A penny a share was the usual charge. If 15 shares were
> issued the winner would receive a shilling. This form of gambling
> spread very quickly.

This system has now been superseded by a worse one, coupon betting.

In the greater number of cases the backer has no knowledge of his principal, who is usually a small bookmaker regularly following his calling during the ordinary racing season.

The coupons are printed very cheaply by small local printers and handed practically to anyone who will consent to act as an agent. An agent is not hard to find since he gets from 1s 8d [approximately 9p] to 2s [10p] in the pound for all bets received.

He issues the forms wholesale, it may be in the great ironworks in which he is employed . . . or sometimes he will take his stand at some particular street corner to issue the coupons and receive them back signed.

They are not issued until Thursday each week, and the speculator hands the coupon with his stake to the agent not later than 2.30 p.m. on the Saturday. The bookmakers are usually honest men and pay out the right amounts to those who win, but as they offer only short odds for likely results and more attractive odds only for more unlikely events, there are not many winners. Few youths will risk 6d [2½p] to win 4d [1½p] – the odds offered to anyone backing a home team to win – while there are many always ready to expend 6d [2½p] to win 20s [£1] on the probability of having prophesied three matches to be drawn.

Mr Russell did not seem too enamoured of this trade: 'I am inclined to think this constant practice of betting is doing not a little to affect the general steadiness of character among young workmen.'

'Sufficiently alarmed by the spread of coupon betting', the FA appointed a commission which recommended the permanent suspension of any official, referee, linesman or player proved to have taken part in such an activity. Clubs were also to be required to include a clause in agreements with players, warning that their contracts would be terminated if they were proved to have taken part in coupon betting.

On 23 July 1913 in the House of Commons, the Rt Hon. W. Hayes Fisher presented a Ready Money Football Betting Bill on behalf of the FA. He declared: 'The FA has long been determined to endeavour to free this game from the excrescences which have grown upon it in connection with betting and gambling.

'If this Bill becomes law, no man will be prevented from or penalised hereafter from making any bet as to the result of a football match, but penalties will follow those who hereafter indulge in promoting this ready-money coupon betting business.'

It seems as though the Bill was aimed at killing off fixed-odds betting on a number of games without affecting the ability to bet on single matches, when one might have assumed that any FA objections on the grounds of potential match rigging would have been more effective the other way around.

The Rt Hon W. Hayes Fisher described coupon betting as 'a very pernicious and wasteful habit' and went on to detail a police raid at Newcastle where 51,528 filled-in coupons were seized, amounting to £19,476 13s 7d upon which there was a profit to the firm of £7,229 4s 9d over a four-month period.

He described a coupon: 'If you pay down 1s [5p] we will give you 50s [£2.50] if you have three winners at home, and five away out of, say, 40 matches to be played that day; or you pay 1s [5p] and we will give you £50 if you name six winners at home and ten winners away out of, say, 40 matches.'

He is clearly describing a fixed-odds coupon. The main difference between fixed odds and pools at that time was not so much the format of the coupon but that with fixed odds the potential winnings were known in advance – and guaranteed – but on the pools they were declared as a dividend after the results were known.

Bizarrely, Hayes Fisher alleged that 'the Turf Guardian Society, which contains the best of the bookmakers and the betting fraternity, have passed resolutions against their members indulging in this form of betting.'

One wonders just why they would take such action if it involved turning down good betting money – not a trait often associated with any bookies of my acquaintance.

The Bill did not become law until 16 August 1920.

In 1913, the *Morning Post* estimated that two million football coupons were circulated nationally on a weekly basis.

1914 'Football Betting – A Pernicious Practice' raged the *Glasgow Herald* in a series of articles in March, which warned:

> The extraordinary growth in betting on [football] results is causing considerable apprehension, not only on the part of police and other authorities, but among large employers of labour and prominent leaders of the sport who regard it as fraught with serious damage to the prestige of the pastime. A prominent member of the Anti-Gambling League, accepts responsibility for the statement that £10 million is the amount gambled away on football alone in this country last year. Others consider this a gross exaggeration.

The *Herald* dismissed the newspaper coupons, which 'have as much resemblance to gambling as a turkey (*sic*) carpet to an oil painting', although they might well have had a vested interest in this conclusion. Oddly, too, given the general tone of the piece, the paper seemed to be presenting players as paragons of virtue:

> There is no suggestion that the professional player is mixed up in any dishonourable way with coupon betting. His sense of fair play is beyond question. But he may, and frequently does, 'put a bit on' coupons.

The *Herald* considered the derivation of football betting:

> Apparently, continental bookmakers were the first to realise the potentialities of football betting, and before bookmakers had grasped the situation the continental fraternity had devised an elaborate system. As the transactions were made through the Post Office they were considered to be outside the scope of the law.

Not that the locals were slow to catch on, though: 'In Glasgow district, about 30 turf commission agents and scores of non-professional bookmakers are actively engaged in it.' They estimated that . . .

> one bookmaker distributes a weekly average of about 40, 000 coupon cards in Glasgow and district.
> Occasionally there are prosecutions where an agent is discovered, but in football the agent does not really suffer financial loss, the fines in such cases being paid by the employer.

Originally the coupon contained a list of nine matches 'selected by an expert as being those in which the result was dubious'. These offered odds of 200/1 and were almost impossible to win on, but continental bookmakers soon introduced a 'Pick Where You Please' coupon, offering the chance of tipping four home winners at odds of 2½/1. When all the fancied games went the right way for the punters some of the smaller and less scrupulous bookies had to resort to welshing on payments.

1919 'Football has been turned into a sordid trade by it', according to the NAGL's *Bulletin* report on 'Gambling in Great Britain AD 1919'.

1920 Largely at the instigation of the FA, which had been campaigning for its introduction since 1913, the Ready Money Football Betting Bill was introduced, as a result of which punters now had to pay for their coupon and pools bets a week in arrears, effectively turning them into credit clients. It was remarkably ineffective in deterring people from betting on football, however.

In *The Itch for Play* (1962), L.J. Ludovici commented:

> The Ready Money Football Betting Act [was] designed to prevent the writing, printing, publishing or circulating in the UK of any ready-money football betting. The bookmakers evaded the provisions of this Act by marking their coupons 'by credit only'.

Here is an extract from the Act:

> Any person who, in the United Kingdom (1) writes, prints, publishes, or knowingly circulates any advertisement, circular, or coupon of any ready money football betting business, whether such business is carried on in the United Kingdom or elsewhere, or who (2) knowingly causes or procures, or attempts to cause or procure any of those things to be done, or who (3) knowingly assists therein, shall be liable on summary conviction to a fine not exceeding twenty-five pounds or, in default of payment, imprisonment for not exceeding one month, or, in case of a second or subsequent conviction, to a fine not exceeding one hundred pounds or imprisonment for not exceeding three months.

By this time the first football pools operator of significance, a Birmingham firm of bookmakers named Jervis, had launched a coupon on which customers could forecast for guaranteed prizes the outcome of groups of matches – eight homes and four aways, for example. *BOS* magazine's George Turner believed that

> . . . football pools betting first appeared on the scene in the early part of this century and is thought to have been introduced many years after the first 'fixed odds' football coupon.
>
> Also around this time newspapers ran competitions with prizes of £1,000 or more for correctly forecasting the results of a dozen games – the equivalent of contemporary tabloid bingo games, perhaps. These competitions were eventually outlawed.

1921 Irish club Glentoran invited Football League clubs to join a sweepstake it was involved in. The League Committee forbade any club to enter.

1922 On 7 November, *The Times* newspaper, in its leader column, called for the 'suppression of the football bookmakers who . . . prey on the gullible public.'

In the same year Crystal Palace became the first club to fall foul of FA rules banning advertisements for bookmakers, and pools companies from advertising in club programmes or on ground-side hoardings. Palace were ordered to remove such a sign.

1923 Three wireless telegraphists, Colin Askham, Bill Hughes and John Moores, put £50 each into launching a new football coupon betting business. They operated out of a small office in Church Street, Liverpool. As all three were employed at the time by the Cable Company, they decided they needed a name other than their own for the new enterprise. Askham had been adopted and was known by his aunt's surname. His real name was Colin Henry Littlewood and the partners decided that their new venture should be called Littlewoods Pools. They started business in February and distributed 4,000 coupons outside football grounds in the Manchester area. Only 35 were returned and total stakes were £4 7s 6d [£4.37½p], of which £2 12s [£2.60p] was paid in winnings. Of their next batch of 10,000 coupons, just a single one came back. The partners had to put more resources into their fledgling business, but they were far from wealthy, although Moores, whilst working as a telegraphist in Southern Ireland had saved up a reserve of capital which he now used to buy out his partners. Moores gradually built up the company and by 1926 20,000 coupons a week were being received and the weekly turnover was almost £2,000. At this point the company became involved in a legal wrangle over accusations that it had contravened the Ready Money Betting Act, but the attendant publicity boosted business and by 1929 the weekly turnover was £4,500. In this year Vernons was founded, followed by Zetters in 1933. Empire Pools appeared in 1935, at which stage there were half a dozen sizeable companies dominating the business.

At around the same time that John Moores was launching Littlewoods, two well-known northern names appeared on the fixed-odds scene, Albert Crossley and Ernie Peters. Both competed fiercely with each other for business, both had many agents and eventually both ran their fixed-odds businesses on a national scale, long before William Hill came along.

1925 Arsenal international John Rutherford was almost suspended permanently from the game after a football-coupon promoter called J. A. MacWeeny claimed that Rutherford was vetting coupons sent in to his company, Turf Publishers Ltd. The FA was not amused, but it emerged that MacWeeny had 'deceitfully laid a trap' for Rutherford, who was exonerated as a result of proceedings during which MacWeeny passed away.

1926–8 A series of unsuccessful Bills endeavoured to prohibit betting on an event in Britain with an overseas bookmaker. A great deal of postal betting activity was still emanating from Scotland where such business, although not strictly legal, had traditionally been tolerated, as the 1932–3 Royal Commission on Gambling would confirm.

1927 Newport FC were forced to remove an advertisement for a football betting company from their programme by the Football League. A Hartlepool FC director was quizzed by the League over his alleged links with a betting company.

1928 Football coupon betting competitions in newspapers, which had become so massively popular that some people were buying up vast numbers of papers just to cut out and circulate the coupons, was outlawed. At this time the coupon betting industry was estimated to produce a postal revenue of £36,000 per annum.

1933 The Report of the Royal Commission on Lotteries and Betting recommended that all forms of off-course pool betting, including betting on football, should be prohibited. The Commission was not so much influenced by the nature of pool betting itself, and actually acknowledged that football pool betting was a harmless form of gambling for most of those who engaged in it. However, members of the Commission were impressed by the view that betting on football was a means by which new punters, and particularly young ones, might be introduced to a gambling habit, and also apparently by the fear that this form of betting was open to fraud which would be difficult to detect. In this opinion they were supported by the football authorities who, in evidence to the Commission 'urged strongly that steps should be taken to suppress football coupon betting altogether.'

1934 The Pools Promoters Association (Littlewoods; Vernons; W.P. Murphy; T. Strang; Copes; I.T.P.; F. Jervis; London & Provincial; Western Pools) was founded to lobby on behalf of the industry. It was also very useful for the companies to be in a position to exchange information about bad debtors and defaulters.

A Welsh railway engineer, whose name is lost in the mists of time, came up with a device designed to ensure that bookmakers could know with certainty that the bets they were dealing with had been placed before the event in question had begun.

The clockbag, adapted from a device used by pigeon fanciers, consisted of a small metal box which contained two clocks, a key which remained in the possession of the bookmaker at all times, and two pouches. The bookmaker's agent would take the metal box and the pouches and collect betting slips and money to cover the bets and put both into the pouches. When the pouches were full he would attach them to the metal box, and in so doing would automatically start the timer. When the clockbags were returned to the bookmaker he would open them with his key, and at a glance would see at what time the pouches had been locked on.

The clockbag was widely used for illegal cash betting by bookies' runners who collected bets in working men's clubs, factories and on selected street corners.

Vernons, founded in the '20s, became the first pools company to erect and equip a purpose-designed building for processing pools coupons. The building, in Ormskirk Road, Liverpool, became their HQ.

1935 Seven of the largest pools companies got together to sponsor radio broadcasts by foreign stations including some in northern France and, inevitably, Radio Luxembourg. The 50 hours being broadcast per week was excellent publicity.

Vernons launched a weekly 'Bulletin' for their 'investors', from which the words 'gambling' and 'betting' were conspicuous by their absence.

The *Economist* estimated pools turnover at £30 million per year, based on sales of postal orders, but a more accurate figure for the 1935–36 season is now reckoned to be £17.5 million rising by 1938–39 to £22.5 million.

1935–36 During this season the Football League made a farcical effort to scupper football betting – in particular the pools – by introducing a system whereby fixtures would be arranged on a week-by-week basis with clubs being informed at the last moment. Clubs and officials were sworn to secrecy so that pools promoters would be prevented from preparing coupons in time for distribution.

This somewhat over-the-top reaction marked a watershed in the ongoing relationship between the FA, the Football League, and the by now multi-million pound pools business. Both the FA and the League had been consistently and implacably opposed to the pools, which they saw as potentially damaging to the integrity of their sport. Everton Chairman Will Cuff declared that the pools were 'a menace to the game'.

'The hostility of the FA arose not just from a lack of commercial sense but from a more profound belief that gambling was wrong,' declared Lecturer in History, Richard Holt, in his *Sport and the British* in which he discussed why 'instead of profiting from the enormous interest in gambling on football results through the "pools" system, the FA's puritanism led to a futile and absurd confrontation.'

In a bid to smooth out this strained relationship, Liverpool accountant Watson Hartley came up with a scheme for pools promoters to pay a fee to the football authorities for the use of their fixtures on the coupons. Many believed this to be an excellent compromise with the cash thus generated being used to benefit the game, instead of, as under the then current system, the pools firms making large profits without contributing anything in return. Hard-liners in the FA and Football League, though, were determined to put the pools out of business.

The ill-fated, badly thought-out idea of obscuring fixture information was consigned to the rubbish bin after just a couple of weeks. Fixtures were invariably leaked to the press and other interested parties, while attendances dropped as spectators were thoroughly bewildered by the whole business and could not plan arrangements in advance. Club officials were saddled with unwanted and unnecessary inconveniences. What's more, the Scottish League, displaying rather more common sense than its Sassenach counterparts, had declined to join in with the fixture secrecy scheme, which came into play for the first time for fixtures due on 29 February 1936. By 14 March the normal fixtures service had been resumed, causing the *Oxford Times* to encapsulate the whole episode in the headline 'Result: League 0, Pools 1'.

Later that month, Richard Russell MP introduced a private members Bill to make pools betting illegal. He was supported by the Church, representatives of which wrote to MPs declaring 'there is imminent danger of the permanent establishment of a new vested interest claiming an unconditional right to make money by inciting others to gamble.' The proposed Bill was discussed in the House on the first Friday of April, but was crushed by 287 votes to 24.

1936 A *Sporting Chronicle* survey suggested that the average weekly football pools stake was 2s 6d [12½p], although the majority of individual stakes were for between 1s and 2s [5–10p].

The FA published a report on 'Pools Football Betting':

> The evil influence of Pool Betting on the actual results of matches is probably less obvious, but more insidious than that of other forms of gambling.
>
> Barracking has frequently occurred at matches where the home team – forecast as an easy winner – has been a possible loser. This tends to discredit the honesty and fairness of the game.
>
> When it is remembered that sixteen and a half times as many

people gamble on football as watch it (average gate money on 44 English league matches each week, £48,125 – total into the Pools, £800,000), there is a danger that football will be regarded as having more importance as a gambling opportunity than as a sport.

1937 R. Levy of London won a record four-away dividend, courtesy of Littlewoods, collecting £30,780.

1939 William Hill launched his first Fixed-odds Football Coupon in September, taking just £6 18s 6d, not even enough to cover his printing and postal expenses.

Vernons introduced a pool based on jockeys to fill the summer football close season. The war intervened before it could catch on.

1939–45 During the Second World War the major pools companies amalgamated under the umbrella name Unity Pools, while the facilities of the individual companies were handed over to boost the war effort. During the war an Edinburgh company, Strangs, introduced the treble chance pool and in 1946 when Unity Pools was disbanded, the large companies began to cash in on the popularity of the treble chance in their own right.

Unity was an amalgamation of Littlewoods, Vernons, Copes, Shermans, Socapools, Bonds, Jervis and Screen, and it was launched after the postal services refused to deal with the mail from the various pools companies, despite the strenuous lobbying of the Pools Promoters Association, who had announced as early in the war campaign as 20 September 1939 that 'public demand and the desire of members to give employment to as many as possible had led them to decide to reintroduce the pools from 7 October.' Matches to be used would be English and Scottish fixtures, supplemented where necessary with Irish league games.

However, the new enforced structure of the game did not make it easy for the pools companies to retain the loyalty of their clients. War had broken out on 3 September and the next day's *Daily Mail* reported under a banner headline: 'All Sport Brought to a Halt'. This was, though, an over-exaggeration of what eventually happened. League matches were initially suspended but on 16 September, 31 'first class' friendlies took place, attracting 120,000 spectators. In one game, Peterbrough, then of the Midland League, beat Nottingham Forest 4–3.

Regional league competitions were soon introduced, although some clubs like Villa, Sunderland, Derby, Exeter and Ipswich refused to participate. There were eight regional sections – South A (London teams), South B (south London and south coast) South Western, Western, Midlands (Luton to Leicester), East Midlands, North Western and North Eastern.

Competitive soccer returned on 21 October, but attendances were down to around one quarter or less of the previous season's rates. Many players had enlisted, guest players were permitted, training was reduced, players' payments were minimal (£1 10s [£1.50] per game) and matches were less competitive – none of which was designed to encourage punters to speculate on unfamiliar players contesting unknown competitions.

Following the arrival on the scene of Unity Pools, business was slow to pick up – the first week of December produced a first dividend of just £250, compared with the £10,000 which had become a regular occurrence. As punters became more familiar with the new system, Unity's takings picked up and by April 1940 were up to a third of their pre-war level, with a 44,000/1 four-away dividend giving punters a boost.

Without being able to make use of postal facilities following the GPO snub, Unity advertised in newspapers, even instructing clients not to fill in their entries in 'blotty ink'! Part of the takings were earmarked for charities.

A Unity Pools coupon for matches on 10 January 1940 offered '9 Results, 3 Draws and 4 Aways pools, plus The Easy Six and a 2d [about 1p] Points Pool'.

The effects of the Ready Money Betting Bill meant that punters had to sign the coupon agreeing to 'promise to remit next week' the relevant stake. Minimum investment per coupon was one shilling (5p).

An interesting box on the coupon pointed out that 'Members of H. M. Forces will appreciate that in the interests of NATIONAL SECURITY coupons can only be accepted from HOME ADDRESSES.'

1942 With English law forbidding cash bets through the post, William Hill formed a company called William Hill (Glasgow) Ltd, operating from Scotland, to enable clients to send such wagers through the mail system 'legally'. Within a few months, Hill's football business was on a par with its racing turnover.

The fixed-odds coupon was issued from both Glasgow and London where the new William Hill (Football) Ltd company was based in Ludgate Circus. But for his Glasgow set-up, Hill, who was twice prosecuted for receiving cash bets through the post, could well have been jailed.

1944 Inviting potential clients to apply to receive their fixed-odds football coupon for season 1944–45, the company said:

Under the Control of Paper (No 48) Order, 1942, all coupons must be obtained by purchase payable in advance, at a price of ½d per coupon. We are compelled, by Law, to make this charge, and on no account can coupons be sent until the necessary pre-payment has been made. Two coupons will be sent each week – one for submitting your instructions and the other for clients to retain a copy of their instructions.

In order to save unnecessary work in these days of staff shortage we should appreciate clients paying a full season's fee in one amount.

The William Hill fixed-odds coupon for 4 November 1944 ('Smooth Service, Swift Settlement') makes for intriguing reading. It features 55 matches, including Newcastle v Hull, Hearts (NE) v Falkirk (NE), Liverpool v Manchester United, Lovells v Bath, Aberaman v Cardiff, Rangers (S) v Morton, Aberdeen v Rangers (NE). There were ten different sections, including nothing barred, quoting 9/2 for seven results, 50/1 three draws; triple chance at 20,000/1 for finding the correct outcome of 13 games; a lucky seven at 300/1; snip six, 120/1; favourite five, 55/1; fair four 22/1 and trim three at 10/1.

Another section, a correct score on a selected game, in this instance Manchester City versus Everton, offered some generous-looking prices, ranging from 12/1 for 1–0 and 0–1 to 100/1 for 4–4, but specifying: 'In the event of the result being a score other than any of those priced above, all bets are lost.'

1945 Advertising of pools in newspapers for the distribution of coupons was declared illegal after an action was brought against the UK Totalisator Co Ltd.

1946 Unity Pools disbanded and normal commercial competition resumed. Paper supplies were severely restricted, though, and prospective clients were asked to pay a registration fee of two shillings [10p] for a supply of coupons. The most popular pool featured on coupons at this time was the penny points pool which required a correct forecast of 13 or 14 selected matches for up to £30,000.

A small sign of dissension in the ranks emerged when the London FA proposed that 'since there is no evidence that Football Pools have the slightest influence on the results of matches', it would be reasonable to suggest that the government could organise the financing of sports facilities via pools money. The full FA toed the party line, feeling it 'inconsistent and illogical' to ask for a share of the proceeds and confirming that 'its policy remains as complete opposition to all forms of betting on football.'

1946–47 At the start of this season, Vernons introduced the first nationally available treble chance, paying three dividends.

1947 With no advertisements taken by the BBC and no commercial radio in this country, William Hill came up with a cunning plan to push their fixed-odds football betting facilities. They sponsored a weekly programme on Radio Luxembourg, which could be picked up in Britain, even though the signal was notorious for fading in and out of earshot. An advert to plug the service read: 'On the long wave 1293 metres – next season the William Hill programme will again bring you all English and Scottish league football results, and a summary of the day's matches, every Saturday at 5.30 p.m.' On a Sunday, the company were also broadcasting the 'William Hill Half Hour' which apparently featured Billy Ternent and his orchestra, Val Merrall and the Beverley Sisters.

In March, *The Times* carried a report which highlighted the condescending and barely tolerant attitude which the authorities had towards the pools companies. The Ministry of Labour, reported 'The Thunderer', 'proposed to discuss with the organisers of the football pools what might be done by agreement and co-operation to limit the amount of manpower employed by them and to secure for them the employment of the type of labour least suited for manufacturing industry'. In other words, the pools companies should only be permitted to employ the very lowest quality personnel available on the job-market. Commented writer Mark Clapson in his *A Bit of a Flutter*, '*The Times* report clearly illustrated the dislike many Labour MPs felt towards the pools as a massive gambling enterprise, and the consequent low priority they afforded to the pools as an employer.'

1948 Pools Betting Duty, at 10 per cent was introduced in January, and was raised to 20 per cent in October. At the time the duty was first imposed there were reportedly 231 pools firms in operation; by 1951 only 42 survived, with three firms, Littlewoods, Vernons and Shermans accounting for 85 per cent of the business.

In April of 1948, Littlewoods' client, Mr F. Chivers of Aldershot had become the pools' first £75,000 treble chance winner.

1949 The Scottish FA proposed a scheme for control of the pools, with profits going to fund football facilities.

The FA gave evidence to the Royal Commission on Betting, Lotteries and Gaming, reporting:

> The Association believes that betting has no influence whatsoever upon the result of any matches played under its jurisdiction. Nevertheless, it is mindful of the fact that if betting

were to gain a hold on the game, the present position would be seriously undermined.

Here it is appropriate to distinguish between three types of betting – ready money, fixed odds and football pools. The potential danger of each may be summarised as follows:

Ready-money betting: this is by far the most dangerous . . . Whereas the Association has no reason to believe that the results of any matches have been affected by this type of betting it is recognised that it might prove a very real danger to the game should the law ever be relaxed in its favour. Quite apart, however, from the possible effect on individual matches, this type of betting would bring within the environs of football clubs all the appurtenances usually associated with ready-money betting.

Fixed-odds betting: this Association has no information as to the extent to which it exists, but is satisfied that it has no influence upon the results of matches. Indirectly, however, this form of betting undoubtedly affects the attitude of certain sections of spectators at matches in which they have a financial interest. It may well result in barracking of players, abuse of the referee, or other unsavoury incidents. For these reasons alone the Association is rigidly opposed to fixed-odds betting, and will enforce the full vigour of its rules against any offender within its jurisdiction.

The football pools: there is no reason to believe that football pools can in any way affect the result of any individual or group of games. The interest of the 'punter' is so dissipated over a number of matches that it would be mathematically impossible to 'arrange' results to ensure a correct coupon.

In its own memorandum, the Scottish FA stated that it had no reason to believe that there was any substantial amount of direct betting at any match; that they were satisfied that 'amongst those who play and those who control matches, betting on the matches in which they are engaged does not exist.'

The Football Association of Wales commented that 'when a section of spectators does infrequently become abusive and difficult, it is possibly due to the fact that when the home team loses when considered a certainty to win and entered as such on the spectator's coupon, the conduct referred to is due to a feeling of being let down by the home team.'

The Churches Commission declared that, 'No ground whatever

exists for allowing football pools to continue. They constitute a menace to social and personal life and are a form of exploitation for which there is no justification.' Representatives of the Roman Catholic Church told the Royal Commission that they regarded pools as 'a relatively harmless form of gambling'.

Australian matches were first used on British coupons in May. In October, pools betting duty was raised to 30 per cent.

A statistical survey by Research Services Ltd revealed that 33.1 per cent of adults entered the pools, with an average stake of 3s 2d (16p). The survey also broke the population into classes, purporting to show that 15.1 per cent of the 'upper middle class' participated, 23.7 per cent of the middle class, 28.9 per cent of the lower middle class and 37.3 per cent of the working class. Either the upper class did not participate at all, or the organisers of the survey did not dare ask them! 18.8 per cent of women were said to enter the pools, with an average stake of 2s (10p), which was 1s 10d (9p) less per week than the 49.5 per cent of men who gambled on the pools.

1950 Mrs E. Knowlson of Manchester became the first Treble Chance £100,000 winner. Football pools companies had been using horse racing lists on their summer coupons, but Littlewoods dropped them in 1950 as 'the appeal of these pools was minimal'.

1951 The Royal Commission of this year suggested more severe controls should be introduced to the pools 'to obviate the risks of fraud and to curtail operators' ability to offer promotional inducements by artificially inflating the larger prizes.' They also called for a maximum first prize – a recommendation not given the support of the law, although in November 1951 Littlewoods decided to impose their own treble chance first-dividend limit of £75,000. In May of that year the same company had used Aussie matches on its coupons for the first time.

1953 Former MP and author, A.P. Herbert, summed up 'the crazy state of Britain's betting laws' in his book, *Pools Pilot*:

> Messrs Z do football betting at fixed odds only. They have a large office in London, and another, it is said, in Scotland. If you send them a bet in London you must not send the money with it – that would be 'ready money' betting which (off the course) is illegal. You may send it next week, for then it will be credit betting, which is all right.
>
> The moral principle behind this distinction is hard to discover. A man who bets with ready money is at least betting with money he has got, but a man who bets on credit may not have it when

the time comes to pay and may be driven to steal to get it.

Exactly the same law (the Betting Act 1853) applies to Bonny Scotland. But, to put it mildly, it does not carry the same weight in those far parts. Our friend and neighbour, Mr Blanket, like many other Londoners, sends his money with his bet to the Scottish office of Messrs Z every week. This suits Messrs Z, for it means they are sure of getting Mr Blanket's money; but you and we may, for all they know, default next week. The volume of default, we gather, is 'appreciable'.

We are lawfully doing credit betting. Mr Blanket believes that he is lawfully doing cash betting in Scotland.

Mr Blanket's bet on the Obvious Eight, with its humble shilling, is carried to Bonny Scotland by train. But it is not then hurried to Messrs Z's great Scottish office; for Messrs Z have no great Scottish office, though they have a small one. The sack of wagers is now transferred to an aircraft and conveyed back to London. Mr Blanket's little ready-money bet is deemed to have acquired legality by its brief visit to Scotland. This, we think, is about the funniest thing that happens in this island, and it happens every week.

1954 The Pools Betting Act made it legal for stakes to be sent in with current coupons. Previously, all stakes had to be paid a week in arrears. The Act also required Pools Promoters annually to make a return to the relevant authorities of their turnover and the amount deducted for expenses.

Gambling authority L.J. Ludovici explained further in his *The Itch for Play:*

In 1954 the Pools Betting Act was passed. A court decision of 1944 held that football pools were competitions within the meaning of the Lotteries and Betting Act of 1934. They continued to be excluded from newspapers. Nevertheless, football pools still came within the purview of the 1853 (Betting) Act and the Ready Money Football Betting Act of 1920. Coupons merely had to be submitted 'on credit' and paid for the following week in order to comply with the 1934 Act. The Pools Betting Act allowed pool betting for cash; but promoters now had to be registered and had to publish accounts indicating the total amount of the stakes, the total amount paid out to winners, and their own expenses and commissions.

1955 Writing in *Soccer from the Press Box,* respected journalists Archie Ledbrooke and Edgar Turner commented:

> British football has turned out to be an admirable means for pools wagering. Despite any criticism which may be made about such things as under-the-counter payments and so on, there is not a sport of such magnitude in the world which is run straighter.

1956 Vernons introduced a collector service for clients.

1957 Having stood, albeit in modified forms, since 1892, the FA rule preventing club officials and players from wagering on football matches was lifted in respect of betting on authorised football pools. Directors, players and officials discovered to be involved in the organisation of gambling or bookmaking, though, were liable to suspension.

Littlewoods lifted their £75,000 treble chance first-dividend limit in September. Shortly afterwards, Mrs Nellie McGrail of Stockport became the first £200,000 winner, receiving her cheque from comedian Norman Wisdom. This established the fashion for inviting celebrities to make such presentations, a clever public relations innovation, adding a gloss of respectability and acceptability to the perception of gambling.

1958 Legendary England and Preston winger Tom Finney gave his verdict on the pools controversy in his autobiography, *Finney on Football*:

> The pools companies should not be blamed for any reluctance to assist the game which supplies them with their bread and butter – and a fair share of the jam: indeed their offers, sometimes exceedingly large ones, have in the past been virtually thrown back in their faces. Gambling has always been regarded as taboo in football, even though such strict adherence to principles meant the rejection of pools offers, one of which was of not less than £100,000 a year made just after the war. It is a strange anomaly that the same gentlemen who, for years, would have nothing to do with pools money, were at the same time tolerating, even encouraging, lotteries in their own supporters' clubs to raise much-needed revenue.

1959 In May, the Football League were successful in obtaining a judgment in the Chancery Division to the effect that their fixture lists were copyright. In July, four members of the Pools Promoters

Association signed a ten-year agreement to pay the Football League and the Scottish League a royalty of one half a per cent of gross stakes, to a minimum of just under a quarter of a million pounds. In 1965 the FA and the Scottish FA signed a deal with the PPA for use of Cup fixtures, which earned them £60,000 and £15,000 respectively. They had, at last, bowed to the inevitable.

The Churches Council on Gambling released figures showing the estimated turnover on gambling in Great Britain between 1955 and 1959. The total was £524 million in 1955, £548 million in 1956, £556 million in 1957, £568 million in 1958 and £603 million in 1959. The fastest-growing section of the market – which was divided into horse racing, dog racing, football pools, premium bonds and other forms – was football pools. Fixed-odds betting was included for the first time in 1959, estimated on its own at £45 million.

The horse-racing turnover grew by just over 10 per cent from £330 million in 1955 to £365 million in 1959. Dog racing increased only very slightly, from £120 million in 1955 to £124 million in 1959.

The increase in football pools betting leapt spectacularly from £68 million in 1955 to £98 million in 1959, almost a 50 per cent rise.

1960 In December, the FA relaxed its betting ban by permitting clubs to run their own pools competitions to raise money.

In March of this year, Littlewoods' founder John Moores became a director of Everton but had to resign his pools and bookmaking directorships to do so. He later became the club's chairman.

1961 The Churches Council on Gambling revealed that the turnover on football pools betting had dropped from £111,135,000 in 1960 to £101,448,000 in 1961 – but fixed-odds turnover was up from £45 million to £50 million. In the same years horse-racing turnover rose from £385 million to £440 million.

In July, the pools betting duty was raised to 33 per cent.

Fixed-odds betting was an extremely competitive business – to the great benefit of the punters, who were able to take advantage of some extremely generous, not to say over generous odds as bookmakers battled to win a greater share of the market. A great bone of contention amongst fixed-odds companies was the price available for selecting three draws, which had been lengthening from 40/1 and was now widely offered at 60/1. A meeting was called at London's Connaught Rooms. Over 100 bookmakers engaged in fixed-odds betting attended, recalled Richard Kaye, 17 years a director of the company, in his 1969 book, *The Ladbrokes Story*.

Archie Scott was in the chair, and began by saying that the

meeting had been called to put a halt on the competitive nature
of fixed-odds betting which had developed, and which it was felt
could only harm bookmakers themselves.

Kaye, who attended with Ladbrokes' top man, Cyril Stein, recalls that
the smaller operators at the meeting were the ones keenest to limit the
odds offered and that a resolution was passed that three draws should
be limited to 40/1. This was passed, despite the fact that all the major
companies voted against, with William Hill commenting that it was 'a
question of the tail trying to wag the dog'.

Both William Hill and Cyril Stein's Ladbrokes, who had only entered
the football betting market at the start of the 1960–61 season, declared
that they had no intention whatsoever of adhering to the meeting's
resolution, which would have been tantamount to forming a cartel
operating a restrictive practice entirely against the interests of
consumers, i.e. the punters.

'The meeting had been entirely unrealistic,' remembered Kaye. 'It
was as if an amalgamation of village drapers had told Lord Marks at
what price his goods could be sold.'

On 1 May, licensed betting offices became legal. It was easier for the
man in the street to place a cash bet without running the risk of
breaking the law.

For the first time, William Hill paid out over £1 million to fixed-odds
coupon winners, on 9 September. The actual total was £1,118,983,
including a single payment of £43,392 to Alfred S. Miller of Stoke,
near Andover in Hampshire, who had a series of 2d (just under 1p)
bets on the correct scores list.

1962 In June, a big match was played out in the High Court between
William Hill and Ladbrokes, with the latter being accused of infringing
the former's copyright on their fixed-odds coupon. Ladbrokes
launched their coupon in August 1960. According to former director
Richard Kaye, they 'admitted copyright to an extent, but claimed that
there was no copyright in such a piece of work as a football coupon'.
Hill's were claiming that although others had copied their style, none
had done so as much as Ladbrokes. William Hill were now clear market
leaders even though fixed-odds betting had been in operation long
before the eponymous Hill had even been born. In the High Court Mr
Justice Lloyd Jacob ruled that there had been no infringement of
copyright, but the case went to appeal where the judgment was
reversed. It then went on to the House of Lords, by which time the
Ladbrokes' coupon had been redesigned. The House of Lords – Lords
Reid, Evershed, Hodson, Devlin and Pearce – ruled that there had been

a breach of copyright and Hill's were awarded damages of £1, which was all they had claimed in trying to establish a principle. The legal costs, though, were estimated at around £30,000. The two companies went on to battle for supremacy in the market, still trying to outdo each other in the odds they offered. Former Ladbrokes' director Ron Pollard claims that after one fortnight of bad results Ladbrokes lost the equivalent of £3.5 million.

'It was touch and go whether they would survive,' he commented. They did, though, and flourished.

1962 All previous fixed-odds payout records were broken on 13 October as 26 draws turned up on the coupons. The biggest company of all, William Hill, paid out a record £1,312,810 to winners, amongst them Lyle Gough, managing director of a Coventry wholesale fruit firm, and James Sharman, a Fleckney, Leicestershire newsagent, both of whom won £20,000 for single bets on seven draws. Another client, Mrs H. Ettles, a Brighton doctor's widow, won £8,000 for a shilling stake and her son, a medical student, won £2,333. The top dividend paid on the pools that week was £2 12s 6d (£2.62½p) for 2d (under 1p) for eight draws. At the same time, the average odds paid for three draws on the pools was 5/1, against the 60/1 paid on the nothing barred list by Hill's, and the 75/1 paid on their restricted draws list.

There was a noticeable impact on football betting as many pools punters switched their loyalties to fixed-odds coupons, although perhaps the compiler of the *Hill's Sporting News Annual 1963–64*, was a little biased when he claimed:

> Disappointed pools punters in their thousands now realised the truth that pools cannot lose. They can only share out what they have in. Fixed odds offers better value, for if the week's form runs true and YOU win – and everybody else does, too – you are paid the full guaranteed odds and do not have to share your winnings with anybody.

Essentially accurate, but given perhaps the slightest of 'spins'.

However, fixed odds was facing a threat to its future, for on 10 July 1962 the management committee of the Football League had drawn attention to the fact that football pools firms paid some £270,000 a year for use of copyright fixtures and had asked members to lobby their MPs to support the introduction of legislation compelling bookmakers to pay a levy to the Football League's funds for the same purpose.

There was further fragmentation amongst the big fixed-odds

companies, with Coral's taking out a large advertisement in the November 1962 edition of *The Licensed Bookmaker* magazine to tell the trade:

> We Do Not Approve of the Fixed-odds Price War – We have never started the increased offers, but will always make available on our coupons odds to equal our competitors. Any bookmaker who feels that it may no longer be worthwhile to run his own coupon is invited to contact us and we will print his own heading free of charge and provide a really efficient service on a 50/50 sharing terms or commission basis . . . The fact must be faced that odds may be forced even higher by our competitors in the near future and the safest policy for a bookmaker to adopt, whether or not he is running his own coupon, is to rely upon the experience of the Coral Service.

Make your own judgement about whether Coral were seriously condemning what was going on, or attempting cynically to exploit it for their own good.

It was estimated that 12 million people were entering the pools each week – nine million of them men – half the adult male population. The average stake was seven shillings (35p); one in ten letters posted (or over 600 million) was a coupon; and 60 per cent of all postal orders purchased were for pools.

1963 The Pools Panel was introduced to decide the results of postponed games after a severe winter wiped out matches for weeks on end. They sat for the first time on Saturday, 26 January and received a mixed reception from the betting public. The Panel included players Tom Finney, Ted Drake, Tommy Lawton and George Young, as well as referee Arthur Ellis. Each was paid £100 for their efforts, and of the 38 games upon which they deliberated, they nominated seven draws, eight away wins and 23 homes.

Next day, the *News of the World* reported that 'people were calling it a farce' and they ran a cartoon in which two characters were comparing their fortunes on that week's pools entries, with one saying to the other, 'We were right on all our selections – it was the Pools Panel who mucked it up.'

On 5 February William Hill guaranteed odds of 80,000/1 for eight draws on a restricted list on his fixed-odds coupon – the first time any fixed-odds company had done so. He also made the first-ever quote of 25,000/1 for eight draws from a complete nothing barred list.

The Hill's fixed-odds coupon featured an interesting section, the

treble odds list which gave 36 matches to pick from. For six selections
punters were offered 25/1 if tipping the correct half-time outcome; 25/1
if correct at full-time, and 75/1 if correct at both half-time and full-time.

The FA approved a scheme for establishing its own football pool, but
this was never implemented.

1964 William Hill boasted an annual turnover of £50 million of which
around one third was fixed odds. Incredibly, Hill's had a file of five
million football clients, from which they received an average of two
million coupons per week. However, in this year a damaging blow hit
fixed-odds betting as a 25 per cent tax was levied by the Chancellor of
the Exchequer, Reginald Maudling, effective from August. In his
Gambling: Hazard and Reward, published in 1972, Otto Newman
speculates on the true reason for the imposition of this tax on a type of
gambling previously benefiting from tax immunity.

> Partly in an effort to bring it into line with tax regulations on
> pools, but chiefly, it is being held, in order to nip in the bud
> emergent manifestations of bribery and of corruption.

It should be remembered that ten footballers had recently been charged
with having deliberately thrown matches for betting purposes and the
media was rife with speculation that the scandal was even more
widespread. The effect of the tax was felt almost immediately as the
odds offered to punters 'previously not ungenerous to the true initiate',
were trimmed to reduce the tax burden to the bookie. Turnover on
fixed odds, an estimated £65 million in 1963 fell to no more than £15
million in 1965, a fall of some 80 per cent, then collapsed to £7 million
in 1967 and £5 million in 1968, with the pools at £128 million in 1967
and £126 million in 1968. Newman wrote:

> If any lesson in strategy may be learned from this operation, so
> successful in the achievement of its objective, it may well lie in
> the direction of the vastly greater effectiveness of shock treatment
> and in the far greater efficacy of one single heavy blow upon a
> single limited target in preference to dispersion over a wider
> diffuse area.

An initial slump in consumption of a product affected by the imposition
of a tax, e.g. alcohol and tobacco, has often been followed by a gradual
return to previous levels of use. This did not happen with fixed-odds
betting, and the slump proved long lived. Economist Alex Rubner
looked at this situation in *The Economics of Gambling*, and declared:

When the 25 per cent tax was put on all stakes in 1964, the acute competition between the betting companies prevented an upward adjusting of the odds to take full account of the new situation. As a result, at the end of the 1964–65 season the big three fixed-odds firms all recorded net losses and gave up this business altogether – Holders' Investment Trust, which owns William Hill, lost £2.7 million on fixed odds in that one season.

Rubner also considered that the decline in turnover of the fixed odds once its advantage in tax over the pools was eliminated, was proof that much of its appeal was based on the tax-free nature of the product. 'Once the Treasury equalised the duty, relatively few punters remained loyal to a type of betting in which skill is less unimportant than in treble chance.' I would not go along with that entirely and suspect that it was a combination of worsening odds and desire to invest in a less taxing (literally) gamble which may well have turned fixed-odds punters either towards horse racing, possibly to illegal football betting, or even to temporary hibernation from betting. But I find it difficult to accept that the more sophisticated fixed-odds punter would submit to the brasher, more superficial, less satisfying wiles of the pools coupon, although the new tax did mean that fewer fixed-odds coupons remained on which to bet.

As William Hill himself lamented at the time: 'The Pools Promoters will be celebrating, and thanks to their lobbying they will be drinking wine mixed with blood – bookmakers' blood. Fixed odds are finished. In order to keep my staff, my plant and my offices occupied, it will be necessary for my firm to enter the pools field. Only when we cannot lose will we be happy to pay 25 per cent duty. For that reason, we shall direct all our energy into building up a pool.

'I shall carry on the fixed-odds business for a while to see if there is any hope, but I very much doubt whether we could manage to break level in a season.'

In his biography of his older brother, *The Betting Man: A Racing Biography of William Hill*, Joe Ward Hill wrote: 'Whatever the tax was intended to realise, it raised in fact barely £4½ million, of which William Hill (Football) Ltd, contributed £2½ million, according to the *Financial Times* of 11 August 1965.'

Ward Hill records William's conviction that the levying of the fatal tax was the result of constant lobbying by the Pools Promoters, worried about the competition to their own business. Robert Sangster, now a major player in the horseracing world, and once head of his family's business, Vernons, told me that Vernons' credit betting and fixed odds operations were introduced for the 'convenience of clients', but that they were never built up to any great degree, partly due to the vagaries and difficulties of postal betting, and partly due to the difficulty of appointing sufficiently capable and trustworthy management staff.

Mr Sangster did recall a meeting with the then Chancellor, Reginald Maudling, at which he and other executives advanced their case for equality of taxation between the Pools and the Fixed Odds companies. Mr Maudling asked them whether they were hoping for a comparable rate of tax for the two businesses – and they said they were. They duly got the requested equality – only what they had actually been looking for was that the Pools would be given the tax exemption enjoyed at that time by the Fixed Odds. 'William Hill always seemed to be very aggressive towards me after that!' remembered Sangster, 'As if he thought I was responsible for the imposition of tax on fixed odds betting.' He confirmed that fixed odds betting was a very low profile section of Vernons' business.

Littlewoods had a similar division, which was certainly in operation during the 1952–53 season as I possess a copy of the *Empire News Football Annual* for that season, which contains an advertisement for 'The Best Fixed Odds Coupon: Littlewoods'. And the business was still extant at the start of the 1961–62 season when it was promoted in the *Daily Mail Football Annual*.

In June 1997, Littlewoods FA Cup sponsorship manager, Paul Hughes, told me: 'Littlewoods had a Racing division, operating credit betting by phone and post. This company ceased in the late 1960s, and I would guess it ran for 20 years or so. 'We also operated a fixed odds football coupon, which if I remember rightly, ceased in 1969–70.' Actually, I should imagine that Mr Hughes' memory is at fault, given that he believes it was the tax imposition which 'killed it off'. However Roger Munting's *An Economic and Social History of Gambling in Britain and the USA*, published by Manchester University Press in 1996, gives a date of 1970 for the withdrawal of the pools companies from the fixed odds scene. 'Unfortunately the 1970s was not noted for the preservation of company archives' admitted Mr Hughes, 'and I can't easily think where more detailed information might come from.' Ironically, as fixed odds faced its death throes, British Rail welding inspector Arthur Wyles of Nottingham, won a world-record payout of £100,000 for just £1 after finding nine draws on the William Hill coupon. Said William Hill as he handed over the cheque, in a reference to the 25 per cent tax, 'The more money we take, the more we lose.'

1964 Pools betting duty was lowered to 25 per cent in August.

1965 William Hill suspected that the 25 per cent tax on fixed-odds betting may have been prompted by a hidden agenda. Speaking at a press conference, he declared: 'I visualise the whole betting industry being nationalised, perhaps within five years. The tax of 25 per cent on fixed-odds football betting levied by Mr Maudling in his budget of 1964 deflecting, or so he must have hoped, all the wagers with Messrs Hill, Ladbroke, Coral etc, into the hands of the Pools Promoters was, in my view, the first move in this direction.'

One of William Hill's top executives, director Charles Layfield, addressed the Annual General Meeting of the National Sporting League on 29 June 1965, and told them that Mr Maudling lost the General Election by imposing the fixed-odds tax.

'He antagonised millions and killed an industry in three months,' he said.

The impact of that tax was perhaps not fully realised until in November 1965 it was revealed that William Hill (Football) Ltd's parent company, Holders' Investment Trust had lost over £2½ million in the 12 months ending 31 July 1965. No dividend was paid to shareholders who had received 25 per cent in the previous year for which profits of £1¼ million had been achieved. The loss, said the company, was entirely due to the payment of fixed-odds betting duty of £2,572,000. The decision by Reginald Maudling's Labour successor as Chancellor, James Callaghan, to increase the tax to 33 per cent had virtually read the last rites over the already terminally ill business.

Despite this evidence, football writer 'Midas' disagreed in his book published in 1965 by the *News of the World, How To Win at This and That*:

> At the end of the 1963–64 season there was something of an outcry from the fixed-odds bookmakers, who said that their business would be crippled by the new tax arrangements. In my view, this is not by any means the case; it is true that they do not now have the margin of the pools tax, by which to offer relatively inflated odds (as against the pools dividends), but they should still be in a position to compete with such items as the 3 Draws, 4 Aways and 9 Results on a basis that will give fair average odds.

On 20 July 1965, William Hill chaired a press conference at which he announced that his company was to launch a pools coupon. It did not prove to be a success. By the end of November 1965, turnover was running at just £60,000 per week – £40,000 a week below break-even level. By August 1966 the venture was finished.

1965 The second division match between Cardiff City and Coventry

City, played on the evening of 6 October, opened the way for a betting boom on soccer. It became the first match to be shown on closed-circuit television. Viewsport, already well-known for showing big fights, broadcast the game live to 10,295 fans paying £3,500 (no, not each) at Coventry's Highfield Road ground. They watched their side, on three 40ft by 30ft screens, win 2–1 at Ninian Park where 12, 639 supporters were in attendance. Closed-circuit prices varied between four shillings (20p) and 15 shillings (75p). Single bets were not accepted on closed-circuit or televised games at that stage, but it started the demand which would eventually be satisfied over 20 years down the road.

Also in 1965, the FA came round to believing that pools firms were under a 'moral obligation' to pay for the use of FA Cup fixtures on their coupons. The Pools Promoters Association agreed that £75,000 was an acceptable fee.

1966 In January, William Hill surprised the football betting world by announcing that he was to re-enter the fixed-odds betting business which he had only recently discontinued in protest at the tax level. Other companies had continued issuing coupons and the previous market leaders explained, 'It is precisely because of these other fixed-odds coupons that Hill's have now to provide a similar service for their clients.'

This explanation failed to impress the *Sporting Life* which sniffed:

> The news that William Hill Ltd are to re-enter the fixed-odds field is surprising to say the least of it.
>
> They were foremost in condemning the 25 per cent tax, as they said that it made such betting impossible. But unless they resign themselves permanently to the role of public benefactors, one must conclude that they have found that a 25 per cent tax is NOT impossible.

On 5 July the *Sporting Life* reported on an apparent tax anomaly: 'According to Customs and Excise, singles on fixed odds are tax free. Doubles and accumulators are taxed – but not if the games are played on different days.'

On 6 August Hill's confirmed that they were closing down the pools business they had only recently launched but declared that the re-introducton of fixed odds had proved such a success that they were now planning to issue a full coupon.

1968 A survey conducted by Research Services Ltd revealed that 45 per cent of pools gamblers staked between 12½p and 25p per week. The average stake per gambler was 21½p per week which represented, in terms of expenditure patterns of the day, no more than half the average individual outlay for 1949 when an earlier survey had been carried out.

In March, pools betting duty went up to 33⅓ per cent.

1969 In April, Littlewoods introduced Trap-the-Ball, the first ball-spotting competition. In August, they differentiated between points awarded for no-score draws and score draws on the treble chance.

1970 The minimum age for entering the pools was reduced from 21 to 18 in January by the Family Law Reform Act. In August, the pools points system was modified to differentiate between a home and away win, awarded 1 and 1½ points respectively.

1971 William Hill, who created the biggest fixed-odds betting business of all, died on 16 October, aged 68.

A national postal strike meant that the pools companies' collector services – Littlewoods' service was launched in 1957 – came into their own. At their peak, prior to the arrival of the national lottery, some 70, 000 collectors nationwide were responsible for handling over 80 per cent of all coupons.

The introduction of decimalisation in 1971 was also a watershed for the pools business. Commented Vernons' own publicity material:

> Vernons' minimum stake moved from 1s 4d to 1s 8d, which actually represented a stake increase of 20 per cent and resulted in collector stakes alone increasing by £50,000 during the first week of decimalisation. Hence the pools companies inadvertently discovered that punters would readily accept increased prices, and stake increases became a necessary occurrence to help offset inflation.

Quite an admission about the gullibility of pools punters!

1972 Mr K. Grimes of Liss in Hampshire became the first pools half-millionaire.

Chancellor Dennis Healy increased the tax on fixed-odds betting to 42 per cent, which just about administered the final *coup de grâce* even to those hardy few who had continued to provide this type of betting for their football-enthusiast customers.

Pools betting, though, showed no signs of slumping. In 1972, Vernons reported record stakes of £43 million, an increase of 34.8 per cent in one year. Throughout the '70s the popularity of the pools strengthened with record dividends. A 1972 Gallup Poll on gambling stated that 69 per cent of all men took part in some form of gambling, football pools being the most popular, with more than half the men surveyed regularly betting on the pools. In the same year Vernons introduced a 'ladies coupon'.

1973 Spotting the ball was introduced by the PPA. Of all stakes, 12.5 per cent was given to an independent trust to help implement safety work at football grounds. In 1979 this trust became the Football Ground Improvement Trust and by 1997 was receiving 15 per cent of turnover.

1974 Pools betting duty was raised in April to 40 per cent. A £500,000 limit was imposed on the treble chance first dividend by Littlewoods: 'The company felt £½ million was a sufficiently large prize for one client to win.'

In August 1974, football fixed-odds betting rose from the dead, reincarnated as individual-odds betting, largely thanks to the persistent efforts of one man, albeit in collaboration with the big four bookmakers – Coral, Ladbrokes, Mecca and William Hill. John MacFarlane was the managing director of the 22-shop Scottish firm Queen Bookmakers which, prior to the imposition of the swingeing tax, had enjoyed a substantial fixed-odds turnover. After months of political wheeling and dealing, MacFarlane and his fellow bookmakers secured a meeting with Clifford Cross, at that time a Commissioner of Customs and Excise.

Initially Cross rejected the idea of a new-style fixed-odds football coupon which could become a test case. He continued to turn down the idea on several more occasions before the intervention of a sympathetic MP secured John MacFarlane a meeting with the Minister of Finance, John Gilbert, at which the determined bookmaker explained that he intended to produce a fixed-odds coupon which would qualify for general betting duty only. He explained to the Minister that the new- style coupon differed from the traditional fixed-odds coupon in that it quoted a separate, flexible, price about each eventuality – home, away and draw. This would make it 'individual-odds' betting and therefore no different from any other type of bet.

Gilbert told MacFarlane that if the proposed coupon was introduced at the 1974 betting duty rate of 7 per cent, Customs and Excise would make it a test case which would proceed straight to the Court of Sessions.

The coupon was duly produced and subsequently challenged by Customs and Excise in Scotland's Court of Sessions, equivalent to the English High Court. The case was heard by three Law Lords: Lord Emslie, Chief Law Lord of Scotland, assisted by the Lords Cameron and Greer. Customs and Excise were represented by the Scottish Solicitor General and Queen Bookmakers by J.P.H. Mackay QC, an

English Lord Chancellor. The case lasted a day, with the historic decision being delivered three weeks later, on 6 June.

The Law Lords' decision was unanimously in favour of Queen Bookmakers. Individual-odds football coupons could be offered and treated in the same manner as any other bet for betting duty purposes. Within months the coupons appeared throughout the land.

Whilst relating this story to me when we met during my research for this book, John MacFarlane told me that his initial idea for individual odds was still-born. The plan was that separate companies would come up with odds for each match and an industry starting price would be arrived at by taking an average of the odds on offer. These would then be announced via Reuters. John also swore that whilst he agonised over the new individual-odds format he paced up and down on his office carpet so often that he literally walked a groove along it!

1976 'Gambling in Britain', a Gallup survey, found that 37 per cent of the adult population (defined as aged 16 and over) took part in football pools at some time, and that 89 per cent of those did so weekly.

1978 Taking evidence for their report, the Royal Commission on Gambling – whose members included David Coleman and Marjorie Proops – heard from the Pools Promoters Association, who told them that up to 17 million people took part each week during the British football season, and 12 million in the summer months. At the time score draws were worth three points each, and eight of these were required to hit the jackpot. With 55 matches to choose from, the Commission heard that there were 1,217 million different possible combinations of eight matches which might be selected. The Commission concluded: 'The football pools are a well-established feature of the British scene and are not only popular but widely accepted as a harmless activity.'

Despite this, the Commission understood that 'the punter gets a very low rate of return: only 30 per cent or less of his stake finds its way to the prize pool and is paid out in winnings . . . A relatively low rate of return is common for this form of gambling. Nevertheless it is notable that in none of the comparable long-odds operations abroad on which we gathered information – mainly national lotteries – did the prize fund form so low a proportion of stakes.'

Discussing the question of whether a limit on the maximum payout was necessary or desirable, the Commission came down in favour of an 'upper limit' payout of £500,000 'with a provision for periodic adjustment, to take account of inflation'.

The Commission also looked ahead to a situation which has since occurred – the arrival of a national lottery: 'If the pools were forced to compete in the long-odds market with such a lottery, some limit on maximum prizes should be imposed as a sensible rather than a necessary restraint. The object would be not to handicap the pools to help the lottery but to avoid a situation, which we believe would be undesirable, where each side sought to outbid the other in a scramble to secure a share of the long-odds market . . . this limit should apply equally to a national lottery for good causes.'

During the year Littlewoods raised their first-dividend limit to £750,000.

1978-79 This season saw Vernons introduce Matchplay, asking punters to find 12 match results plus two jackpot games at 10p per line. It was soon phased out.

1979 In March, unemployed Port Talbot hairdresser Irene Powell filled in a pools coupon for the first time, and promptly won a record £882,528.65p for a 45p stake.

1982 In April, the pools betting duty was raised to 42½ per cent.

1984 In November, Littlewoods raised their treble chance first-dividend limit to £900,000.

The Football League negotiated a deal with the PPA, increasing their income by £1.3 million to £5.5 million annually.

However, the League were not in the bookmakers' good books. The *Licensed Bookmaker* magazine reported that BOLA – the Betting Office Licensees Association – had informed the English and Scottish Football Leagues that the various bookmakers' associations were unhappy about the way their meeting with the Leagues in late summer had been conducted. In a letter to the League, the content of which was approved by the National Association of Bookmakers, the National Sporting League, and the Scottish Starting Price Bookmakers' Association, BOLA expressed extreme dissatisfaction both at the outcome of the meeting and at the League's refusal 'to enter into any sort of negotiations'.

BOLA said, 'As all bookmakers are painfully aware, the Leagues decided just over a year ago to increase the fee paid by bookmakers for the right to reproduce the fixture list from £10 per bookmaker, plus £4 per thousand coupons used, to £50 per betting office and £1,000 for each pure credit business.

'This massive increase was pushed through in spite of the strongest possible protests . . . in fact the Associations were told they should be grateful that the charge was only £50 as some of football's hard-liners wanted to go for double that amount.' BOLA were, though, happy to have been given permission to conduct correct-score betting on single matches in the approaching season.

The NSL attacked the rise in fees as 'a sick industry trying to obtain easy money for nothing' by forcing bookmakers to 'subsidise them'.

1985 It was revealed that during the 1984–85 season, the English and Scottish Football Leagues had collected £345,000 in licence fees from bookmakers, even though BOLA calculated that this meant 'that 37 per cent of bookmakers did not pay', although some of them may not have taken bets on football. The Leagues had reiterated that their charges applied to all bookmakers, even those who did not use coupons.

1985–86 Crystal Palace chairman Ron Noades was amongst the leaders of a group of 75 clubs on both sides of the border who wanted to launch their own pools competition. Top Score, boasting winnings of £600,000, was introduced at the start of the season – and had collapsed within three months, with reported losses to league clubs of over £1 million.

1986 A quarter of a century after they were legalised, betting shops were at last permitted to install TV screens.

Nursing Sister Margaret Francis and ten colleagues from Roundway Psychiatric Hospital, Devizes, Wiltshire, became the first million-pound pools winners in April when their 8 from 11 perm costing £1.32p brought them £1,017,890. They revealed that the winning numbers had been selected by their patients.

On 15 November Littlewoods raised their treble chance first-dividend limit to £1 million.

Philip Carter, Everton chairman from 1977, became the 12th President of the Football League. Ironically, given that body's determined stance against the football pools companies over the years, Carter was a former Littlewoods managing director. He also became an FA vice-president.

In December, Vernon Sangster, joint founder and life president of the company to which he gave his name, died. His son, Robert, took control.

1987 Fifty-one-year-old lorry driver Jimmy Anderson won a record £1,339,358.30p from Littlewoods.

A Key Note Report on Betting and Gaming revealed that 39.2 per cent of all men and 18.3 per cent of all women participated in football pools. The lowest age group percentage participation was 13.4 per cent of men aged 15–19, and 3.4 per cent of women in that age span; highest was 49.5 per cent of men aged 45–54, and 23.2 per cent of women in the same age group. 45.8 per cent of socio-economic group D men participated and 22.3 per cent of women in that group. Lowest percentages were in the AB group – 28.1 per cent of men, 11.1 per cent of women. In 1987, £4,743,000 was spent on advertising by Pools Promoters, showed the report, up from £4,098,000 in 1983, but down from £5,267,000 in 1984.

1988 Figures showed that £648 million was gambled on pools, an increase of 8 per cent from £598 million in 1987. In 1982 it had been £444 million and had been rising – to £473 million in 1983; £486 million in 1984; £513 million in 1985 and £554 million in 1986.

A Mintel report entitled *The Gambler* declared:

> The most popular form of gambling in the UK is the football pools with, according to research commissioned by Mintel in March 1988, 34 per cent of all adults 'doing the pools' in the previous month. The second most popular form of gambling is the one-off flutter on the Grand National or Derby with 19 per cent of all adults in Mintel's survey betting on these races.
>
> Despite being the most popular form of gambling, the pools offers the lowest returns in the form of winnings to the gambler at 30 per cent of all takings.

1989 Littlewoods raised their first-dividend limit to £1,500,000.

Restrictions were relaxed by the Football League and the Scottish Football League, with the result that bookmakers were granted permission to accept single-result betting on live televised matches for reception within the United Kingdom, subject to annual review, from the start of season 1989–90.

Ladbroke Group plc acquired Thomson T-Line, the holding company which had purchased Vernons for £90 million in February 1988, making Vernons part of the Ladbroke Betting and Gaming Division.

1990 Single-result betting was permitted on Football League Cup and Skol (Scottish League) Cup matches, from season 1990–91.

The copyright fees for betting offices to use league fixtures rose from £80 to £100 for the 1990–91 season, with agents paying £100, printers £250 and credit businesses £2,000. All fees to be doubled in the event of late payment. The fees were to remain the same for two seasons.

1990 In March, the then Chancellor of the Exchequer, John Major, reduced pools betting duty to 40 per cent, with the proviso that the 2½ per cent reduction be given to football through the Pools Promoters Association's Football Trust. Figures quoted in the budget claimed this would amount to £100 million over five years, covering the bulk of the cost for Football League clubs to make their stadiums all-seater, following the recommendations of the Taylor Report into the Hillsborough Disaster.

Following the announcement, the Football Trust and Football Grounds Improvement Trust were amalgamated under the new title of the Football Trust (1990), chaired by Lord Aberdare, to administer the £30 million a year now to be given to football by the PPA (£10 million from the Spot the Ball competition).

1991 In March, Littlewoods approached the Chancellor of the Exchequer with a proposal for a new £60 million-a-year foundation to promote sport and the arts. The Chancellor agreed to provide £20 million by further reducing pools betting duty to 37½ per cent, subject to agreement being reached on the provision of the other £40 million by the members of the Pools Promoters Association.

In September, three betting kiosks run by William Hill operated at Wembley Stadium for the England v Germany international. It was a successful innovation – bets were even taken in marks – and has continued ever since.

In October, Romanian-born Rodi Woodcock became the first person to win more than £2 million, when her 8 from 10 perm, costing 54p, netted her £2,072,220 from Littlewoods.

1992 The English and Scottish Football Leagues were believed to have an income of about £1.5 million per year from bookmakers taking up a licence to use their fixtures. Almost 9,000 betting offices were paying fees, although the number was down by 100 from the previous year, and 32 were the subjects of legal action for failing to pay. *The Racing Post* reported that betting offices were charged a copyright fee of £300 per shop, payable to the Football Leagues, for season 1992–93 while bookmakers operating credit businesses would pay £5,000. Both sets of fees were subject to a 50 per cent discount if paid by the end of September.

1993 In February, to increase the frequency of big winners, Littlewoods introduced a new jackpotting system, with 1–1 draws carrying three points, any other score draw being worth 2½ points, no-score draws worth 2 and any other result being valued at 1½ points.

In April, Ladbrokes opened a credit betting facility in Gibraltar, enabling them to accept bets – predominantly on football – from high-rolling foreign-based clients, without those wagers becoming liable to any tax deductions. Today a number of other companies offer a similar service.

In December, Vernons became the first betting and gaming company to gain sponsorship on the ITV network, via a deal with the *Wish You Were Here* travel programme.

An entirely new way of placing a football bet was launched by the International Bet-Exchange (also known as Bet-Ex), a Brussels-based off-shoot of sports bookmakers, SSP. Bet-Ex describes itself as 'an exclusive, members-only club for serious gamblers the world over, and simply works as an intermediary, allowing its members to bet anonymously against each other.'

By 1997 the minimum stake was $500 (US), with no maximum bet. A charge of 10 per cent per transaction is levied, plus a commission of 5 per cent of net winnings, with no further bookmaker's charges or taxes deducted. Only single bets are permitted, generally for single matches taking place on the day of the bet. Bets can be placed by phone or fax, and winnings are paid 'automatically and immediately after the conclusion' of each event, either to a bank account or credit card account. Membership of Bet-Ex is free. An account is opened and payments can be made via major credit card or debit cards, or by transferring funds to Bet-Ex's bank account in Brussels. Bet-Ex will fax a daily update of bets on offer to members, and members can make their own bet offers.

This is how the system works: Member A calls or faxes Bet-Ex, wanting to bet $2,000 on Newcastle to win at home against Blackburn in the Premiership at odds of 5/4. Bet-Ex will now offer their members the option to bet from $500 up to $2,500 on Blackburn to win, or the match to end in a draw; at combined odds of 4/5. As soon as the bet offer is 'sold' Bet-Ex will send confirmation to member A, or will confirm how much of the offer has been 'bought' by another member or members. Alternatively, the member will see an offer on the faxed list and contact Bet-Ex to take the whole or part of that offer. Obviously the drawback with this system is that it may not always be possible to match up buyers and sellers. As Bet-Ex warn: 'Theoretically you can offer bets on anything, although there is no guarantee that your bet offer will be taken up. Bear in mind that odds will have to be realistic in order to attract take-up.'

1994 In February, the first-dividend pools limit was raised to £2¼ million, and within two weeks Littlewoods paid father and son Harry and Barry Mallet of Harwich, Essex, £2,255,387 with a 60p, 8 from 10 perm.

In September, Littlewoods announced that they were to become the first-ever sponsors of the FA Cup in its 123 year history. The sponsorship deal was worth £14 million over four years, with an associated spend of a further £6 million. The sound of scores of now deceased Football Association worthies, who had so vehemently opposed the pools, spinning in their graves could be heard from

Wembley to Lancaster Gate. Littlewoods managing director Colin Thwaite declared: 'Undoubtedly, a moment of sporting history and one of great importance. Our four-year sponsorship links the name of the country's biggest football pool with the most prestigious trophy in our national sport.'

Others were less than ecstatic, wondering whether this move heralded an era during which the name associated with the FA Cup would change on a regular basis, eventually devaluing and demeaning the hard-won and richly deserved reputation of this fine old tournament.

Is it not the case that the League Cup, alias the Milk Cup, Rumbelows Cup, Coca-Cola Cup and so on, has suffered adversely since it sold its soul? Isn't there a feeling abroad that the FA Cup ain't what it use to be – no one knows when the draw is made, games are strung out over a number of days, clubs switch home draws to the away venue, replays take place over a week after the original game? Or is it just me being old-fashioned?

Commercial director of the FA at the time Trevor Phillips had no such doubts: 'Both parties in the new partnership are very pleased with the outcome,' he insisted.

In November, the National Lottery was launched, and it had an immediate, adverse effect on all the traditional forms of gambling, including the pools and football betting. Some concessions were made to the pools companies – entry age was lowered from 18 to 16, although there was no suggestion that a similar lowering of the age at which it is legal to enter a betting shop should be made. Pools companies were permitted to roll-over the first dividend in certain circumstances in weeks where no client achieves maximum points. This proved far from popular with punters. Coupon collection was permitted from retail premises, including betting offices, allowing clients to place their bets up until kick-off time on Saturdays.

Pools firms paying 37½ per cent tax claimed the 12 per cent tax level enjoyed by the lottery gave it an unfair advantage. The bookmakers made a similar point about their tax liabilities.

In November, regulars from the Yew Tree pub at Worsley, Greater Manchester, won a record £2,924,622. At this time, Littlewoods were receiving over seven and a half million coupons weekly, estimating that as a result of shared entries 'well over 12 million people have an interest in the Saturday results each week'. The company boasted that it was paying out £6 every second, £350 a minute, £21,000 every hour, £513,000 each day, over £4 million weekly and more than £200 million a year.

HM Customs and Excise Notice 147: Excise Pool Betting Duty explains quite clearly the difference between fixed-odds football betting and individual-odds football betting in terms of their liability to betting duty. It asks:

> What is fixed-odds coupon betting? This is where bets are invited by *the issue of a coupon; *a blackboard list; or *a newspaper advertisement.
> It is a type of bet not usually made without such an invitation and not usually made with a totalisator. The betting offers the punter stated odds for a choice of bets (e.g. 30/1 for 3 draws). Fixed-odds coupon betting is liable to pool betting duty.

The question: 'What other bets are not liable to pool betting duty?' is posed, and answered:

> Individual-odds coupon bets. These vary from fixed-odds coupon bets because the coupons provide sufficient variety of odds to give different accumulative results. For example, if two punters place bets of, say, two home wins, two draws and two aways they must be able to obtain different odds if they bet on different teams. Bets made on individual-odds coupons are liable to general betting duty.

It was announced that bookmakers would be permitted to take doubles on Football League (including Premier League) matches when one of the games was screened live, from season 1994–95. Punters were also now permitted to bet singles on the half-time/full-time double-result bet, which had been restricted to doubles unless there was a live TV match.

A request to the Football League from the Betting Office Licensees Association for an official to be appointed to identify the first goal-scorer (and the time the goal was scored) in live TV matches was turned down.

1995 In January, continued pressure from pools companies persuaded the government to lift the ban on broadcast media advertising, paving the way for pools to advertise on TV and radio for the first time in April. The very first TV ad for Littlewoods was screened at the end of part one of *Coronation Street* on 29 April, and featured comedian Frank Carson.

In March, a new 3–2–1 points system was introduced to simplify checking of coupons and increase the number of winners.

In April, Littlewoods announced a Quick Pix 10 coupon, offering a greatly simplified entry form with single perm entries.

In May, following a successful lobbying operation, citing tax advantages enjoyed by the National Lottery, pool betting duty was reduced by 5 per cent to 32½ per cent. At the previous, higher rate, the PPA had estimated that they were paying over £310 million a year in tax.

In November, Chancellor Kenneth Clarke reduced pools betting duty by 5 per cent to 27½ per cent in his budget speech. A further 1 per cent was offered, providing the cash generated was divided equally between the Football Trust and the Foundation for Sport and the Arts.

During the year both Littlewoods and Vernons announced substantial redundancies, which were blamed on the adverse effects of the National Lottery. The Lottery was believed to have hit turnover by some 15 per cent. Pools turnover for 1995 was later reported to be £723 million, with £172 million returned to winners.

The budget also brought good news for football punters in betting shops when the Chancellor reduced the rate of betting duty with the result that from 1 March 1996, deductions were made at 9p in the pound, down from 10p.

A survey of betting shops compiled by William Hill market research executive Brenda Hammonds, showed that just under 63 per cent of Hill, Ladbroke and Coral customers also did the pools, the incidence increasing with age, from 36 per cent of under 24s, to 70 per cent of over 55s. The survey also showed football as the second most popular sport with William Hill customers, of whom 53 per cent bet on it at some stage, compared with 93 per cent who bet on horse racing and 41 per cent on greyhounds. Football and racing had both increased by 1 per cent in popularity year on year, whereas the dogs had slumped by 10 per cent.

Only 21 per cent of Hill clients said that they would never bet on football, compared with 2 per cent who said that about racing; but 56 per cent would never bet on American football, 50 per cent on tennis and 47 per cent on rugby union.

As the National Lottery began to bite at the football pools, and other forms of gambling, Littlewoods public affairs director, Mick Casey, announcing 520 job losses, said: 'We estimate that 12 million people have a regular interest in the Saturday football results. But faced with the reduction in income caused by the National Lottery, and our commitment to maintaining the same level of prize money, we have reluctantly been forced to shed jobs and cut costs.' Littlewoods Chairman, Leonard van Geest added: 'The pools division has lost its previously pre-eminent position in the soft gambling market.

Football punters were offered decimalised odds for probably the first time as bookmakers Eurobet opened for business in time for the 1995–96 season. The company, which also takes bets for matches in lesser known footballing lands such as Portugal and Norway, price their games in a format including stakes. For example, the home team maybe on offer at 2.10 (11/10 in traditional odds), with the away side at 2.85 (37/20, a price never seen in conventional odds), and the draw at 3.25 (9/4).

1996 As a concessionary move because of the impact of the National Lottery on their business, the pools companies had been permitted to advertise on TV. Littlewoods captured the public imagination with some humorous offerings. In one, the scenario was the last minute of a big match with the team a goal down taking a last-chance corner. The ball comes over into a packed goal area only for the ref to leap and head it in before awarding a goal and rushing off on a lap of honour, waving aloft his pools coupon which, obviously, has just won him the jackpot courtesy of the 1–1 result.

In 1997 they involved former Liverpool star turned TV soccer pundit, Alan Hansen, famous for his scathing comments about the defensive frailties of various teams which come under his scrutiny. Hansen was seen looking somewhat disconsolate after a score draw between Liverpool and Nottingham Forest.

'Last Saturday was the worst night of my life,' he said. 'Okay, so I won £1 million, which I suppose for some people is cause for celebration, or something like that . . . but I tell you what, the sloppy defending that led to the equaliser really took the shine off it for me. No one tracked back, men were left unmarked . . . '

Advertising specialists analysed the ads: 'You can see what Littlewoods game is,' said Robert Campbell, a creative partner at agency Rainey, Kelly, Campbell, Roalfe. 'Persuade the punter that the pools has a noble, heroic "added value". Football is more important than money. Frankly, I think it's a long shot.'

Dominic Mills, editorial director of the advertising business's trade magazine, *Campaign*, added, 'Research by Littlewoods' ad agency DMB&B revealed a simple truth; that there is a moment for every fan when the game comes together with the pools, and that is the results. Thus the agency's game-plan has been to concentrate on this moment.'

At the time of writing, bookmakers are still prohibited from advertising on TV and radio.

From 20 June betting shops were allowed to accept Spot the Ball coupons and to pay out football pools winnings.

In August, Littlewoods cut the number of matches on their coupon from 58 to 49. Why? 'To improve the odds of winning by 20 per cent,' they said. Nothing, of course, to do with the National Lottery having 49 numbers, one presumes!

1997 In February, England keeper David Seaman launched Top Spot, a new Littlewoods 'skill-based' football game, offering £100,000 for correctly predicting the position of the ball in six photographs of football action. Would you call that betting?

Graham Jenkins, a 56-year-old Bournemouth cabbie, won a record £292,000 with a £10, 14 match accumulator individual-odds bet from Ladbrokes.

On 14 January it was announced that football pools companies were to be given the green light to launch competitions based on midweek matches under deregulation measures. The Government, though, stopped short of permitting pools competitions based on horse racing. Home Office Minister Timothy Kirkhope declared: 'The proposal which would allow shops, pubs, clubs and other premises to sell pools competitions on horse racing will not be taken forward. This is due to concerns that it could change the pools into a harder form of gambling with frequent opportunities to place bets and chase losses.'

A House of Commons committee criticised the Advertising Standards Authority, expressing surprise that it had not up-dated its code to take account of advertisements for football pools. They said they were worried that the code did not address 'the need to protect children, to discourage excessive gambling in general and to prevent gambling being seen as a way out of financial difficulties'.

In March, Littlewoods announced that over 400 staff were to be made redundant, with the company placing some of the blame on the National Lottery's recently introduced midweek draw.

'Trading conditions are difficult and this is partly due to intensified competition from the midweek lottery,' a spokesman told the media. The loss of jobs meant that Littlewoods would be down to a staff of around 1,000 compared with 4,000 prior to the launch of the National Lottery.

The adverse affect of the lottery on the fortunes of the pools produced an income reduction for the Football Trust, whose chairman, The Rt Hon Lord Aberdare KBE, warned: 'The decline in the Trust's income is a cause for real concern. Before the introduction of the National Lottery our reduction in pool betting duty was running at about £23 million a year and our Littlewoods Spot the Ball at about £14 million a year. In 1995–96 our RPBD income was £16 million and STB £6 million.'

In February 1997, income from Spot the Ball was withdrawn. In the *Nationwide Review* magazine, distributed in programmes to spectators at first, second and third division games, David Harrison of the *News of the World* wrote that income could suffer even further:

> . . . Once the impact of the new midweek lottery draw is known. It is a depressing scenario for football. The downturn in pool company income has had a crippling knock-on effect for an organisation which provides finance, practical support and advice for football at every level.

Lord Aberdare added: 'Sadly we have had to withdraw support from many grass-root areas. We are no longer able to support local authority projects, Football in the Community schemes, and the many charities which include football initiatives amongst their activities.

'We are proud of our achievements. In 20 years the Trust has, with the help of Government, distributed £256 million from Littlewoods, Vernons and Zetters pools and Littlewoods Spot the Ball. This has ushered in a new age in the quality of our football grounds and provided essential support for our national game at all levels.'

Lord Aberdare called for consideration to be given to additional forms of income for the Trust, although David Harrison warned: 'Next year the most optimistic forecast suggests the Trust's income will be down to £9 million from reduced betting duty.'

In August the Tote introduced their first Individual odds coupon.

In September 1997 the pools panel sat to adjudicate when coupon matches were re-scheduled following the tragic death of Diana, Princess of Wales.

Also in September two new opportunities for football punters to win 'big money for a small stake' were launched – Jackpot Football, a weekly Internet game, and Football Forecast, a score-prediction contest.

A survey of William Hill credit clients revealed football, with 54 per cent participation to be the second most popular betting sport, behind horseracing's 90 percent.

Ian Wright of Arsenal became the star of a new Littlewoods TV advertising campaign.

In October an international game appeared on a football pools coupon for the first time when the England *v* Italy World Cup qualifier was included by Littlewoods.

CHAPTER THREE

Match-Fixing Scandals? Don't Bet On It!

Players striking bets during the course of a game would rightly be frowned upon, you would think, at any time during the history of the sport. An early example of such goings-on is recorded in a March 1878 edition of the *Darwen News*, which described a football match between Darwen and local rivals, Turton, whose 'goalkeeper did pretty well, but we should recommend him to cease his contention with the spectators and keep his money in his pocket.'

When Manchester United played Liverpool at Old Trafford on 2 April 1915, several players had plotted to ensure that the result would be a 2–0 win for United, thereby landing them a successful betting coup; they had wagered on the pre-ordained scoreline at odds of around 7/1 or 8/1. It was probably not the only game thus influenced around that era but became by far the most celebrated case.

However, although the central issue of the game being deliberately manipulated was never seriously challenged by those involved, the case may still have involved a major miscarriage of justice. Close study of the events surrounding the game suggest that the Manchester United One may have been as harshly treated as those whose convictions have been declared unsafe in recent high-profile criminal cases.

Enoch John West, known as Knocker, was the only Manchester United player actually taking part in the game who was punished. But he went to his grave in September 1965, aged 79, declaring his innocence.

To put the incident into perspective, the game was taking place in an atmosphere at which we can only guess these days – against a background of the First World War and with pressure being brought to bear on the authorities to ban the game for the duration of the conflict. Players must have been fearful for their futures – both financial and physical. Many would have been fully aware that they faced joining one of the forces and their lives being placed in considerable danger.

Prior to this match, two others involving Liverpool had been the subject of some speculation – a draw against Newcastle in 1911 actually resulted in an enquiry, while in March 1913 the Liverpool versus Chelsea game, which ended in a 2–1 win for the Londoners, caused Arsenal chairman Henry Norris to comment in print that Liverpool could have won if they wished, 'quite readily'. Again, an enquiry failed to unearth anything untoward.

When Liverpool came to Old Trafford on that fateful Good Friday, United were in relegation danger, Liverpool in mid-table. Knocker West, born in 1886, had joined United from Nottingham Forest, for whom he had scored about one hundred goals, for a fee of £450. He was top scorer three times in four seasons for United who, perhaps significantly, had promised him a benefit match worth up to £500 in the 1915–16 season. Would he wish to jeopardise this? Or did he, perhaps, fear that the war would scupper it? In his book *A Strange Kind of Glory*, Eamon Dunphy says: 'For days before the match, rumours had circulated in Manchester that the result was "squared"'.

The game was duly played, but a contemporary report from the *Sporting Chronicle* describes it in less than glowing terms:

> In the second half [by which time United were a goal up through George Anderson] the play fell off greatly, the forwards being slow and unenthusiastic. The Liverpool forwards gave the weakest exhibition in this half seen on the ground during the season . . . the play in the concluding stages [by this time United had, oddly, missed a penalty but gone two up through Anderson] was too poor to describe. Beale, in the home goal, had not a good shot to parry in all the match . . . the proceedings in the second half reflected no credit to either side.

Other reports said that elements in the crowd voiced their opinions that the game was rigged, while Liverpool's Fred Pagnam hit the bar only to be chastised by a colleague for shooting. Even the referee, John Sharpe, was moved to call the game 'the most extraordinary match I have ever officiated in'.

Suspicions about the game began to circulate, and became public when the *Sporting Chronicle* carried an appeal from an anonymous betting firm declaring that players had placed substantial bets on the game, and offering £50 reward for further information. Whether that reward was ever paid is not clear. The Football League appointed a commission to investigate, which began to speak to players involved.

On 29 November 1915, *Athletic News* announced: 'We are told of clubs making huge profits and growing dissatisfaction amongst players' on the same page as it announced news of the United–Liverpool enquiry.

In December 1915, the commission finally issued its report:

> The allegation of squaring the match carried with it a charge of conspiracy by some of the players, and as a result of long and searching investigations we are satisfied that a number of them were party to an arrangement to do so, and joined together to obtain money by betting on the actual result of the match.
>
> It is proved that a considerable sum of money changed hands by betting on the match, and that some of the players profited thereby.
>
> Every opportunity has been given to the players to tell the truth, but although they were warned that we were in possession of the facts some have persistently refused to do so, thus revealing a conspiracy to keep back the truth.
>
> We are satisfied that the allegations have been proved against the following: J. Sheldon, R.R. Purcell, T. Miller and T. Fairfoul (Liverpool); A. Turnbull, A. Whalley and E.J. West (Manchester United) and L. Cook (Chester).They are therefore permanently suspended from taking part in football or football management, and shall not be allowed to enter any football ground in future.
>
> There are grave suspicions that others are also involved, but as the penalty is severe we have restricted our findings to those as to whose offence there is no reasonable doubt.
>
> F. Howard (Manchester City) is suspended until the expiration of 12 months after the registration of professional players has been resumed by the Football Association, for the unsatisfactory and contradictory manner in which he gave evidence before the Commission.

Athletics News examined these findings on 27 December 1915:

> A plot to cheat the public, to sell to the faithful followers of football a sham instead of the genuine article, to rob bookmakers

by criminal fraud and to conspire for the suppression of the truth has been revealed.

Had it not been for the bookmakers, corroborated in the most emphatic and extraordinary manner, the collusion between the culprits could not have been proved.

There was a carefully worked out plan by which the bookmakers in whole districts were filched at such odds as 7 and 8 to 1 against the actual result.

In one or two instances, the suspicion of the bookmakers was aroused by the insistence upon betting on the actual result, and the amount of money tendered.

Generally speaking, the bookmakers paid their clients although they discovered they had been 'rooked'. A few refused to disgorge.

There was general incredulity that only one of the United team (the other two listed had not played) had been singled out. West was working as a mechanic at the Ford works (which was why he had not been required to join up) where he protested his innocence, no doubt to the healthy scepticism initially of his work-mates. The *Sporting Chronicle* commented on 29 December 1915: 'Sympathy on E.J. West would be wasted, but it does not seem right that he should bear all the burden of this infamy and that his accomplices, because he must have had them, should be free.'

In 1917, West attended a match between, ironically, Manchester United and Liverpool, where he handed out leaflets offering a £50 reward to be donated to charity, to anyone who could prove he had placed a bet on the outcome of the rigged match. No claims were forthcoming.

In April 1917, one of the other suspended players, Sandy Turnbull, who had been banned despite not playing in the game, died in action.

On 5 July 1917, West went to court to claim damages for libel against the FA and E. Hulton & Co. – the latter over articles which appeared in the *Sporting Chronicle, Athletics News* and the *Daily Dispatch*. He was also asking for his playing ban to be overturned.

West defended his play during the game in question and denied having known that the match was 'squared' or that he had told another player that he had bet £10 on the 2–0 scoreline. He did admit that it was odd that heavy betting on the game had been reported from Hucknall Torkard, his own birthplace, where he still had relatives.

Liverpool winger Jackie Sheldon, then in the Army, who had played, told the court that he had fixed the game with players from his own side, but declared that he had met with West, Turnbull and Arthur Whalley in a Manchester pub where they had agreed on a 2–0 scoreline, with a goal either side of half-time. George Anderson also appeared and repeated the claim that West had placed a £10 bet. Anderson said, though, that he had refused to join in with the scheme. This was despite initially denying all knowledge of a fix.

Part-time bookmaker E. Giles said that the volume of bets he had been offered on the game had made him suspicious and he had lost £150 but had turned down enough business to have lost £500.

FA commission member Charles Sutcliffe appeared and gave his opinion that West had given contradictory evidence to the commission and was definitely prominent in the affair, although he wouldn't accuse him of placing a bet.

Justice Ridley, despite mentioning in his summing up that the commission had not originally been intending to implicate West by name, found no libel proved and that the ban should stand.

West was soon called into the forces and became a driver in Ulster – where he was prevented from playing football under an alias.

By February 1918, West was in the Court of Appeal where he received a small boost to his campaign when a new trial was ordered over the newspaper comments.

In March 1918, George Anderson, still only 26, was charged by the police with 'having conspired with persons unknown who had made bets on the results of various matches'. Anderson denied the charges but was found guilty and sentenced to 18 months' imprisonment with hard labour, although no proof that games had actually been successfully fixed was produced. Anderson's conviction must have cast some doubt on his apparent condemnation of West.

On 15 January 1919, West returned to court to try to win his libel damages. West, in his defence, raised the question of his potential benefit earnings, which he put as high as £2,000, and alleged that Manchester United could have supported the allegations about him to avoid paying out such a sum.

Charles Sutcliffe appeared again, admitting that at one stage the commission had removed West's name from the list of guilty players, but did accuse him again of giving contradictory evidence. West lost again and was ordered to pay costs.

The four Liverpool players also banned were now offered a chance to apologise for their behaviour, in recognition of their Army service. All four did so, their bans were lifted, and all of them except Fairfoul resumed their careers. No such opportunity was offered to West, who now cut himself off from football completely – either in disgust at his inability to get justice or because he realised it was useless to protest further. As late as 1945, though, he declared of Old Trafford: 'I don't want to go near that place again.'

Author Simon Inglis, who studied West's case in great depth was forced to concede, 'Nor can we ever dismiss the possibility that despite all the evidence West may indeed have been innocent.' Not, though, that he believed this in his heart of hearts. I talked to Inglis in March 1997 and told him that I believed West could just have been hard done by. Not a bit of it, was the gist of Inglis's reply. He went on to tell me that he had seen 'secret letters' about this and other cases, suggesting that he was confident that the alleged crookery had definitely taken place.

Fair enough, I said, but poison pen letters are far from being an unknown phenomenon and if these letters were, or had been, so convincing, how come they were never produced as evidence?

But I digress somewhat. To return to the theme, in 1927 West left his wife and six children to move south to a new Ford factory in Dagenham, staying there until he retired after the Second World War, when he moved back north to Walnut Street, Salford. In October 1945, when West was aged 59, the FA issued a general amnesty and West's ban was lifted.

In October 1960, when another match-rigging scandal was emerging, 74-year-old West told the *Manchester Evening News* he had been innocent all along and that 'if a player is approached and asked to fix a game he should agree and then go straight to the FA' – which was not precisely his own *modus operandi*.

'He still maintains that he had no part in fixing the Liverpool, or any other game,' reported the *News*, quoting West as saying: 'There was still four months of my three-year contract to go when I was suspended, so United still owe me a benefit match.'

West died of cancer in Eccles Hospital, aged 79, in September 1965.

Such persistence against all the odds prompts the question: why? West was either a stubborn old cuss who had managed to convince even himself that his motives were exemplary and that he had done nothing to warrant punishment – or he was totally innocent all along.

In March 1997, I spoke at some length to Roger West, grandson of Knocker West who, perhaps inevitably, is a Manchester United fan himself – 'although I can always see two sides playing, unlike some.'

'As far as I am aware,' said Roger West, 'Knocker never admitted to anyone, including his family, that he was guilty.'

He wasn't a popular man within that family – which, of course, is hardly surprising, considering that he dumped his wife and kids to go to London – and Roger said that he was variously described as 'stubborn, arrogant, and a boozer', but even though 'none of his sons liked him' – indeed, he recalls one of them knocking him down in a fight when he returned following his flit to London – neither did they ever accuse him of having resorted to match fixing.

'Knocker reckoned he had been set up,' said Roger West, whose own father, Albert, was also known as Knocker. 'And even though he could probably have earned a pardon by standing up and admitting his guilt – tugging his forelock, as my Uncle Eric, who played for Grimsby, put it – and it could all have been forgiven and forgotten, he never even considered that option.'

Who can entirely rule out the possibility that, being less than overwhelmingly popular in the dressing-room amongst his team-mates, they decided to stitch him up when the time came for the final reckoning? After all, they may well have reasoned, 'It'll be water under the bridge when we all go off to the war.'

In the Football League's official 50th anniversary publication, *The Story of the Football League*, published in 1938, there is a reference to the United–Liverpool game, which declares:

> The reason being certain of the players were satisfied that football would be discontinued during the War, and that by betting on the correct result they put handsome sums into their pockets at the expense of bookmakers, without fear of discovery.

The book also refers to West's action for libel, but states erroneously, 'In the long run, after losing his case, West admitted the truth of the charge.'

This reads like history being re-written to suit the current regime, similar to the cold-war days of the iron curtain.

A somewhat less than sophisticated attempt to persuade a number of Lancashire-based players to rig matches was made in 1918 when players from four different teams received letters purporting to be from two firms of Scottish turf accountants. The letters began in flattering terms: 'I understand that you are a reliable man – one whom I can trust' before offering a £50 payment for helping to throw a particular game. The Football League was informed and made a great show of announcing that 'this canker of corruption must be kept at bay' and stridently declaring that the FA and the League would 'do all in their power to protect the players and thwart the evil designs of these fraudulent swindlers'; although one wonders quite how they intended to do this when the companies and their addresses turned out to be non-existent. It smacks more of a hoax, despite the authorities using it to demonstrate their supposed vigilance.

Alan Hardaker used this episode in his 1977 autobiography, *Hardaker of the League,* to show how firmly the League had acted – without mentioning the bogus nature of the correspondence, thus allowing another slur against bookmakers to appear on the record.

Considering the number of football matches which have taken place since the game became organised and subject to strict rules, the percentage proved to have been manipulated, rigged or fixed is so tiny as to be virtually imperceptible. But naturally, those cases which have come to light have been sensationalised in lurid headlines.

Betting has sometimes proved to be behind games which have produced pre-ordained results, but it is far from being the only reason. The days of maximum wages (finally overthrown in 1961) provided plenty of opportunity for less than honest players, tempted by under-the-counter payments, to go along with the deliberate throwing of games in order to influence promotion and relegation issues which might have had drastic financial implications for those clubs involved. Such shenanigans are outside the sphere of discussion of this book, but many examples of such chicanery may be found in other books, including Simon Inglis's *Soccer in the Dock.*

During my researches for this book, I have come across a great many references to betting and the fixing of matches which have rung less than true to me, as someone with over a quarter of a century's practical experience in the world of bookmaking.

It is impossible to deny that match rigging has taken place, but perfectly possible to argue that the betting influence has often been over-played and supported by evidence which does not stand up to close examination. You can draw your own conclusions, but I have stated my doubts where they have made themselves apparent as we trawl through the admittedly murky waters surrounding some allegedly bent games.

Bent games weren't on the agenda, but the reputation of Sheffield United and England goalkeeper Billy 'Fatty' Foulke – 6ft 2½in and 20 stone when he played for United in the 1901 Cup final – was severely dented when, in his retirement, he made the news rather than sports pages of the *Sheffield Telegraph,* on 30 September 1910.

Sheffield police had made a raid on the Duke Inn, run by Fatty, and taken him into custody along with one Frank Greaves, described as a bookmaker. Fatty was duly charged with allowing his premises to be used for the purposes of betting.

In 1912, 27-year-old Richard McNeall was jailed for two months after admitting to writing to Burnley FC and Norwich City, purporting to be the goalkeeper of teams they were to play and offering to throw the games for £20!

In 1913, the FA set up a commission to investigate coupon betting. Players' Union representatives, officials and directors were involved and it alleged that betting on the game was 'prevalent throughout the country', even though it was unable to come up with any serious evidence of match rigging related to betting. It recommended permanent suspension for anyone in the game found guilty of an involvement with gambling.

Around about the same time, in March 1913, Charles E.B. Russell was blaming betting for unrest at games and hinting at skulduggery. Writing in *The Spectator* he suggested:

> Sometimes the violent scenes which have taken place upon football fields may be traced to large numbers of spectators having lost money owing to the favourite team not having won, and to there being a general suspicion that the goalkeeper or some other member of the losing side has sold the match.

In 1914, a bookmaker's father was imprisoned for five months after being found guilty of offering £55 to a player to influence the outcome of a match. The man convicted was named Pascoe Bioletti, whose son William Alfred Bioletti of Hove in Sussex operated a football coupon betting business based in Geneva.

The player approached was, bizarrely, the Bobby Charlton of his day, the entirely incorruptible England and West Bromwich Albion skipper, Jesse Pennington. The £55 sum on offer represented a fiver per player to ensure that his side did not win their imminent game at home to Everton on 29 November 1913.

The incident was reported and the police called in. The game went ahead and ended in a draw, after which Pennington approached the man and asked for his 'bung', at which point the law intervened and the bad guy was taken into custody. It was later alleged that he had also endeavoured to 'get at' Birmingham captain Francis Womak.

These bungling efforts to fix games do not carry with them the overwhelming impression that here was a well-organised, ruthless syndicate in action. Rather that an individual had made a rather naive and hopelessly ill-targeted bid to influence the outcome of one or two games, which had inevitably been rumbled almost immediately and properly and promptly dealt with.

An unnamed Norwich City player was discovered to be distributing football betting coupons at the factory where he worked in 1923. The FA suspended him permanently and passed on details to the local constabulary.

Demonstrating the game's determination to avoid all contacts with gambling, Sheffield United forced former international Ernest Needham, who was working for them as a scout in 1926, to give up his other little earner as a newspaper forecaster of soccer results.

Football and social historian Nicholas Fishwick captured the dilemma facing the game's authorities when he wrote in his *English Football and Society 1910–50*:

> The football authorities were hostile to betting on football, they claimed, because it damaged the sport's reputation and threatened the fairness of the game. This involved taking every possible step to prevent betting from influencing football, whilst strenuously denying that any such influence existed.

In actual fact there is precious little evidence to suggest that such an influence *did* exist to any significant degree during that 40-year period.

In another example of the ridiculous, hypocritical stigma which could still attach to an association with gambling, the front page of the *Swindon Evening Advertiser* – and much space inside – was devoted on 1 November 1934 to the scandalous tale of former Swindon star player Bert Denyer. Now the publican of the Running Horse Inn, he was charged with using that inn for the purposes of betting. He was fined £30 with four guineas (£4.20p) costs.

The story was headlined across the front page: '£114 Fines in Swindon Betting Prosecutions'.

During the case, Mr H. Dale, appearing for the defendants, said: 'Football betting was carried on everywhere and their worships could see from the totals paid out, the enormous proportions to which it had attained.' It had been revealed that £7,064 was being distributed 'to those taking bets' in the pub.

Sir Stanley Rous, then Secretary of the FA, admitted in 1949 in a statement to the Royal Commission on Lotteries, Betting and Gaming, that he had evidence of just one case of a player receiving money from a bookmaker to share among the teams if a certain match was fixed. Details were, to say the least, sketchy. Whether Sir Stanley believed that the 'fix' had actually taken place is not clear, but the president of the Scottish FA, J.A. Lamb stated to the Commission that 'many years ago' two players were permanently suspended after being found guilty of accepting a bribe – presumably for betting purposes, and presumably in Scotland.

It is likely that he was referring to a 1924 incident, as a result of which former Scottish international John Browning and Archibald Kyle, once a Rangers player, were both sentenced to 60 days hard labour for attempting to influence the result of a second division game between Bo'ness and Lochgelly. The pair were accused of handing over an inducement of £30 to Bo'ness players, Peter Brown and Thomas Anderson. The two players reported the approach to their manager and police were called in.

It was alleged that Browning and Kyle were acting on behalf of an unnamed bookmaker who had sent £200 to Browning. That seems to be a great amount of money to devote to rigging the outcome of what, with due respect, was a pretty obscure game which would be hardly likely to attract huge betting interest. Why would a bookie want to do such a thing? So that he could take bets on what he knew to be losing outcomes of the game, perhaps? Or so that he could place money himself on what he knew to be the likely winning outcome? The latter seems the more likely scenario but surely even in those days any hefty amount of money placed on such a low-profile game would attract suspicion and almost certainly be turned down. No definite proof seems to have been produced in any case to confirm beyond doubt that a bookmaker was involved.

In November 1925, Stenhousemuir goalkeeper Joe Shortt claimed that he had been offered a payment of £50 by a bookmaker to throw a match against bottom of the table rivals Broxburn United. He reported the incident and played in the game which his side won 6–2. Subsequently a bookmaker was charged and sentenced to three months in prison. Once again the evidence suggested that this was an ill-conceived, one-off opportunistic plan by an itinerant occasional bookmaker.

Despite these admissions, though, the FA themselves told the Commission that it was confident that betting had 'no influence whatsoever upon results of any matches played under its jurisdiction', but added that it was always mindful that if betting were to gain a hold on the game the present position might well be seriously undermined.

In 1936, there were reports that a Sheffield-based fixed-odds bookmaker stood to lose £75,000 if Sheffield United beat Fulham in the FA Cup semi-final. Rumours circulated that 'fixers' might be out to target United players, but they duly won the Molineux semi by 2–1, only to be beaten 1–0 by Arsenal in the final.

Even during those periods when there was precious little concrete

91

evidence to suggest that any untoward practices related to gambling affected football in any way, there were still those on the scene who were anxious to infer otherwise.

Striker Ken Chisholm turned out for several sides between 1947 and 1957, during which time he scored 132 league goals. He was playing for Leicester in 1949 when, as he would later allege, he was told that his side's game in May against Cardiff, in the second division, was rigged. Leicester needed a point to avoid relegation, Cardiff needed a point to finish fourth, which would gain the players much needed bonus money.

Chisholm was not alleging that the game was rigged for betting purposes but, being a man who enjoyed a flutter, he claimed in his autobiography, *There's Another Way to Live*, that he took advantage of his inside information by staking £250 with a Glasgow bookmaker on the game to end in a draw at odds of 5/2. Despite the pre-arranged result being 0–0, the game ended 1–1 – apparently a Cardiff player scored an own goal by mistake and Leicester had to be assisted to an equaliser.

Chisholm said that he had advised the bookmaker with whom he had placed his bet to hedge the bet on to another bookmaker. That would be the only explanation to account for a bookie even considering accepting a bet of what was, for those days, a pretty hefty amount on a game in which the punter had a direct interest – normally a recipe for disaster from which most bookies would run a mile.

No inquiry into the game was ever launched by the FA or Football League despite disquiet being voiced; nor, apparently, did Nottingham Forest, relegated as a result of Leicester getting the point they required, make any official complaint.

Anti-gambling campaigner E. Benson Perkins, a former official of the Temperance and Social Welfare department of the Methodist Church, and chairman of the Committee of Churches on Gambling, was never short of a critical word or several thousand as he churned out a series of less than complimentary-to-betting tomes such as *The Problem of Gambling, Gambling and Youth* and, in 1950, *Gambling in English Life*. In the last he cast a few aspersions:

> The danger of football being seriously affected by the betting on the game was greatly increased with the development of the now familiar Football Coupon. It was different from the Football Pool Coupon of today in that it was betting on definite odds offered by the bookmakers.
>
> Coupons of this type are still current, the bookmakers offering specific odds for certain selections out of given lists of football

matches, such as 2/1 for selecting two wins, 10/1 for four home wins, 50/1 for five away wins.

The circulation of these coupons was largely carried out by agents of the bookmakers inside the factories. The Football Association had, from the first, viewed this development with alarm as they were concerned for the genuine character of football as a popular sport.

One or two cases came into the Courts in which the evidence revealed the fact that a certain match had been scratched in the interests of betting, and in other cases that bribes had been offered to the players.

Rumours of bribery and corruption appeared again in 1960, says Maurice Golesworthy in his *Enyclopaedia of Association Football*, adding 'but although evidence was placed in the hands of the Director of Public Prosecutions this was apparently inconclusive, for no further action was taken.' These would almost certainly have been the allegations which made headlines in the *Daily Mail* for a ten-day period beginning on 10 October 1960, when the paper's front-page headline was: 'Big New Bribe Shocks by *Daily Mail* Investigation Team'. It began:

> Small groups of soccer players and gamblers have been scheming to fix the results of matches on which they have laid heavy bets.
>
> In one weekend last season attempts were made to fix four games and bets totalling several thousand pounds were laid on the results.

The article went on to pinpoint two games which were the subject of alleged outside interference. Swansea Town wing-half Roy Saunders was alleged to have offered 27-year-old Bolton skipper John Higgins £200 to 'see that Bolton lost' a game against Manchester City. Higgins would have nothing to do with the scheme and Bolton won 3–1. Two Scottish internationals, Bobby Collins and Alex Parker, who played for Everton were allegedly offered cash to lose to Chelsea – a game they won 6–1.

The *Daily Mail* declared that they had set their investigative team to work three weeks earlier after the Football League had expressed concern about information which had reached it concerning allegations of match fixing.

'The team travelled thousands of miles and interviewed scores of players, former players, club officials, backers and bookmakers.'

On 11 October, the *Mail* named Chelsea's Scottish international centre-half Bobby Evans as the man who had allegedly 'tried to bribe Everton star Alex Parker to lose against Chelsea last season.' Evans, who had 72 caps to his credit, reportedly told the *Mail*: 'I had read rumours about rigging games. Another Scottish player and I decided we would try it ourselves.' They apparently offered Parker £500 in a phone call, planning to 'win some cash on the fixed-odds pools by betting on this game.' They would have had to go some to win £500.

Also on 11 October, another *Mail* article revealed: 'This IS the Way Soccer Matches ARE Fixed'.

> When a footballer runs on to the field with the aim of fixing a game, his own bet is probably no more than £20 to win £30. But by throwing the game he may win £3,000 for his fixed-odds gambler contacts who have staked £2,000.

An unnamed commission agent, allegedly acting as the middleman to put the bets on with bigger bookmakers, was quoted as saying. 'I try to spread my bets between the six leading fixed-odds bookmakers in Britain, who specialise in singles and doubles. But it's not easy. The weight of money soon puts them wise. After the first £300 has gone on they begin to smell a rat.'

Indeed they would. Even today when millions of pounds are being gambled, sometimes on one game, the bookmakers have such a well-developed early warning system that any unusual pattern of bets will soon be spotted. Whether it is a comparatively small number of large bets, or a larger number of modest wagers, the pattern will be detected and alarm bells will begin to sound.

Maybe the bookies were less efficient or their sense of self-preservation was less well developed back at the end of the '50s and beginning of the '60s, but somehow I doubt it and one just has to wonder what proof existed of these alleged hefty bets actually being placed. The *Mail* certainly didn't produce much evidence of that type.

Simon Inglis in his *Soccer in the Dock* seems confident, though, that large winnings were there to be had. Despite admitting that punters had to know their bookmakers well to be able to place bets on single matches and that the average stake for such a bet would be 'below ten shillings', he commented, 'with a national network of middlemen placing the same bets the profits could be enormous and very difficult to trace.' I would still maintain a healthy scepticism about that, myself.

Rather worryingly, the *Mail* of 11 October declared:

One disturbing feature disclosed by the inquiry is that it is exceptional to find a professional soccer player [who] does not bet on match results. It is the sinister minority who are involved in the scandal of match rigging on a big-money scale.

This suspicion would apparently be confirmed years later by Football League secretary Alan Hardaker. In *Hardaker of the League* he said: 'They would bet against their own team. If they won their match they picked up their £4 win bonus, but if they lost, their bet meant they did not lose financially as well.'

Let's just think about this for a while. Presumably, if this problem was as widespread as Mr Hardaker would have us believe, it couldn't have produced that much of a problem. Surely, you would then have had players on side A backing side B to win and players on side B backing side A. The most likely outcome in this instance would be a draw, so the bookmakers would be quite happy!

Perhaps he wasn't implying it was that widespread. Perhaps it only happened with certain teams on a regular basis. Where did these players place their bets? Four pounds would be a sizeable bet on its own – if all the team members were doing the same thing, there'd be bets of nearly £50 to get on. Did they place the bets with a local bookie? If so, word would soon have got round about whose money it was, especially if they were doing it every week and especially if they were going out of their way to ensure that, when the odds on the opposition were attractive, the bets became winners.

Local bookmakers might fall for that once, but never twice. So perhaps it was larger bookmakers who were targeted. But, in general, the larger the bookie, the more suspicious he will be, and the quicker he will pick up on untoward betting patterns, or look closely at clients who win regularly.

Alan Hardaker claimed that

. . . bookmakers began to get in touch with me, first a trickle, then a stream, all complaining that a lot of money had been won and lost on games which had finished with very unexpected results. The suspicion was growing fast that the whole business had gone far beyond players 'insuring' their win bonuses. It looked now as if a few players were after bigger money by committing the unforgivable – they were throwing matches.

So, despite his original claims not standing up, Mr Hardaker escalated the problem to match rigging. Incidentally, Alan Hardaker had already pointed the finger at bookies allowing punters to stake bets on single games, pointing out that it was against FA rules for players to make such wagers. 'But many players did not seem aware of this and the rest just ignored it.' Surely they should have been *made* aware of it, and shouldn't the FA and/or the Football League have refused to permit legal bookmakers to accept such wagers if they wanted to make an effort to stamp out this apparently rapidly growing problem?

The *Mail* allegations had suggested that there was no honour amongst thieves – some bookies in the know, it said, were cashing in by placing bets with not so well-informed competitors. The paper claimed: 'We also know that a southern bookmaker was responsible for placing the bets for four footballers after a goalkeeper had been fixed for £1,000.' Names forthcoming were there none.

The article went on to describe ways of throwing a game – bad or misplaced passes, deliberately conceded penalties, injury-faking (no substitutes in those days), or own goals. The Football League had asked to see the *Daily Mail* dossier on the match-fixing scandal, said the paper on 12 October, adding that they now knew of three players who had been forced to take orders from 'unscrupulous match benders' because of the heavy gambling debts they had acquired through betting on horses. Perhaps they should have stuck to football 'good things'!

Meanwhile, it emerged that Oldham player Jimmy Ferguson had been commended by the Football League for bringing to light an attempt to bet, (presumably by players involved) on the Oldham v Crewe match the previous Good Friday.

Suggestions that an amnesty for anyone involved in the match-fixing scandal may be the best way of bringing all the details out into the open were floated in the *Mail* on 13 October while the paper's star sports columnist, J.L. Manning, linked corruption in the game's hierarchy – e.g. illegal payments to players still subject to maximum wages – to players being tempted to throw games: 'The only difference between directors bribing players to join their clubs, and players taking bribes to lose their matches is that directors bear a heavier guilt because they have a greater trust.'

The next day the *Mail* moved on to report allegations of bribery to secure promotion – Brighton players had paid Watford players to go easy in games which helped the seaside club to clinch the third division championship in 1957–58. They quoted Watford skipper John Meadows as confirming that £110 had been paid over.

'We wouldn't have beaten them anyway,' he allegedly said, even though they had lost the first game just 1–0. They lost the second 6–0.

There was no allegation of any betting angle here, oddly enough, although you may think that if it were so easy to get such lumpy bets on with the bookies, players involved in two games in which they apparently knew precisely what the results were going to be would have found it difficult to resist the temptation of cashing in.

Other betting allegations had begun to appear. Stoke's Eire international keeper Jimmy O'Neill had been offered cash to ensure Stoke were beaten at home by Norwich in August 1960. O'Neill reported the approach and the story soon made the papers.

Bury winger Johnny Hubbard revealed in October 1960 that he had been offered a staggering £3,000 to fix a game in February 1960 against Barnsley – an amount equivalent to more than a year's wages even for a top player. Hubbard alleged that the approach had come from a Scottish first division player whose name he would not reveal.

Bookmakers would not object if the Football League decided to ban fixed-odds betting on single matches, reported the *Mail* on 15 October, quoting Joe O'Gorman of the Bookmakers Protection Association: 'At the first sign of any unusually big bets on one particular game members will be wary. They will contact one another to see if the bets are being spread with other bookmakers.'

During the course of the series of articles, it transpired that internationally famous referee Arthur Ellis had been asked to fix a match. He told the paper that prior to a 1959–60 FA Cup tie between Preston and Stoke he was offered £35 to make sure that Preston won. He reported the incident, but it was not clear whether there was any implication of a betting motive. Stoke went through after a replay.

By 20 October the *Mail* obviously believed that the shark of match rigging had been scared off by their investigative lifeguards and that it was safe for the sunbathing punters to go back in the water for a dip, as their back page carried this headline: 'Try This Bet on your Fixed-Odds List'.

The bookmakers themselves did not seem over-concerned that their livelihoods could be at risk if the *Mail*'s stories were accurate. On 26 October 1960, both Hill's – 'The Best Bet in Football' – and Nufsed – 'Britain's Best Bet in Fixed-Odds' – were running large back-page adverts in the paper, both apparently quite happy to accept doubles i.e. bets on two matches. Surprising, surely, in view of the *Mail*'s fears that riggers were producing pre-ordained results week in, week out.

Even if this exposé had been somewhat light on detail, it would subsequently become obvious that the seeds of a far greater scandal had been well and truly sown and that within a very few years they would sprout prominently and threaten to overgrow the garden in which they had taken root, at least according to the lurid media coverage given to events which soon came to prominence.

The Football League had been receiving allegations of match fixing as well as the press. One correspondent had pointed the finger at a West Ham player, declaring that he had taken £1,000 to lose three matches, and it was true that the Hammers' shock 5–3 home defeat by Newcastle in February 1960 had been heavily backed, along with a similarly unlikely away win at Brentford by Grimsby on the same day, with fixed-odds bookmakers.

Another day, 23 April 1960, had also produced a number of suspicious results – Arsenal, out of form, beating Manchester United, unbeaten in five recent games by 5–2; Derby winning 1–2 at Swansea; Bolton beating Chelsea 2–0 and Nottingham Forest defeating Newcastle 3–0.

Five Oldham players had apparently made allegations following a game they played against Crewe, whose games were being monitored by the League.

The Football League, who had consulted with the FA and invited observations from certain players, had submitted their findings to the Director of Public Prosecutions but were ultimately advised by their lawyers that there was insufficient evidence available to justify starting proceedings.

Football League secretary Alan Hardaker made efforts to set up a full investigation via his management committee and won support from the likes of Manchester United manager Matt Busby. Incredibly, though, no such investigation ever took place, suggesting either that there really was no hard evidence available, or that the authorities preferred to try to sweep the matter under the carpet. It could have proved an embarrassing testimony to their own inefficiencies and to the iniquities of the game's current policies regarding payments to players, who were feeling inadequately rewarded. The structure of the game was still governed by a maximum wage system which, in June 1958, had been raised to £20 in the playing season and £17 in the close season – hardly a king's ransom, even with the addition of bonuses of £4 per win or £2 per draw. After Jimmy Hill led a threatened players' strike in January 1961 the maximum wage was finally abolished.

Returning to the vexed question of alleged match fixing, Hardaker gave full vent to his frustrations and suspicions in his 1977 autobiography:

> There are many men in football today, among them respected
> and celebrated managers, who have good reason to remember

the great bribery scandals of the early 1960s. They were deeply involved in the mess but escaped because the Law and the League could not get the evidence to nail them.

Once more, fine sounding rhetoric which makes it sound as though Hardaker and the League were well and truly on the case. But the plain truth remains that no action was taken, even though Hardaker was now insisting to his management committee that at least 20 clubs were involved in bribery, that betting on single matches was common and that fixing games was becoming so. Hardaker continued:

> Widespread gambling by footballers leads to them getting deeper and deeper into debt with the bookmakers, and sooner or later they are tempted to indulge in the fixing racket in order to square their outstanding debts.

More arresting words but with little to bolster them up. Hardaker alleged that the fixing was going on with the full knowledge of managers.

Some of his committee members just didn't believe him. One of them was Dr Andrew Stephen, Sheffield Wednesday chairman. Wednesday were one of the teams Hardaker was accusing, justifying his claims by pointing out that,

> It is now a matter of record that early in 1965 Tony Kay and Peter Swan, both England internationals, and David Layne, were all gaoled for four months for conspiring to prevent their team from winning a match in order to pull off a betting coup.

Indeed they were, but that was several seasons later, and involved only one game.

Hardaker contradicted himself in his own book when, having declared that fixing was rife, he later averred: 'One match can be fixed, two are difficult but three are just about impossible because of the number of people involved.'

However, in 1965, ten players were jailed for conspiring to rig matches, including the three mentioned by Hardaker. On 12 April 1964, the *People* carried a story headlined, 'The Biggest Sports Scandal of the Century', which named three first division footballers, two of them internationals, as having been involved in the fixing of a match, each of them having had a bet of £50 which included their own side being beaten. They were David 'Bronco' Layne, Peter Swan and Tony

99

Kay, and all three had played for Sheffield Wednesday in a 2–0 defeat at Ipswich on 1 December, 1962. They each made £100 profit on their bets which also depended on Lincoln losing at home to Brentford and York being beaten at Oldham.

The *People's* story was the culmination of investigations which had been continuing since 1960 when, as already recorded, Stoke's Jimmy O'Neill had reported being approached to throw a match against Norwich.

The key man in the whole saga turned out to be Jimmy Gauld, a Scottish player who had suffered a broken leg whilst playing for Mansfield Town. He had apparently set up a network of players paid to rig games on which he then bet. He claimed in 1964 that his syndicate had been netting £1,000 a week by betting on fixed-odds coupons.

The Sheffield Wednesday trio, and several other lesser-known players, were duly charged, along with Gauld, and on 26 January 1965, at Nottingham Assizes, they were amongst ten players sent to prison for conspiring to defraud bookmakers by fixing the results of matches.

Layne, Swan and Kay – the latter pair internationals – were each given four months imprisonment and were banned from soccer for life. Swan and Layne subsequently had their bans lifted and they played again in 1971. Kay emigrated to Spain and had no further involvement with the professional game. Gauld was sent to jail for four years and ordered to pay £5,000 costs.

Brian Phillips of Mansfield and Jack Fountain of York both received 15 month sentences; Dick Beattie (Peterborough) got nine months; Sammy Chapman (Mansfield), Ron Howells (Portsmouth) and Ken Thompson (Hartlepool) all received six-month sentences.

The method used by Gauld to work his system was to post coupons from different locations to several different betting companies in the names of different people, who included shopkeepers, a recruiting sergeant, a gas company worker, an electrical engineer and a long-distance lorry driver. Investigators working on behalf of the Football League but actually employed by the pools companies, supplied the League with vital names and evidence. This, together with the evidence turned up by the *People*, whose team was headed by investigative reporter Michael Gabbert, eventually gave the police the necessary ammunition with which to prove their case.

It transpired that as early as November 1961, Jimmy Gauld had been interviewed by Alan Hardaker and his investigators who, although not being entirely happy with his responses, had insufficient evidence with which to charge him. He was free to continue his wheelings and dealings for the best part of another two years, during which time, it emerged, 11 of the 14 allegedly crooked games were played.

Gauld had played for five different clubs during his career and he began to recruit personnel for his betting syndicate from personal acquaintances and friends of friends, ensuring that each new recruit knew as little as possible about the extent of his operations.

All went well for Gauld until April 1963, when Bristol Rovers goalkeeper Esmond Million conceded two goals against Bradford Park Avenue in such a suspicious manner that his boss, Bert Tann, confronted him, whereupon Million confessed what he had been up to. In July 1963, Million and team-mate Keith Williams were both fined £50 along with go-between Brian Phillips, who had played with Million at Middlesbrough. The three were banned permanently from football.

Gauld's name came up during the case at Doncaster Magistrates Court and the *People* were quickly on his trail. Once approached, Gauld readily admitted everything and agreed to co-operate with the *People* in return for a payment of £7,000. Gauld's co-operation and certain dubious set-up meetings and hidden recordings produced the evidence which incriminated many of his contacts.

Other suspect games mentioned during the case included a 1960 Swindon v Port Vale game and a Scottish fixture between St Mirren and Dundee.

Although not disputing their guilt, Layne, who once played with Gauld at Swindon, claimed: 'Gauld was just an old colleague. I went to a match at Mansfield and bumped into him in the car park. The irony was that I was never a gambling man. We had this bet as a result of his suggestion. There was never any question of throwing the game, and anyway the way things went our side was never in a position to win that day.'

Swan commented that when the other two discussed the scheme with him he told them, 'We'd got nothing to lose as Ipswich were really on song at that time. I told them we should just play our normal game, because we were going to lose anyway. I don't know what I'd have done if we'd been winning. Whether I'd have conceded a penalty or scored an own goal, I just don't know.'

In actual fact, Ipswich won only five home games that season and finished four points clear of the relegation zone while Wednesday finished in the top six. Ironically enough, in the game against Ipswich, Tony Kay was rated Wednesday's best player of the match by the *People*, who gave him an eight out of ten mark.

In 1997, the Sheffield Wednesday trio were thrust back into the limelight by a BBC TV programme about the affair, *The Fix*, written and directed by Paul Greengrass who said, 'The essential tragedy of those guys, was that they were caught just on the cusp of the change between two eras. If it had happened five years before, journalism would not have been like it was and they would never have been caught. There would have been far too many people in the game not willing to talk.

'Equally, if it had happened five years later they wouldn't have been caught because they would have been too cute.'

I'm not sure I can go along with that – after all, the *Mail* and the *People* managed to pick up on plenty of earlier possibly rigged games and I can't really see that five years down the line they would have been any more likely to get away with it. I don't think it is really possible to present these lads as the innocent Sheffield Wednesday Three but it is certainly possible to have some sympathy for the way in which players must have felt that they were being exploited in those days. Huge attendances were the norm yet the players were kept in their place and, even after the abolition of the maximum wage, still very much under-valued.

Tony Kay was asked in 1997 why he had become involved. He replied: 'I've asked myself why a thousand times and I haven't yet come up with an answer. I just thought we'd get beat.'

At the age of 60 in March 1997, Kay was still turning out in games – I even played against him myself a few years back in a fund-raising game for a team in Bushey, Herts, against an Arsenal celebrity side. I was playing for a team made up of fathers and friends from a local school and I think I was the only person on our side who knew Kay's background. When I mentioned it to one of my team-mates during half-time – we were taking a beating – he dared me to offer Kay a few quid to go easy in the second half. I didn't, of course, but it demonstrates the stigma with which he must have had to live for many years, and which he has clearly never been able to live down.

One angle on the whole affair which has been rarely if ever reported is the bookmakers'. One who was directly involved was Jack Pointer of Norwich, now retired, who told me: 'One Saturday, customers – mostly trade [other bookmakers] – all wanted to back against Sheffield Wednesday. We then barred this match.

'I was certain some defenders at Sheffield Wednesday were trying to fix their matches. I reported this to Alan Hardaker of the Football League, by phone and letter.

'Frankly, he did not want to know. The following week he visited Norwich for Anglia TV to take part in a sports programme. He stayed at a Norwich hotel overnight, but did not even wish to make contact with me.

'I phoned the BBC who asked me to appear on their sports programme at 6 p.m., on which I stated the game between Ipswich and Sheffield Wednesday was fixed. The following day a reporter from the *Sunday People* was in my office and I gave him all the details. Incidentally, the BBC paid me £50 for appearing.'

Jack also had his suspicions about two Irish defenders playing for another first division side. Regardless of this, there were certainly a considerable number of games implicated in the affair.

On 21 October 1961, Tranmere won at York and Bradford City at Mansfield. Odds of 10/1 were apparently offered about the double, although with both games reportedly looking like home bankers one might have expected double odds of nearer 20/1.

A number of winning bets on these two games were, it transpired, placed in Yorkshire and, more suspiciously, in the same names. A bookmaker investigation allegedly revealed that a dozen punters had placed bets with 20 betting companies – winnings were withheld. These punters were identified and interviewed by Football league investigators but were believed to be largely genuine – to the bizarre extent that they were reported to have agreed to forfeit their winnings when told that the games were suspected of being fixed. They were obviously not out of the same mould as every punter I have ever met!

One, though, was not so co-operative. He kicked up a fuss and demanded his winnings. His name was Jimmy Gauld, an injured Mansfield Town footballer. He was given a clean bill of health by investigators, even after being interviewed again by Alan Hardaker himself.

In April 1963, bookmakers were again reported to be feeling aggrieved as some £100,000 was said to have been lost on a 6/4 home double, with Derby beating Scunthorpe 6–2 and Stockport seeing off Hartlepool by 4–1. At 6/4 that suggests that at least £40,000 was staked on this combination of games – an extraordinary sum. Some bookmakers refused to accept further wagers, amongst them a certain Jack Pointer, who was quoted in the *People* at the time as saying: 'There is likely to be such a stink that the FA will have to investigate.'

In the same article, the *People* also commented: 'Bets of £50 to £1,000 a time were placed at the same time with bookies all over Britain. Desperate bookies tried to lay off . . . and by mid-afternoon on Friday it was impossible to bet on the two games.' A close look at these two games suggests that their outcome would have been no great surprise to form students. Hartlepool were rock bottom of division four, having lost 14 of their 19 games, while Stockport were well-placed in mid-table. In the other game, Scunthorpe were notoriously unreliable on their travels, losing ten of their 17 outings, although as Derby were fifth from bottom it might seem somewhat bold to risk massive amounts on them winning – and the 6–2 margin may well have raised eyebrows.

Then came the Million affair which ended up in court as we have already seen. 'These are isolated cases,' claimed the FA.

In May 1963, the Football League banned fixed-odds bets on doubles, making trebles the minimum acceptable wager. Escaping horses, stable doors and locks must have come to mind.

In August 1963, Ken Thomson of Hartlepool confessed to betting on his own team losing (as they almost always did in those days) at Exeter. He won £200 and admitted to taking bribes, but denied that he had actually to do anything to collect. Thomson was also guilty of being involved in attempts to rig games against Stockport and Crewe, winning £327 on the first game and losing £50 on the second. Thomson, it transpired, knew Esmond Million and Brian Phillips. He was banned for life by the FA.

On 11 August 1963, the *People* named Jimmy Gauld as the mastermind of the betting syndicate. He said that he first got involved in match rigging when playing for Swindon in 1959–60 when he heard that Tranmere and Mansfield players had agreed that Rovers would win the match between the two sides, with Mansfield already sure to go down. It was suggested to Gauld that if he could arrange for his own team to lose to Port Vale on the same day they would have a good double to bet on. Mansfield lost 2–0, Swindon lost 6–1, but Gauld only managed to make a £40 profit on his wagers, he later alleged.

During the next season, Gauld really developed his syndicate, and claimed that players even began to contact him unsolicited.

'I was amazed by the number of players who were eager, not just willing, to get into the act,' he said.

On 18 August, the FA revealed that it knew of nine crooked players and that 'there will be a further enquiry'. Bookmakers announced that they were arranging to set up an early warning system to detect possible coups. In the autumn, Gauld was fined £60 by Rochdale magistrates for offering bribes to footballers.

He now began to deal with the *People* to entrap others involved, apparently without any qualms. By the spring of 1964, the paper was ready to go public with more allegations, and on 12 April the Sheffield Wednesday revelations stunned the sporting world. On 19 April the *People* 'outed' several more players, including Scottish Under-23 keeper Dick Beattie, described by the paper as 'an artist at deliberately letting in goals while appearing to have unluckily missed making a miraculous save'.

An FA commission held in Sheffield on 2 May banned Gauld for life from the game. By this time bookmaker Joe Hancock, believed to be involved in Gauld's syndicate, had committed suicide by drowning, fearing that he was about to be exposed.

With the 1966 World Cup looming, everyone was keen to put this scandal behind them, although Barnsley MP Roy Mason and his Stoke counterpart Ellis Smith encouraged the Government to investigate the whole question of football bribery.

In his *A Strange Kind of Glory*, about Sir Matt Busby and Manchester United, controversial author Eamon Dunphy reveals that 'there is no doubt in my mind that Manchester United players did conspire to fix the result of at least three games during the 1960–63 period.' Dunphy alleges that former United keeper Harry Gregg told him that although he had refused to participate himself, matches were thrown by some of his colleagues. Dunphy says that although the media had got wind of the story, Matt Busby managed to persuade the *Daily Mail* not to publish the allegations, after which he had a showdown with his players.

By 1977, Alan Hardaker was able to declare that he believed that only one further attempt to fix a game had been made, and rejected.

Author Simon Inglis believed in 1985 that 'with players' wages so much higher nowadays the relative demands of a "bent" footballer would be high enough to make such a gamble [rigging matches to win bets] comparatively unprofitable.'

A shady, underworld figure claimed that a 'ruthless gambling gang' had twice pulled off a daring coup during the late 1980s by deliberately sabotaging the floodlighting system at grounds when matches were going the way they had bet on. Self-confessed fugitive Harry Rogers revealed details of the affair to *People* journalist Brian Radford in September 1995. He claimed that he had become involved because the gang knew that he could place hefty bets for them and they wanted him to put £50,000 on the outcome of a game which would not go the distance.

In those days bookmakers had a rule which said that bets on abandoned games would be settled on the score at the time of abandonment. Today, the vast majority of bookies will make such a game void for betting purposes.

The gang allegedly took Rogers to Brighton for a dress rehearsal and he watched 'as they poured a can of sulphuric acid over power cables' with predictable results. Claimed Rogers: 'They pulled it off twice. On the second occasion they discovered the football ground had a stand-by generator, so they had to sabotage that as well.' Rogers was only prepared to add that both games 'were played in a low division'. The games were both played prior to August 1989 when Rogers, 49, quit the country – he was being sought by police investigating a massive fraud.

John Johnson of BOLA (Betting Office Licensees Association) commented: 'If the bet was shrewdly placed and the football element was included with other events, there's no reason why they shouldn't have got away with it.'

The *European* newspaper disclosed in March 1997 that UEFA had set up a 'top secret, anti-corruption committee' in 1996, charged with keeping tabs on allegations of match rigging, bribery and corruption. Secretary of the committee, Rene Eberle was quoted as saying, 'We are actively pursuing a number of cases. In a lot of cases we run into a dead end and sometimes we get furious.'

Amongst his fellow committee members were Norway's Arnold Nilsen, a former high-ranking police officer, and Wilhelm Hennes of Germany, a former chief justice.

One area on which the committee may have to keep an eye is spread betting, warned *Guardian* journalist Julian Turner in his 1995 book, *Gambling*:

> On a smaller scale, spread betting may offer more innocent opportunities for stealing a march on the bookies. It has been suggested, for instance, that certain professional footballers with a gambling bent have taken a particular interest in some of the less central indexes: a player who has bought a spread on the number of times a trainer visits the pitch or sold one on the time of the first booking, has both the incentive and ability to influence the action without risking disaster.

Three big-name footballers and a Malaysian businessman twice stood trial during 1997 over allegations that large sums of money changed hands in order to influence the outcome of important English matches.

The prosecution in the first trial claimed that goalkeepers Bruce Grobbelaar of Liverpool, Southampton and Zimbabwe, and Dutch-born Hans Segers of Wimbledon, had taken cash to throw matches, while striker John Fashanu of Wimbledon and Aston Villa, was a go-between. Businessman Heng Suan Lim was the link between the players and a Far Eastern-based betting syndicate that allegedly master-minded the scam. The case against the four was based on evidence of huge cash transactions said to have been made by Indonesians.

Grobbelaar was accused of taking a £40,000 bribe to throw a game in November 1993 when Liverpool, for whom he was playing, lost 3–0 to Newcastle. It was alleged that he could also have collected £125,000 for throwing a game against Manchester United, but the match ended 3–3 in January 1994.

Hans Segers was accused of taking large sums to throw matches involving Wimbledon, in deals set up by Fashanu, then his friend.

Fashanu, also well known as a host of TV gameshow *Gladiators*, was accused of handing £40,000 to Grobbelaar following the Liverpool–Newcastle game, and receiving £20,000 from Indonesian sources.

Heng Suan Lim was said to have contacted the three men on numerous occasions via mobile phone calls.

During the first case, heard early in 1997, 25 Liverpool, Southampton and Wimbledon matches, played between November 1993 and November 1994, were named as being the subject of match-fixing allegations. However, after 34 days, the case ended sensationally on 4 March when the jury of eight men and three women was discharged after telling the judge, Mr Justice Tuckey, that they could not reach a verdict, even when permitted to reach a 10–1 majority decision. The trial was re-scheduled for June 1997.

The case had been triggered in August 1994, after the *Sun* newspaper carried allegations that Grobbelaar had accepted bribes. The keeper's former friend and business partner, Christopher Vincent, had told the *Sun* that Grobbelaar was involved in match rigging for a Far East gambling syndicate. Meetings were arranged between Grobbelaar and Vincent, monitored by the paper's investigators, during which Grobbelaar was filmed on video, allegedly accepting a £2,000 payment from a bogus betting syndicate. Grobbelaar later claimed that he, in turn, was trying to entrap Vincent.

During the first trial, Fashanu declined to give evidence; Grobbelaar claimed that he had been stringing Vincent along in order to discover who was behind the attempted rigging; Segers denied all allegations of match fixing, but admitted receiving £45,000 for forecasting the outcome of Dutch matches for Lim. Counsel Jerome Lynch said: 'Mr Lim did no more than forecast for his benefactors in Indonesia.' Lim admitted paying Grobbelaar and Segers for giving match predictions, and also mentioned other players, current and former, as being advisers. Lim told the court that an Indonesian 'benefactor', Johannes Josef, would bet up to £50,000 a week on English matches.

The re-trial produced a climax even more dramatic than the original. It began at Winchester Crown Court on Wednesday, 4 June 1997 and finally ended on Friday, 8 August 1997 when, after two trials, lasting 17 weeks and costing more than £12 million, Grobbelaar, Fashanu and Segers were found not guilty of conspiring with Heng Suan Lim to receive and give corrupt payments from a Far Eastern betting syndicate.

Grobbelaar was cleared of a charge of corruption after he was filmed accepting £2,000 allegedly to influence the outcome of a match. The jury could not agree a verdict on the charge after lengthy considerations, and Mr Justice McCullough formally entered a verdict of Not Guilty.

The Football Association immediately ordered a review of its rules on betting and forecasting relating to those within the game. Said Director of Public Affairs, David Davies: 'It is essential that nobody is in any doubt that players have only one motive in every game and that is for their team to win.' The FA had invited evidence of match fixing when allegations were first made against the defendants in the Winchester trial, but said that none had been forthcoming. Mr Davies reiterated the request, asking for 'any evidence of wrong-doing to be brought to our attention immediately.' The FA investigation was set up under the former Metropolitan Police Deputy Commissioner, Sir John Smith.

After the case Fashanu said: 'I was dragged into this storm two and a half years ago. I have maintained my right to silence. I'm not bitter at all.'

Grobbelaar said: 'You should never have doubted me. There's never been a game thrown in the past and there won't be in the future.'

Segers commented: 'We got the verdicts we wanted and deserved.' By late August Segers was signing for Wolves, while Grobbelaar was once again involved with the Zimbabwe national side and then signed for Sheffield Wednesday.

Controversially, the judge refused a plea for costs from Fashanu and Segers, saying that 'Mr Fashanu brought suspicion on himself' and accusing Segers of telling 'lie upon lie upon lie' when offered the chance to explain £104,000 paid into a Swiss bank account.

Reaction to the verdicts was mixed. The *Daily Mail*, in an opinion column, declared: 'The Mandarins of our national sport . . . are merely deluding themselves if they think that 'the stench of suspicion has gone away.' Stan Hey, in the *Independent on Sunday* said: 'If the notion took hold that games themselves might be influenced by outside elements such as betting, football would become a pariah sport.' A *Sun* opinion column on 9 August 1997, said 'The fans . . . are entitled to know that the game is cleaner than clean. The evidence that came out of

Winchester Crown Court over the past ten weeks did little to allay their fears.'

The bookmaking industry was relieved that the case produced no evidence to back up frequently reported allegations that domestic football was being targeted by match riggers. It is worth recording here that I am not aware of any suspicious betting patterns associated with the matches mentioned during the course of the Winchester trial, nor with any other domestic matches of recent years. Bookmakers are not complacent but the feeling within the industry is that in the event of match rigging being attempted, evidence would soon emerge of untoward betting patterns centred on the games involved. Bookmakers have a strongly developed sense of self preservation and would soon draw attention to such a phenomenon.

I deal in greater detail with the relationship between the FA and betting in the opening chapter of this book, but I should like to consider the question of forecasting, which has never previously been referred to in FA Rules.

Following the Court cases, Grobbelaar and Segers were, on 18 September 1997, charged by the FA with breaking their Rules on betting. As this book went to press the pair were facing the possibility of a lengthy ban from the game if found guilty.

Grobbelaar had recently joined Sheffield Wednesday for a limited spell and Hans Segers had signed for Wolverhampton Wanderers.

The charges were apparently made as a result of evidence the pair had given at their trial regarding the forecasting of match results. If the FA charge were to be based on this 'forecasting' element of the Grobbelaar/Segers defence it would appear to open a potential can of worms with regard to football figures – such as West Ham manager Harry Redknapp, who had a tipping column in the *Racing Post* – even offering an opinion as to the outcome of matches.

Taken to its logical conclusion, a ban on forecasting could result in the ludicrous situation where a non-League manager or player facing a 3rd Round FA Cup tie away at Old Trafford, or Anfield, would be unable to admit the likelihood of defeat lest he face a penalty for contravening the forecasting rule, if such should be introduced. Basically, rules on forecasting must, by definition, endeavour to quash speculation – which would be a nonsensical, unenforceable situation. Horse racing rules ban jockeys (but not owners and trainers) from gambling – but even this authoritarian sport has never sought to crack down on forecasting – even if the passing of information could be construed in certain circumstances as contravening regulations. It is common practice for jockeys to appear on TV programmes like

Channel Four's *Morning Line*, a gambling-based show, and to predict the outcome of races in which they are riding. They don't always predict that they will win these races, but I have never heard anyone accuse them of conspiring to lose deliberately if they subsequently are beaten. I should also mention the self-evident truth of the long-standing adage, which would no doubt apply to footballers, that jockeys make lousy tipsters!

Writing in his 1997 book *To Win Just Once*, jockey Guy Lewis admitted that some of his colleagues can and will bet. He pointed out: 'There are ways of backing a horse which don't necessarily involve going round the betting ring in your riding silks with a wad of fivers in your hand.'

In my opinion, the FA inquiry into gambling and forecasting was little more than a cosmetic, face-saving exercise to avoid having to give direct and possibly embarrassing answers to awkward questions in the immediate aftermath of the match-rigging trial. No one could support a situation in which players were rewarded for forecasts only on the basis that the ultimate outcome of the matches met with the satisfaction of the forecast purchaser. You might also believe it would be circumspect for players/managers/officials not to accept payment for information involving games in which they have a direct interest and which they might believe could be used in order to encourage bets to be placed against the teams with which they are involved. You might also believe that it would be very difficult to prevent such activities by means of an FA rule. Those who wish to do it are unlikely to be deterred by such a measure. Forecasting, like betting, is in 99.9 per cent of instances entirely harmless and highly unlikely to represent a risk to the integrity of the sport.

Have a rule, by all means – but be prepared to enforce it on every relevant occasion, or just don't even bother with the rule. Better still, do not have a specific rule to cover forecasting but make sure a mechanism for dealing with undesirable incidents of such a type exists in the 'disrepute' section of the game's laws, because forecasting in itself is not a problem for the sport, although the misuse or potential abuse of it could possibly become so in an extreme situation.

CHAPTER FOUR

Of Tipsters and Systems

Some of my longest-standing professional friends make a living out of trying to predict the outcome of soccer matches. I believe that football tipsters have been around since well before 1925 when the *People* became the first national newspaper to introduce a column predicting the outcome of football matches. But, notwithstanding the fact that people like Derrick Shaw of the *Sporting Life* and Derek McGovern of the *Racing Post* may decide to cut me out of their wills, I feel I have to pose the question: football tipsters – why?

I mean, horse-racing tipsters have a tough enough job trying to sort out the winner of every race, but at least they have a comprehensive form book to work with; and, with the invaluable assistance of the Racing Channel, Sky TV, Channel 4, BBC and SIS, which broadcasts the daily racing programme into the nation's betting shops, they can watch every race as it happens – and file it for future dissection and analysis. How many games can football tipsters possibly watch in full every week? Maybe a dozen? How can they hope to know those little bits of inside information and outside influences which can determine the outcome of a match? Yes, the papers give details of injured players and behind-the-scenes wrangling, but how accurate is that kind of media information? And how often do clubs deliberately spread dis-information in order to disguise the real situation from the opposition?

Take, for example, a game I went to see in January 1997, between 'my' team (since 1959!) Luton Town, and Wrexham. This was a match which virtually every so-called tipster was giving as a banker home win.

You could work out the logic of their selection process, which had probably taken them a few seconds to put in action. Luton had a lengthy run of successive home victories to their credit and were sitting in second place in the second division table. Mid-table Wrexham were suffering from a certain inconsistency of late – easy, banker home.

Life just isn't like that. I could have told them that Luton without skipper Gary Waddock, out injured, were nowhere near the same force. The game was coming after a big freeze which had left the Hatters without a match for almost a month, while Wrexham had played recently. Luton were notoriously slow starters after a lay-off and had lost their first three games of the season to prove it. The game ended 0–0.

These were factors which the so-called experts would be extremely unlikely to have taken into account; nor would they have been aware that I had altered my own pre-match preparation for the game – which was bound to affect the result. All right, I'm exaggerating slightly – but only a little. It is just not possible to forecast with any degree of certainty the outcome of a football match, *unless* you get together a genuine fan of each of the sides due to play and quiz them about their gut feeling on the result. (An Internet site is planned to exploit this system for the 1997–98 season.) Nine times out of ten I believe a real supporter just knows instinctively what will happen to his or her team on a given occasion. If the two supporters agree, then you've got a banker result.

As for the chances of a chap with just the bare results to go on, and a little bit of team information, being able to tip you worthwhile results – just forget it. Let's face it, if there was genuinely a way of accurately forecasting results, those same tipsters would be helping themselves to large amounts of cash, courtesy of philanthropic bookies and generous pools companies. Within a week or two, any turf accountant foolish enough to continue to advertise odds about matches would be out of business. Oddly, though, that doesn't seem to happen, does it?

This line of thought seems to have occurred to Messrs B. Seebohm Rowntree and G.R. Lavers, way back in 1951 when their *English Life and Leisure* was published, in which they pointed out: 'If by relying on form sports writers could win football pools, they would probably prefer gambling as a career to journalism.'

However, in defence of the tipsters I have just been rubbishing, I should point out that the greatest obstacle they face is that they are expected to offer an opinion on every match played throughout a season. This gives them a task on a par with the weather man who is burdened with the job of telling us what the elements will get up to everywhere, everyday. It can't be done.

However, as punting meteorologist Piers Corbyn, who makes a healthy profit from staking £10,000 per annum on the selective vagaries of the British climate, will attest, some make a better fist of it than others – and the methods the tipsters or forecasters use can vary dramatically.

The majority just opt for the straightforward analysis of current form from which to make a prediction – nothing which anyone with access to the league tables and the last couple of weeks' results couldn't do.

Others are more devious. Kevin Pullein of the *Sporting Life* is always looking for significant pointers overlooked by others – teams who regularly lead at half-time, only to be pegged back, for example; or those who consistently concede goals in the last five minutes; or those who never beat certain opponents.

Another popular method is deliberately focusing on the odds available and tipping on that basis, e.g. in a match where the home team has the best form and is odds-on, but the away team has a good record against them over the years, select the draw as the most likely outcome.

Still others go for the *Boston Globe* school of tipping – always go for the unconsidered outsider because no one will notice when you get it wrong, but everyone will pay attention when you are the one who correctly goes for Hartlepool to win away at Manchester United. This technique is inspired by and named in honour of the one newspaper bold enough to back Evander Holyfield to beat Mike Tyson in 1996 – the newspaper will feed off that fact for years to come regardless of whether it finds another winner over the next decade or not.

What's more, you should always beware of claims about the efficiency or otherwise of a tipping service; they will invariably be of a very selective type, if not downright misleading.

Having given a sound coating to the tipping profession, I decided it would be only fair to allow members of the tipsters' union to defend themselves, an invitation which Derrick Shaw of the *Sporting Life*, one of the longest-surviving football pundits in the business, was quick to accept.

'How many matches can we watch a week?' he countered. 'Fair enough, not that many – though satellite coverage has helped with the Premiership. We do have a sort of form book with match-by-match coverage in some of the football weeklies, while we also have access to all the agency reports.

'There's no doubt we are better informed than the average punter and I have an interesting question to put to the author, who is the mouthpiece for William Hill. If, as he suggests, both the press and punters are ignorant of the little things that lead to good forecasting and tipping, why, oh why, does his firm, along with the other bookmaking chains, make a rule on Saturdays of a five-time minimum for selections, when a home is included, in a coupon bet?

'Surely, if we are rubbish, minimum trebles would not be taking much of a chance.

'I know that racing folk have blanket TV coverage on SIS – sad cases, I suppose, watch every race – but give me a home, away or draw choice every time.

'The non-trier element is eliminated in most cases and racing is much more open to "fixing" than football.

'Footballers can perform on most surfaces, and the only thing to get on their backs is the manager, and sometimes the fans.

'The author also refers to "bankers". What does the term mean? How many "bankers" do you find these days on football coupons? Being a bit of an old grunter, with over 20 years of football forecasting under my belt, I remember when there were genuine "bankers" on lists. These were generally in the lower divisions, but these days, with the loan system prevalent and so many footballers seeking employment, clubs dredge the football internet for new faces and ideas. In these circumstances, how can a supporter from each side be certain they have a "banker"?

'Football betting these days, with the arrival of the spread betting firms, is a major industry. This was not always so. Back in the '70s, long before individual-odds coupons arrived *en masse* in the betting shops, the big punting medium was the FA Cup. Just as now, bookmakers took singles for the ties in those days and a betting-starved public piled in. Bets of £5,000 on a single team to win a tie were not uncommon – I reported extensively on these transactions.

'The first match I reported for the *Life* was Arsenal versus Portsmouth in the early '70s, and, not having a telephone, I had to dive out of the ground before the end to find one locally. When I left the scores were level, but Arsenal won with a late penalty. You could rightly accuse me of not seeing that one!'

Racing Post football pundit, Derek McGovern – the brother, incidentally, of controversial TV writer Jimmy – was also quick to rebuff my condemnation of his profession.

'There's little doubt that soccer is the most difficult of all sports from which to make a living by betting,' he said, 'so it follows that soccer tipsters have their work cut out to stay ahead of the game.

'Everything the author of this book says about the difficulties in following the progress of lower-division teams is true. He should also have added that bookmakers handicap punters further still by their demands for minimum trebles or five-timers on weekend coupons. Finding one winner is hard enough: three, a minor miracle.

'But, it's not all gloom and doom for tipsters. There are loopholes we can exploit.

'If it is hard for tipsters to keep tabs on the progress of the Shrewsburys and the Lincolns of this world, it's equally exhausting for the bookies' soccer odds compilers. And their workload is hardly helped by the fact that it is their duty to price up *all* English and Scottish league matches of a weekend – tipsters on the other hand can pick and choose.

'At the risk of sounding arrogant, the soccer tipster's very profession gives him a huge advantage over the deadly enemy.

'Football managers and players are more likely to talk to newspaper reporters than to odds compilers, unless there's a heavy fee involved! We can find out before bookies about injury worries, absences, even suspensions. Some, an unsung full-back for instance, may be irrelevant; others, like a midfield dynamo, hugely significant.

'Odds compilers must also labour under cruel deadlines, often handing tipsters, and therefore punters, a huge advantage. Odds for Saturday coupons are generally compiled the previous Saturday night to be available in betting shops on Monday, or at the latest, Tuesday. But it is conceivable that a team quoted at, say, 11/4 for the following Saturday, could first win a match on the Monday and then again on the Wednesday beforehand. Clearly their form is on the upturn and there's little doubt that bookies, given the chance, would love to shave that 11/4 to something like 2/1. But they can't. The coupons are already printed and in the shops.

'This is the greatest weapon in the tipster's armoury – the inability of bookies, save for live TV matches when betting soars, to change their odds once printed. Hence the name "fixed" odds.

'I'm not suggesting for a minute here that soccer tipping, successful soccer tipping that is, is a doddle. Far from it. Tennis matches, boxing bouts, snooker showdowns, can all go to plan because it is the form of only two players that matters. In football the form of all 22 can have a bearing. That's why we see so many shock results.

'But diligent homework, the opportunities the early show of odds give us to stay a jump ahead of the bookmakers, and the privileged position newspaper tipsters enjoy should all combine, if not to give us an advantage, at least to level the playing field.'

I am grateful to Derrick and Derek for supplying those well-argued defences of their profession. I wouldn't want to put myself in the firing line as a tipster on a regular basis – even though it seems that there is a

gentleman working in the Federal Department of Fisheries in Nigeria
who seems to be convinced that I know in advance the results of all the
football matches played in this country. He's not the only one – on
average I used to receive a letter a month from that country, demanding
that I let them in on the secret. Quite why they believe I am privy to this
useful information, I cannot say, but listen to what the Fisheries
Department man (whose name was illegible) wanted from me: 'Five
draws, starting from week ten until the end of the English season.' In
case I failed to grasp the point of a bookie providing punters with
winners (even if it were possible) he added, 'The business will be done
strictly on a credit basis – and a substantial part of my business will be
sent to you.'

One of my other correspondents guessed that I had 'secret keys to
draws which I can arrange to buy from you. If, on the alternative, you
are not in possession of the keys would you therefore be good enough
to direct me to such addresses.' Then he confided why he wanted these
mysterious keys: 'To enable me to make a fortune.'

In December 1996, another letter from Nigeria arrived, signed by
one Maven Ogbonna from Izombe and headed: 'Request for a Nap and
a Life Key'.

> After several attempts without the slightest success, I decided to
> stop playing the pool game. But when I read your advert in one
> of the pool telegraphs I decided to try to write and ask if you will
> be able to sort out a five draws nap so that I will try again. Then
> when sending the nap, you now state the possible conditions I
> must meet to be able to have a life key so that after playing the
> nap I now write again and collect the key but please make the
> conditions light for me.

I have developed a theory that just as you can go abroad and purchase
'genuine' Rolex watches of dubious origin at cut-price rates, so some
unscrupulous operator in Africa has taken to passing himself off as a
representative of world-famous London bookmaker William Hill and
advertising tipping sheets for sale. Occasionally some disgruntled
customer, almost certainly unable to secure any satisfactory outcome to
complaints at the African address, takes a flyer and sends off a letter
vaguely addressed to William Hill, England. Some of them find their
way on to my desk, but still fail to produce any worthwhile resolution
of the poor pools player's problems. Sorry, chaps.

Well, I'm afraid I couldn't help them, but I do remember someone
who may once have been able to – that legendary gentleman who used

to advertise regularly during the 1960s on Radio Luxembourg (remember listening under the covers as the signal faded in and out of range) that he could predict infallibly the results of soccer matches, and who used to sign off as 'Mr Horace Batchelor of Keynsham, that's K E Y N S H A M. I've no idea what his system was – I could not afford in my early teens to send off the cash to find out – so if you happen to know . . .

I once had to delay my Sunday lunch so that I could appear on a radio programme with an astrologer who was going to predict the outcome of the 1994–95 football season by making deductions from the dates of birth of the players in the various clubs involved in the Premiership, Football League and Scottish league competitions. Yeah, right, that is what I thought, too – and I don't think I was far wrong, either. Terri King, for it was she who was doing the predicting whilst plugging her new book and taking some time out from producing horoscopes for *Daily Star* readers, clearly had not the slightest idea about football. She proved that, in my humble opinion, by predicting that Arsenal would do well because of David Seaman's star sign – as if he could be the only Premiership player born under that sign, whatever it may be.

She's not the first astrologer, clairvoyant, star-gazer, palmist or other would-be Mystic Mug I've met who has claimed to be able to predict the winners of horse races or football matches. When you ask them why they haven't become wealthy by backing their own selections, they become very much holier than thou, and retreat behind a stream of unlikely sounding excuses and reasons which tend to be a variation on the 'I wasn't given this gift to enrich myself' routine. Well, I know that I for one would have no objection if they chose to enrich me by imparting their knowledge in my direction – I wouldn't even insist that they sully their hands by burdening themselves with the problems of what to do with suddenly acquired riches.

He claims to tip guaranteed winners, but I can't help classing Lancaster University statistician Mark Dixon as a definite loser. What do you make of a man who has 'what he claims is a foolproof method of taking money off bookmakers' and even convinced *The Times* to carry a lengthy article by their science editor, Nigel Hawkes, all about it – but who then reveals that he 'has not placed any bets, since the process would be time-consuming' and he 'is a researcher, not a punter'.

Dr Mark Dixon published details of his 'foolproof' football betting plan in an academic journal. However, said *The Times*, 'The only problem is that users of the method need a degree in statistics to understand it – and a powerful computer to make it work.'

Dr Dixon's method assumes that each team in the Premiership and Football League has certain parameters, such as attacking and defensive ability, that can be measured by feeding past results into a computer programme which contains data covering two seasons' worth of games. The programme then predicts the chances of a home win, away win or draw for each fixture and compares its percentage predictions against the bookmakers' odds.

In a small number of games the computer predictions will show that the bookmakers are offering more generous odds than they should be, and a (theoretical) bet is placed on that selection by Dr Dixon, whose results apparently show enough accuracy to turn every £10 wagered into £12 – a 20 per cent profit rate.

To be fair to Dr Dixon, he and I once underwent a challenge on TV's *Tomorrow's World* which put his tips to the test and he did indeed make a profit. But, surely, even the most cloistered or committed of academics could not pass up the opportunity of a regular, guaranteed, non-taxable cashflow, courtesy of the bookies, could he? Sorry, Doc – loser!

One hazard to which most football tipsters would never give a second thought is the danger of being reported to the authorities for doing their job badly. But in October 1992 the Press Complaints Commission revealed that it had received correspondence from a reader, complaining that 'press predictions of the Australian football results were inaccurate'. Fortunately for the unnamed tipster from the unnamed paper, the PCC contented itself by pointing out to the complainant that 'predictions are not always accurate'. Perhaps that adjudication should have said: 'Predictions are almost never accurate.'

I think '60s gambling writer L.J. Ludovici had a somewhat jaundiced view of those who earn a living by advising others how to place their bets. In *The Itch for Play* he was somewhat scathing:

> Professional tipsters tell us how to win our hundreds, our thousands and our tens of thousands.
>
> All tipsters rely upon our gullibility rather than upon their own advice to do that very thing; and there are as many tips and tipsters as there are newspapers. It is like the old story of the expert who guarantees to grow hair on the baldest of pates. When the customer, brimming with hope, rushes in he finds to his consternation that the expert is himself as bald as a coot.

Mr Ludovici would certainly have had a chuckle at the efforts of some of the best-known names in football who were quizzed before

England's home World Cup qualifying match against Italy in February 1997 which England lost 1–0. The *Racing Post* asked how the interviewees/tipsters would advise people to bet £100 on the game: 'England to win 2–0,' declared Mick Channon; 'It would have to be the draw,' said former England international Peter Osgood; 'England without doubt,' England full-back Kenny Sansom; 'I feel strongly that England will win this game,' former international turned manager, Joe Royle, who also confessed: 'I bet quite often but I'm not a big gambler. Certainly no bookie would win a fortune off me.' With tips like that, he would eventually, Joe.

Yes, I know it is eminently unfair to take an unrepresentative example and draw misleading conclusions from it – but I have to confess that I grinned along with the *Guardian* which, on Saturday, 1 March 1997 pointed out: 'And they are supposed to be experts. Because the West Ham v Tottenham 4-3 thriller was moved from Saturday to Monday for television, the Pools Panel had to give their verdict on the score: 0–0.'

Manchester publishing family, the Stoddarts, launched *Sporting Luck* in 1890 at one penny per week, which was one of the first papers to concern itself with predicting the results of football matches, arriving on the scene just after the October 1889 launch of Manchester-based tipster, *Umpire's Football Programme and Weekly Calendar*. Both publications also included free entry coupons inviting readers to predict the outcome of football matches to win cash prizes.

The Weekly Football Star appeared in 1894, offering advice on the likely outcome of matches to betting-minded readers. Five years later a publication called *Invaluable to Couponites* also promised to assist in the quest for riches via soccer wagers, but following the *Excelsior System* in 1910 would have proved a quick route to the poor house:

> You select a Professional Football Team, and back it to draw every week. [Anyone who continued to read from this point for any purpose other than a hearty laugh was destined for financial problems.] The fixed odds for a draw being 3–1 against, a glance at the League tables will show that every team averages a Draw about every fourth or fifth game, now, what you have to do is back it two weeks with an even stake, then double it on the third.

Oh dear – variations on this staking plan, which makes no allowance for an extended absence of draws, are still doing the rounds today, usually amongst impoverished roulette players.

W.J. Duckworth hailed from Padiham in Lancashire – the same part of the world as that other celebrated but unsuccessful punter, *Coronation Street*'s Jack – and in 1914 produced *The Incomparable Football Forecasting System* which promised 'My system has been fully tested' and that it was based on 'the only possible and most profitable system . . . the law of averages'. What it boiled down to, though, was backing any team to have won its last four matches – well, unless their opponents had also won their last four games, in which case you'd opt for the home side. Just *who* they had beaten in their last four matches didn't seem to much concern Mr Duckworth!

In 1932 a book called *Football Betting Systems* came up with a new way of finding winning results: 'The theories are based upon the "permutation" method used by "Senior Wrangler" in the solution of cross-words.' I'll leave you to dwell on the likely chances of success of such a system.

One of my favourite tipping systems was revealed just prior to the start of the 1950–51 season and was available to all for a mere shilling (5p), the cost of buying the *News of the World*'s *Football Pools Guide* in which Adrienne Arden, the paper's astrologer 'outlines an ingenious new System' (note the capital S) which, it transpired, was based on the Planets.

'First, you must know your planet.' To discover yours you had to consult a chart listing birth-dates and linking them to a planet; 23 November, my birthday, linked me with Jupiter. Next, we learned, each day also has a planet which will 'exercise some influence over the day's events'. It follows, then, that if you know your planet, and you know the planet for the day, you can choose the best time to study form or complete your actual coupon. Get the picture? But I can't understand just why the system, sorry System, made no mention whatsoever of . . . Uranus – which is probably the best place to store details of this bizarre scheme.

There is no shortage of tipsters only too willing to part novice punters from their cash – sorry, eager to assist newcomers to invest wisely in the eternal battle with the bookmakers. Just a glance at a publication like the weekly *Racing & Football Outlook* during the 1996–97 season revealed ads like: 'Professional Football Tips – 10 weeks for only £15 – you either want to win or not!' Who are these people who want not to win, one wonders?

Then a philanthropist from Brighton declares: 'Fixed-Odds Blockbuster – Averages ONE BIG WIN a month – Completely FREE to clients who send two 26p stamps. A year's FREE supply if you don't win.' A free supply of what?

'Treble Chance method – has given 8 and more draws every week this season.' (So would my method – tip every game to be a draw.) 'Was £75, yours FREE if you enclose 2x26p stamps.' This from a chap in Gloucester.

Or, what about joining the 'Football Fixed-odds Club'? 'We offer our clients value for money honesty consistency' (and, incidentally, freedom from punctuation). 'Advice with no waffle' (pardon me for thinking that you are actually, er, waffling on a bit already). 'We let others do that. Isn't it time you started winning.' (It clearly isn't time the advertiser started understanding the use of the question mark.) 'We give forecasts for English & Australian football. For a free info pack write . . .'

You will find any number of guaranteed get-rich-quick schemes of this nature scattered around the pages of many football publications and all gambling-orientated magazines and newspapers. If you want my advice, which comes, as a special offer, free of charge (once you have shelled out for this book, of course), it is that whilst you may well find some useful hints amongst the overwhelming amount of expensive dross, you would be much better off making a thorough study of the football pages of the national newspapers, flicking through the freely available text pages on your television and listening to the radio for up-to-date team information, and then trusting to your own judgement to make your selections. At least that way you have no one to blame but yourself. Maybe that is part of the problem for compulsive followers of dodgy systems – they don't have to face up to personal failure. They can excuse their inability to back winners by blaming their 'adviser' who, almost certainly, is taking them for a mug.

Never forget the self-evident truths that any perfect system would soon put the bookmakers out of business and that anyone who had access to such a holy grail of the forecasting world would have to have saintly credentials indeed to wish to share it with losers and no-hopers like you and me. That sort of beatific human being usually ends up following a different calling and moving towards Holy Orders.

And blow me down if, just as I was putting the finishing touches to *Gambling on Goals*, I didn't receive in the post an unprecedented – and, indeed, unsolicited – invitation to hitherto undreamed of football-pools winnings. Good old Edward Wynford of Old Gloucester Street, London, had evidently heard through the grapevine of my inherent inability to dig out even one score draw, for here he was, generously offering to share with me the secret of his own, unparalleled success.

'I've won to date 1,098 FIRST DIVIDENDS' Edward excitedly informed me. 'I have perfected my winning formula over a period of 38 years,' he assured me, suddenly remembering, 'I have also won 9,937 MINOR dividends,' but then becoming a little impertinent – even if accurate – by demanding to know: 'Have you ever won even one first dividend??? I doubt it very much.'

So, friendly old Edward was kindly prepared to do something about this sad state of affairs: 'I shall never disclose my Secret to anyone,' – oh, what a shame. 'However from time to time the formula requires an intake of new Clients, hence my approach to you at this time,' – well, WHAT a stroke of good luck for me. 'My usual charge is a once and for all payment of £500,' continued Edward, 'but now to you, you can enrol for an initial fee of £35 and the balance of £465 if I win for you by 24th May 1997.'

There was more: 'If my Correct forecasts do NOT continue I refund you your £35, what can be fairer?' (Hold on, give me a minute, I'm sure I'll come up with something.) 'I know of nothing. Pay ME THE FULL PAYMENT OF £500 NOW and I'll even make AND PAY FOR your weekly entries.'

Now, how could anyone resist such blandishments and philanthropy? Quite easily, as it happens, and that's just what I did.

Sorry, Edward.

One man – I don't believe there are any women in this line of business – who is right in the line of fire from tipsters and punters who target football betting as their means to a profitable income, is Athos Christodoulou of William Hill, a top odds compiler. He and his colleagues – Richard Browning and Dave Brown – have to price up every game of any significance in domestic and European competitions (even farther afield during World Cup qualification and finals), and also worry about Australian games during our close season.

The punters only have to take them on when they think the odds are in their favour – they can be selective. But, rather like a TV weather forecaster, Athos and Co. are expected to get it right everywhere all of the time.

'How do we price up a football match, what do we look at?' asks Athos. 'The main aspect is current form, usually the last six results is enough. Injuries and suspensions are important. Most of our information is freely available via Teletext, newspapers, the Internet etc, but basically it finally comes down to opinion.

'Long gone are the days when the only live football was on a Saturday afternoon in May – the Cup Final. Rarely a day goes by now when there is no televised football.

'With the introduction of singles betting on live matches, football betting has rocketed to phenomenal heights, and the importance of accurate pricing has increased.

'Liabilities on these matches can be staggering on the bigger, more important games. The biggest gamble in football history, though, went our way. The match was the last Group game in Euro '96, between Russia and the Czech Republic at Anfield. We quoted Russia at 11/8, with the Czechs at 6/4, while all the other firms made the Czechs clear favourites. We laid three bets of £100,000 at 6/4 and numerous other hefty wagers, giving us a total potential payout of approaching £1.75 million if the Czechs won.

'I was working in the office on the night of the game. After forty-five minutes we looked like being hung out to dry as the Czechs were 2–0 up, and to say they were dominating the game is an under-statement, as they had hit the woodwork three times. The atmosphere in the office was grim, as we knew the knives were being sharpened above our heads.

'I don't know what they put in the Russian tea at half-time – possibly Smirnoff vodka – but it certainly sharpened them up. It was as though a different team took the pitch, and before you could say "Perestroika" Russia had scored twice. When they added a third the cheers could probably be heard in the Kremlin and even though the Czechs equalised in the last minute we knew the company's money was safe.

'There was little time for self-congratulation, though, as we then had to price up the quarter-final matches.'

Even so-called 'insiders' find tipping a frustrating task. West Ham boss Harry Redknapp revealed in September 1997 that he had received an irate reaction from a punter who had staked £2,000 on his tip for Sheffield Wednesday to draw with Blackburn – they lost 7–2!

So there you have it – tipsters and compilers alike agree that their's is not an easy calling. Perhaps the last word on the subject should be given to the anonymous author styling himself 'Statistician' who wrote *Betting Systems that Win*, in 1991, in which he perceptively observed: 'The one thing that is certain about football and betting on it is its uncertainty.'

CHAPTER FIVE

Spread the Word

Definitely the newest, and probably the most innovative, advance in football wagering is spread betting, which offers almost endless fascination to both the football enthusiast and the inveterate punter, but which carries with it essential ingredients which will always deter the cautious player. Spread-betting debts are recoverable through the process of law, unlike conventional betting losses. This is because the companies who operate this type of business are members of the Securities and Futures Authority – the SFA – the body which regulates stockbrokers and commodity brokers (the milieu which first inspired this kind of gambling) and monitors the financial integrity of its members. It is also the only form of betting in which, when you place your wager you cannot usually tell just how much you may end up losing.

Nonetheless, it has become an established part of the betting scene with many devoted followers – former England star turned racehorse trainer Mick Channon, for example. In February 1997, Channon told the *Racing Post*: 'I like to have a spread bet on live TV matches nowadays, but I don't think I'm ahead of the bookies. I like to bet on the shirt numbers – you've got to have balls to do that. And I also play the time of the first goal.'

City Index were the first company to realise the potential of spread betting in relation to sports events. City's Jonathan Sparke came up with the original concept for the business when he became frustrated by the queue lengths at the *pari-mutuel* booths when he was in France for the 1980 Prix de l'Arc de Triomphe race meeting. To overcome the

124

problem he and a friend devised a system of spread betting, one with the other, each taking it in turn to quote the aggregate racecard number of the first two horses past the post. Before the end of the afternoon a multitude of similarly frustrated grandstanders were participating in the new game.

From 1981–83, Sparke worked on and refined his idea, thinking of how to relate it to sports like football, then in 1983 he formed City Index in conjunction with his legal adviser, Anthony Wollenberg. They commenced trading in 1984, dealing mainly in financial markets, but pioneering sports index spread betting.

In 1991, after the previous year's World Cup had boosted interest in sports spread betting, City Index created the '100 Index' for knockout sports tournaments, starting with Wimbledon. It rapidly proved their most popular form of such wagers.

Sporting Index and IG Index soon came on to the scene. According to IG's Patrick Jay, putting their spreads on to Teletext gave the companies another major boost: 'We went on in March 1994. Clients could close and re-open their positions, and we found that being able to see the spreads changing in front of their eyes proved to be like a huge orgasm for these customers.'

IG's business grew from taking 'approximately 20 sports bets a day' in November 1993, to '3,500 per week' by spring 1997. Unlike traditional bookmakers, with whom horse racing is still accounting for probably 75 per cent of business, Jay estimates that IG does 25 per cent or less of its trading on racing.

This was backed up by City Index's Paul Austin, who was asked by BBC TV's Julian Wilson in March 1997 what were his company's most popular betting subjects: 'Football first; football second and football third,' was the reply, as he guesstimated an annual total turnover on all sports of some £200 million spread betting. However, senior industry sources I consulted considered this to be an over-optimistic estimate.

In spread betting, the bookmaker absorbs the betting tax within the spread on offer, so there are no deductions whatsoever from the ultimate winnings.

Although spread betting is offered on horse racing it is its ability to give a fresh impetus to wagering on traditional sporting contests which has given it such an impact. Cricket provides an easily understood, basic example of how spread betting works.

Imagine it's the opening day of the first Test between England and the West Indies. England win the toss and decide to bat. How many will they score in their first innings? The bookmaker's 'spread' might be 300–320. This means they think England will score between 300 and

320 runs. If you think the pitch is full of runs and that a total of 400 is nearer the mark, you would 'buy' at the higher quote of 320. If, on the other hand, you think England will be skittled out for nearer 200 you should 'sell' at the lower quote, i.e. 300. In spread betting you always buy at the higher end of the quote and sell at the lower end of the quote. You specify your unit stake, i.e. the amount per run you wish to bet, when you open the bet.

Let's say you are optimistic enough to believe England will do well, and you buy for £5 per run at 320. This means that for every run above 320 that England score, you will win £5. If they make 400, you win (400-320) x £5 = £400.

For every run below 320, you lose £5. If they are shot out for 200 you will lose (320-200) x £5 = £600.

See what I mean about not knowing how much you may end up losing!

Now, if you were confident England would do badly you could have sold for £5 per run at 300. A final score of 200 nets you a profit of (300-200) x £5 = £500.

But every run above 300 loses you £5, and a total of 400 means a loss of (400-300) x £5 = £500.

This demonstrates perfectly the key difference between spread betting and fixed-odds betting. Profits, and losses, are made in proportion to whatever unit stake you choose, but the stake is not the limit of your financial risk.

With a £10 bet on a fixed-odds football bet, that £10 is all that can be lost. A £10 per run bet on cricket can win, or lose, many times more than the £10 unit stake.

Now, let us apply this principle to betting on football. To give you a chance to back your favourite or fancied team to do well – or, perhaps, badly – in the FA Cup, the bookmaker will use a performance index format. For example, they might award the Cup winner 100 points, the losing finalist 75, the losing semi-finalists 50, and the losing quarter-finalists 25. At the time of the third round draw the quote on how well Manchester United will do might be 64–67. This reflects an assessment of the chance of them finishing with 25, 50, 75 or even 100 points, depending on how far they get in the competition.

If you expect them to have a good Cup run, you could buy at the higher figure, 67. If, on the other hand, you expect them to fail in the quarter-finals (a make-up – or final outcome – of 25), or the semi-finals (make-up 50), you could sell at the lower figure, 64. If Manchester United won the Cup, the profit on a £20 buy bet would be calculated as follows:

Opening quote: 67
Make-up: 100
Difference: 33
Profit on £20 buy bet: 33 x £20 = £660

The loss on a sell bet would be 100-64 = 36 times the stake, £720.

Amongst those endeavouring to relieve you of your hard-earned cash by tempting you to match wits with him over the outcome of a football match, IG Index's Patrick Jay is described by the *Sporting Life*'s Alastair Down as 'principal guru in the crucial football market'. Patrick is the son of former ambassador to Washington, Peter Jay, who apparently 'is quite unable to fathom the complexities of spread betting'. He would be well advised to read on.

An advantage of spread betting is that in some events you can bet – or take a profit or cut your losses – in running, or during designated interval periods, for example, half-time. Let's say you have bought Manchester United in the FA Cup index, at a quote of 67. They have reached the final, against Newcastle, and the quote on Manchester United has moved up to 82–84. You think the Old Trafford side will lose, so you decide to close your position at the lower end of the quote, 82.

Opening quote: 67
Closing quote: 82
Difference: 15
Profit on a £20 buy bet: 15 x £20 = £300

You can bet on the total number of goals scored in a game between, for example, Tottenham and Southampton in which the bookmaker quotes the total number of goals in the game at 2.7–3.0. You fancy an attacking match and buy for £15 per tenth of a goal (£150 per goal), at 3.0, expecting a goal feast. The match ends up as a 2–2 draw. The total goals make-up is therefore 4.

Opening quote: 3
Make-up: 4
Difference: 1
Profit on a £150 (£15 per tenth of a goal) buy bet: 1.0 x £150 = £150

Compton Hellyer, chairman of Sporting Index, who claim to be the spread betting market leaders with 45 per cent of the business transacted, told of a customer who regularly bets £10,000 per goal, adding, in February 1997, 'Punters at this level tend to be foreigners or men in the City.'

When I visited the company's London HQ, their football market maker, David Garbacz, the man who devised their markets on shirt numbers and corners, told me of one client who as of May 1997 had lost an astonishing £500,000 by persistently over-estimating the number of corners which would occur in high-profile games.

'Regardless of the game he will buy, but he has a good job in the City and can afford the losses.'

When I expressed surprise that anyone would even CARE how many corners there would be in a game and wondered how you would go about trying to calculate such a total, he pointed out that the size of a pitch could have a great influence on how many corners would be awarded during a game and that his statistical information suggests that it is not an entirely random factor.

Garbacz recalled the time when he introduced a Magic Sponge market, offering it for the first time for a Liverpool v Everton match for which the line was 3–3½ on the number of occasions on which the physiotherapist would come on to the pitch. After some 80 minutes the physio had not been on at all when Bruce Grobbelaar hurt himself against a post and needed treatment. However, he was lying on the touchline and the physio did not actually have to come on to the pitch itself to treat him, although he did rest his bag on the pitch. Sporting ruled that this did not count in terms of the bet, a decision which Garbacz admitted was something of a public relations blunder.

Football now accounts for almost 50 per cent of Sporting's business, estimated their spokesman Wally Pyrah who is in no doubt as to the driving force behind the sport's continued expansion as a betting medium: 'If Sky died, we'd die with it.'

Perhaps you would prefer to speculate on the superiority of one side over the other. In the earlier mentioned Spurs v Saints game, Spurs were at home and the bookmaker made them favourites to score more goals. The superiority quote was Spurs/Southampton 1.0–1.3. A Southampton fan expecting a good result for his team sells at £1,000 a goal (£100 per tenth of a goal). The resulting 2–2 draw (make-up = 0) makes a profit:

Opening quote: 1.0
Make-up: 0.0
Difference: 1.0
Profit on a £1,000 (£100 per tenth of a goal) sell bet: 1.0 x £1,000
= £1,000

Top: Mr Sutton and family receiving a William Hill fixed odds cheque for £16,000, 11 January 1958
Inset: 1936 advertisement featuring one of Vernons' thousandaires (courtesy *Vernons' Handbook 1936–7*)
Bottom: Mr J Ibbs of Wolverhampton won £13,500 on a 3/6d fixed odds bet, 21 August 1954 (courtesy *Express and Star*)

Top: William Hill punters in Lagos, Nigeria
Bottom: Vernons' advertisements from 1948

Top: William Hill employees sorting through the weekly coupons in the 1960s
(courtesy *Bert Hardy Ltd*)
Bottom: The pile of winning coupons grows at William Hill, with one in four being a winner
(courtesy *Associated Newspapers Ltd*)

Arthur Wyles and his daughter Pamela with their William Hill cheque for £100,000, November 1964 (courtesy *Daily Sketch*)

Albert Brown, winner of £22,950 on Hill's 14-match list, 7 February 1967
(courtesy *Matthews' News and Photo Agency*)

Top: William Hill winner Mike Coulson with his cheque for £89,738.96 (courtesy Graham Sharpe)

Inset: England goalkeeper David Seaman teams up with model Joanne Guest to launch Littlewoods' new football-based skills game, Top Spot

Top: Mr A Chee won £16,005.60 on a 1p, 6 match accumulator at world record odds in March 1986
Inset: Terry Venables opening a new Coral shop (courtesy *Steve Daszko Photography*)
Bottom: Frank Bruno presenting a Littlewoods Pools cheque for over a million pounds, December 1987

Top: Costas Constantinou and staff receiving their Littlewoods cheque for £187,650
from Matt Belgrano, 17 January 1987
Bottom: The author receiving a cheque from Blackpool chairman, Owen Oyston on
behalf of William Hill, October 1987

Of course, had Southampton won 3–0, he would have made a profit of £4,000.

Every Saturday during the season, a spread is quoted on whether the home teams or away teams will score more goals in the Premiership. One Saturday the Premiership quote may be: homes/aways 7–8. You believe home sides will outscore away teams by more than 8, so you buy for £20 per goal at that price. In fact, home teams score a total of 20 goals, and the away teams 17, giving a make-up of just 3.

Opening quote: 8
Make-up: 3
Difference: 5
Loss on £20 buy bet: 5 x £20 = £100

In an international game between Italy and Brazil the bookmaker may quote a spread on the total shirt numbers of the goalscorers. The quote is 25–28. You expect plenty of goals from players wearing high shirt numbers and buy for £50 per point at 28. Italy win 2–0 with number 10, Baggio, scoring twice. The make-up is (10 + 10) = 20.

Opening quote: 28
Make-up: 20
Difference: 8
Loss on buy bet: 8 x £50 = £400

In a live televised European game between Bruges and Chelsea, the market on the time of the first goal, in minutes, is 38–41. You fancy an early strike, and sell at 38 for £10 per minute. Unfortunately for you, the opening goal takes 83 minutes to arrive.

Opening quote: 38
Make-up: 83
Difference: 45
Loss on a £10 sell bet: 45 x £10 = £450

At the start of the season your bookmaker may quote a spread on how many points each Premiership (or other division) side will accumulate. The quote for Arsenal is 69–71. You buy at £40 per point at 71, expecting the Gunners to go well. Halfway through the season Arsenal are struggling and looking for a new boss. The quote, updated after each game, has dropped to 54–56. You decide to cut part of your losses by closing half, i.e. £20, of your bet at 54.

129

Opening quote: 71
Closing quote: 54
Difference: 17
Loss on a buy bet: 17 x £20 = £340

You have taken a loss of £340, but still have £20 of your original buy bet at 71 open. Arsenal appoint a new manager, buy two new strikers and their performance improves rapidly – they end up with 73 points.

Opening quote: 71
Make-up: 73
Difference: 2
Profit on a £20 buy bet: 2 x £20 = £40

So, your remaining £20 wins £40, cutting your overall loss to £300.

There are many other ways of placing a spread bet – such as the number of corners or goalkicks, or even free-kicks, in a match; or the time of the first throw-in, settled on when the throw-in takes place, not when the ball leaves the pitch. You can bet on the time of the first goal of the game, or how many yellow and red cards will be flourished by the referee. During the Euro '96 tournament one spread betting company bet on how many times the stretcher bearers would be called into action – and even tried to land a deal to put their company logo on the stretchers themselves.

'The problem was that there were two separate organisations involved and although one of them was quite happy with the scheme, I couldn't get the other one to agree,' Sporting Index's Wally Pyrah told me.

Another opened a 'Duck 'n' Dive' market for Euro '96, based on how many times Jürgen Klinsmann would be booked for taking a dive. You could also speculate on the times of substitutions.

One Euro '96 spread punter lost his bread – literally – when someone threw a sandwich on to the pitch during the Portugal versus Denmark game, played at Hillsborough. Nottingham TV engineer Paul O'Carroll had sold the time of the first throw-in with Sporting Index and was ready to pay out on what he believed to be a make-up of 227 seconds – until Sporting contacted him to explain that they had reviewed that time after being informed that the referee had made a player re-take the first throw after someone threw a sandwich on to the pitch. The result was that Mr O'Carroll was a staggering £400 worse off.

Before the February 1997 World Cup game between England and Italy, IG Index, noticing that the Italians would be fielding Demetrio

Albertini and Gianfranco Zola in their side, offered an A–Z market on the surname initial of the first scorer. They quoted N½–P (14½–16) and bet in-running. Zola scored the only goal of the game, which also saw Sporting Index breaking new ground by trading the total number of bookings in-running.

These entertaining and potentially profitable offerings help to explain why respected *Sporting Life* writer and reformed punter David Ashforth was moved to say of spread betting: 'If you are interested in betting you should make it your business to understand spread betting. It is the most exciting development for a long time.'

Exciting may not be the precise definition used amongst some of the less successful spread-betting punters of whom I have been told whilst putting this chapter together; like the man of whom we have already heard, who lost half a million betting purely on the number of corners in games; the client who lost £100,000 by betting that there would be very few goals in a Premiership game between Chelsea and Sunderland during March 1997 which ended with a 6–2 scoreline for the home side; and the punter who lost £137,000 when Newcastle went down 4–0 in a Charity Shield game against Manchester United.

However, with such unpredictable betting subjects available, the spread companies are very responsive to anything which might suggest or even hint at untoward goings-on.

In January 1997, William Hill Index were taken by surprise at the high level of business they seemed to be attracting for a relatively low-key market on an obscure FA Cup second-round replay between Wycombe Wanderers and Barnet. Hill Index issued a spread on the time of the tie's first throw-in, and they opened up at 60–75 seconds. The great majority of enquiries were from sellers and the quote moved quickly down to 40–55, a very low level for a market which would be expected to trade at around 75–90 for Premiership games.

Just before kick-off, Hill's apparently received a phone call warning them 'to be wary' of certain markets. They removed the line from public display but still received a dozen calls from people wanting to know the quote, including some from people without accounts.

Hill Index's Steve Tucker was quoted in the *Racing Post* as saying: 'The betting patterns on the time of the first throw-in were very irregular. This is a fun market. The bets we have taken on it so far have been of the £1–£10 variety, but we had people wanting to sell for £20 and £30.'

In the event, the ball went out of play after 51 seconds and was thrown in eight seconds later. A section of the crowd was heard chanting 'Out, out, out'.

Leaving aside any question of dodgy dealing here, I have to say that as a regular at Luton Town home games for many years, our regular kick-off tactic under David Pleat was to batter the ball out of play as far as possible down the line into opposition territory, putting them under early pressure. Now, if we had been playing a side with the same tactic in its armoury and a bookmaker had been foolish enough to open up a market on the time of the first throw-in, I would have known that bar some kind of freak occurrence I was going to be betting on a good thing. And had I placed such a bet and the ball had duly gone out of play within six or seven seconds, I would have taken a dim view if a bookmaker had then accused me of taking advantage of inside information or of being involved in some kind of scam. To my way of thinking, that would be taking advantage of unprofessional work by the bookie's market maker.

By the way, before considering how or whether to play this type of market, bear in mind that during Euro '96 in the Scotland versus Holland game the first throw-in did not happen until nine minutes 54 seconds into the match. And in November 1996 an Old Firm derby between Rangers and Celtic cost some punters, who had sold the time of the first throw-in for £20 a second, a huge £9,560 after it arrived well after nine minutes' play, producing a make-up of 548, on a 70–85 spread.

In May 1997, there was another ripple of suspicion over the first throw-in, this time in a nothing-at-stake match between home-side Manchester United and West Ham. The Hammers kicked off and Paul Kitson walloped the ball into touch within seven seconds. Spread firms had reported a large number of sellers at the offered rate of 65–80 seconds. Sporting's David Garbacz said, 'We had one or two interesting calls before the match and took quick evasive action, slashing the line to 50–65.'

City Index, who don't normally take bets on this market because they fear it could be manipulated, said that some of their long-standing clients had been asking for a quote, and their head of sport, Paul Austin was reported as saying: 'The clear inference is that they were desperate to strike a bet at any price.'

It would be difficult to feel too much sympathy for any bookmaker hit financially by betting on such an artificial market – not that that would ever excuse any deliberate collusion designed to exploit such a bet for the gain of participants in a game on which it was offered. West Ham boss Harry Redknapp commented in the *Racing Post*: 'It's a very dodgy bet and I suppose it could be open to manipulation.'

Another facet adding to the appeal of spread betting is the ability often to be able to bet whilst a sporting event is in progress, known as betting in-running. For most live televised matches, this facility is available from all companies. Betting in-running gives the punter control over his betting. He can take a profit, or cut a loss, whenever he choses. It also means he can watch the progress of an event before making a decision on which way to bet.

Another example explains how this facility works. A match between Manchester United and Southampton has a supremacy quote of Manchester United/Southampton 1.5–1.8. You believe that United will win comfortably and bet higher, buying their supremacy for £50 per goal. By half-time, United are 3–0 up. At this stage the Supremacy Spread has moved to 4.0–4.3. The selling price of the Supremacy Spread at 4.0 is now above the price you bought at 1.8, giving you the opportunity to take a profit of £110. The profit is calculated thus:

(Goals Supremacy you sell at) minus (Goals Supremacy you bought at) x your stake
(4-1.8) x £50 = £110 profit

By closing the bet, even if Southampton were to stage a second-half recovery, you have guaranteed yourself £110 profit.

You can also cut your losses. You have bought Manchester United at 1.8 for £50. However, at half-time, Southampton are winning 1–0. Manchester United are still favourites to win the game, but the Supremacy quote has been reduced to 0.7–1.0. If you believe United are unlikely to fight back, you could now close your bet for a £55 loss by betting lower, selling at 0.7. Your loss is then calculated thus:

(Goals Supremacy you bought at) minus (Goals Supremacy you sell at) x your stake
(1.8-0.7) x £50 = £55 loss

Even if Southampton go on to win 3–0, you have limited your loss to £55.

Stop losses/stop wins and maximum make-ups are important concepts operated to give the punter greater control over his betting. Some companies operate either a stop loss/win or a maximum make-up on spreads and therefore you can always work out how much you can potentially win or lose at the time you make your bet. In football supremacy spreads the stop loss/win is likely to be five goals either side of the spread. For the Manchester United/Southampton example this means that if you bet higher, buy Manchester United at 1.8 for £20 and

Southampton win 6–0, your loss would be limited to £100.

Interestingly, although spread betting is receiving wide editorial coverage in many parts of the media, sports editor of the *Sun*, Paul Ridley, was refusing to accept advertisements for it on the pages of his best-selling newspaper, as we went to press. Despite the fact that the spread companies would gladly spend substantial amounts of cash on advertising their wares to *Sun* readers, Ridley believed that this was just too volatile a concept to be dangled before potentially vulnerable readers.

I don't think he was taking a patronising attitude, but that he genuinely believed that spread betting would expose his readers to financial risks for which they may not be properly equipped and thus leave the paper itself vulnerable to damaging criticism should any significant number of readers fall foul of unsuccessful and highly expensive wagers, leaving themselves open to substantial debt.

As this book went to press there were five companies offering spread betting (Coral were set to become the sixth):

City Index; Cardinal Court, 23 Thomas More Street, London E1 9YY (0171 480 5685). Internet: http://www.cityindex.co.uk/city

IG Index Plc, 1 Warwick Row, London SW1E 5ER (0500 911911)

Ladbrokes Sporting Spreads, Imperial House, Imperial Drive, Rayners Lane, Harrow, Middlesex HA2 7JW (0800 130 140)

Sporting Index Limited, Gateway House, Milverton Street, London SE11 4AP (0171 820 9789)

William Hill Index, 1–5 Morris Place, Finsbury Park, London N4 3TF (0800 300320)

SPREAD BETTING TERMS

Arbitrage Relatively rare situation in which conflicting spreads from different companies enable quick-acting punters to place two or more bets which guarantee a profit regardless of the outcome of the event.

Buy Placing a bet when you believe the result will be more than the quote. Sometimes called an up bet, and always placed at the higher quoted figure.

Closing a bet Placing a second bet while an event is still in progress, but in the opposite direction, thus establishing your profit or loss and eliminating further risk.

High/low volatility An indication of the range of possible results in any particular spread. Football matches usually produce less than six goals. Total goals would therefore be a spread of low volatility.

However, the time of the first goal can vary from the first minute to the 90th and would therefore be regarded as of high volatility.

Homes/aways A match bet between the number of goals scored by the home teams against the number of goals scored by the away teams in a specified group of matches.

Index bet Bets constructed around awarding points for performance in an event or for progress in a knockout tournament.

Long-term market A market about an event or competition or tournament whose final outcome may not be known for at least 14 days from its inception.

Make-up The final result of any given bet. The difference between the make-up and the price at which you place your bet, multiplied by your stake determines your profit or loss.

Maximum make-up The maximum number involved in a spread bet, so that if the actual make-up is higher, this maximum number is used to calculate the profit or loss instead of the actual number.

Match bets Spreads based on the relative performance of two participants in an event. This bet is around the margin by which one named contender will beat the other named contender and is independent of the performance of the other participants.

In-running Where spread quotes are changed during a match or event, reflecting its progress and allowing the punter to buy and/or sell at the updated spread.

Numbers spreads Spreads based on the number of runs, goals, lengths, points etc, which will be scored during an event.

Performance spreads Where points are awarded to teams or individuals for their performance in an event, or series of events, or progress in a knockout competition. Spreads are based on how many points the team or individual will achieve. In the FA Cup, 100 points may be awarded for winning, 75 for being runners-up and 50 for being a losing semi-finalist.

Sell Placing a bet when you believe the result will be less than the quote. Sometimes called a down bet; always placed at the lower figure quoted.

Spread The difference between the high (buy) and low (sell) quotes. The prediction of the result quoted as two numbers, e.g. 300–320 runs for a Test match innings.

Stake The amount you bet, in pounds per point, run, length etc.

Stop loss/stop win Maximum levels set to limit the amount you can win or lose on an event.

Supremacy spreads Spreads based on the margin of victory separating the two contenders in a match, race, tournament or event.

Ticks Some spreads are not in whole numbers, but are quoted in tenths, or ticks. For example, total goals in a football match may be quoted as 2.1–2.4 goals.

Your choice (yr ch) This is where in an equal match bet you are invited to select the favourite in making your bet.

CHAPTER SIX

Into the Net

The Internet will undoubtedly have a major part to play in the future development of many aspects of football betting. Already a great deal of information designed to be of use to football punters is to be found on the network.

As a self-confessed computer-illiterate (this book was written on a very basic word-processor) I cannot hope to understand or explain the technological ins and outs of such a facility, but during the compilation of this tome I was contacted by more than one Internet provider. Bill Hunter from Dunfermline in Scotland told me about a new group he was organising, called SAGE – Soccer And Gambling Exchange – which had just acquired a web site, and was designed to attract members with an interest in 'soccer results prediction and all forms of football betting'. The site's index page is located at http://members.aol.com/the12Xpert/sage.htm. Bill also passed on news of a tipsters league on the Web, which includes a weekly consolidated UK pools forecast. Further details available from user@brown.softnet.co.uk.

Echoing an idea which I have been mooting for a number of years, 28-year-old West Bromwich Albion fan Andy Davis revealed in March 1997 that he was attempting to set up a massive network of supporters, linked together via the World-wide Web. Called SIN – the Soccer Intelligence Network – the idea is to 'put punters a step ahead of odds makers.' The *Racing Post* gave the scheme a warm reception: 'The idea behind SIN is simple – fans preview their sides and then predict the outcome. The advantage SINners have over other tipsters and fans of other clubs is they watch their team week in, week out.'

Davis explained: 'There were times when I was certain I knew how West Brom would get on, but I couldn't bet singles on the game.

'I thought it would be a good idea to get fans of clubs up and down the country to come together to share their thoughts and give sensible predictions.'

Post football editor Paul Johnson, was keen: 'I believe the idea has immense merit and is one of the most sensible suggestions made to me during my time at the *Post.*'

William Hill odds compiler, Athos Christodoulou, an Arsenal fan himself, commented: 'I am not sure if they will give each other any more information than is already available.'

The SIN home page is at http://users.aol.com/fdanco/sin.html.

As I write, I do not believe it is possible for the casual punter to place actual bets with any British-based company on football individual odds via the Internet, but an article in the *London Evening Standard* recently predicted that the start of the 1997–98 season might well see such a facility becoming available.

Ladbrokes envisage taking bets via the Internet, but not in the immediate future: 'There's considerable potential in on-line betting on the Internet,' said their Simon Clare in March 1997, 'but there are security and confidentiality issues that need to be addressed to protect both punters and bookmakers.'

Things are moving so rapidly on the Internet scene that instant betting is certain to become available sooner rather than later, probably via one of two methods. Punters will either be able to feed in a Visa card (for example) number and bet directly via that; or punters will open an account with the bookmaker and be given a unique pin number which will give them access to the company's computer system in order to log their required wager.

Security is naturally an over-riding issue which has to be overcome before gamblers can use the Net with confidence. As I write, as well as the major bookmakers, a number of other companies are offering betting facilities via the Internet, although the majority of them involve setting up a credit card deposit facility in advance.

Germany-based Intertops, Ireland's Terry Rogers, Belgian company S.S.P. and Australia's Centrebet all offer a variety of odds, including football, with the Aussie company even enabling customers to bet without deductions. The majority also offer the facility to place bets by e-mail, fax, post or phone. In America, although off-track betting is widely prhibited, bookmakers can take wagers over the web without fear of prosecution.

The legal position on cross-border betting is an extremely grey area. In the US a number of States are trying to introduce legislation to ban it.

An Antigua-based spread-betting company, World Sports Exchange Ltd (WSE), launched in January 1997 and, via a deposit account system, began accepting bets via the Internet, although I am not aware that they currently bet on football. However, Australian companies are accepting bets via the Internet, provided clients first deposit cash with them. In February 1997, they were even quoting odds for a Cambridge United versus Carlisle United third division clash.

The *Sporting Life* has its own Internet site and the paper itself carries a regular column devoted to racing and betting details about the Internet. William Hill has a site, launched for Euro '96, and currently boasting over 100 pages of odds on major football fixtures. In January 1996, the *Independent* reported that Zetters, the smallest of the three British football pools companies, had launched a site on the World-wide Web 'to try and out-manoeuvre the national lottery.' Football fans around the world could now use the Web to gamble on the pools, reported Danny Penman.

> Fans can play the game from anywhere in the world using little more than a computer, modem and a credit card. Punters play by filling in an electronic form, which also contains their credit card details, and then sending it via the World-wide Web to the host computer on Jersey. If they win they are told the following week by e-mail.

Zetters were said to be receiving 'hundreds of bets per week' through the system and their Jamie Easterman was quoted as saying that he 'envisages transactions through the net becoming the company's main source of revenue'. By July 1997 Mahmood Golzar of Zetters could announce: 'The amount of betting generated from our site varies from £400 a week to £1600.'

Littlewoods, who had launched a site in April 1997 reported that it was 'only paying for itself'.

In August 1997, Woking-based bookmakers Eurobet claimed to have become the 'first bookmaker actually taking bets on the Internet', according to director Nico Giovando, whose company estimated that 70 per cent of its business was on football: 'Bookmakers with betting shops have high overheads, but on the Internet all you need is someone to check the bets as they go through automatically. Around 10 per cent of the bets we take are on the Internet.'

Zetters, using a sophisticated encryption system for security purposes, was hoping to capitalise on the global gambling market rather than trying to increase its domestic market share, and Americans and Hong Kong citizens have proved keen. Those who wish to, can do the pools with Zetters, at www.zetters.co.uk.

CHAPTER SEVEN

A Brief Look at Football Betting Rules

Soccer is by far the most popular of all sports for betting. Demand is such that bookmakers produce a variety of individual-odds coupons throughout the domestic season and a special 'Aussie' coupon during the summer. In 1997, William Hill introduced a midweek coupon for the first time, covering only televised matches. Single bets are accepted on live TV games and on Cup matches, but the Leagues require bookmakers to restrict bets on other games to a minimum of trebles, although from the start of the 1994–95 season doubles were acceptable, provided one of the games was televised live.

There is a further restriction on weekend matches, and any bets involving a home selection outside of the Premiership and First Division in England and Premier in Scotland must normally include a minimum of five matches in any one line.

All bets on individual matches are based on the score at the end of normal time and in Cup matches any goals scored in extra-time will not count for betting purposes – although separate odds are frequently quoted for which of the two sides will ultimately progress.

In Cup finals where there is outright betting on which side will win the Cup as well as on the result of the match, anyone wishing to bet outright must state this on their slip, otherwise it will be settled on the 90 minutes odds.

If a match is abandoned or postponed it is void.

First and last goalscorer betting is always popular in live matches but often causes disagreements as deciding the goalscorer is not always clear cut. For instance, a forward will often claim a goal if his shot is heading towards the corner flag and is deflected into the net off a defender. Players on the same side, probably caught up in the emotion of a Cup win, have also been known to 'give' a doubtful goal to a team-mate.

With the decision on who to credit with goals left to the clubs themselves (there is no official goalscorer), William Hill use a consensus of all the national newspapers. When a goalscorer is in doubt, whoever's name appears most in the results sections of the following day's national newspapers will be deemed to be the goalscorer as far as bets are concerned. Other companies may well have different rules; some may award goals in live games to the player credited by the commentator, for instance. You should always check in advance.

In principle, all odds are offered on the basis that they reflect the outcome of a single event. This does not mean that you are unable to do doubles, trebles etc, but the events must be unrelated. For instance, you can back Arsenal, Celtic and Luton in a treble, as one game does not affect the outcome of the others. However, it is not always permitted to place a double on Arsenal to win 1–0 and Ian Wright to score the first goal, as clearly the two parts of the bet are directly related. Up until recently, the stake for the double would be divided and settled as two singles. Nowadays, though, special odds will often be quoted on such related contingencies.

Likewise, expect reduced odds in multiple bets which involve the same side to win more than one event – Liverpool to win the FA Cup, Premiership and Coca-Cola Cup, for example.

Odds about related bets in a single match are now widely available largely due to the pioneering work of William Hill's Operations Research Analyst, Mike Benyon, who explained how this came about: 'I was first asked to look at the possibility of customers betting on first goalscorer–correct score doubles in 1994, in response to the number who were trying to place such bets.

'Odds had never been previously offered, because there is a clear link between the first player and the correct score. If, for example, a customer selects Manchester United to win 1–0 (at 7/1) and Ryan Giggs to score the first goal at 5/1, it is clear that the two are related; he is hardly going to pick Giggs to score first and Manchester United to lose 1–0.

'The basis of calculating odds for the double is to offer the customer the full odds for his correct score and then offer revised odds for the player. In the previous example, the full correct-score odds would be given for 1–0. However, by nominating this score the customer has eliminated from the double the possibility of an opposition player scoring first, and eliminated a 'no goalscorer' outcome.

'By nominating 1–0 he has effectively asked for a double on 1–0 to Manchester United and Giggs being the first goalscorer for United. The odds on Giggs scoring first for Manchester United are more like 5/2 than 5/1, and thus the double offered should be based on 7/1 and 5/2 rather than 7/1 and 5/1.

'A formula to calculate doubles accurately would take into account the odds of the player, the correct score, each team's 90 minutes match odds and the number of goals nominated for each team!

'However, in the cause of simplicity, bookmakers now offer chart odds based on the average deduction required for such doubles. This is not a perfect solution, but it at least gives customers the opportunity to work out their double easily, while ensuring a reasonable profit margin for bookmakers.'

UNDERSTANDING HOW BOOKMAKERS SET THE ODDS

In the early days of horse racing, one owner would pit his best horse against that of a rival owner. They would agree to race their champion over an agreed distance for an agreed stake – perhaps over a mile for 1,000 guineas.

In effect, both owners, in accepting these 'winner takes all' conditions, were taking on a 1,000 guinea bet at odds of even money – or one to one. Whichever horse's owner won would make a profit of 1,000 guineas, also the amount he stood to lose. Fine as it stood, but this type of betting was impossible to widen out and prevented interested observers from becoming involved by backing their own fancy, unless they also bet one against one with another spectator.

Eventually, a few shrewd characters realised that if they were to offer odds about the contestants in a race, whilst incorporating a percentage of profit margin into those odds to enable them to make it pay, anyone who wished to enjoy a flutter, small or large, could be accommodated.

For example, on the two-horse race – or the outcome of any other 'two-horse' event, e.g. which of two football teams would win the FA Cup in the Final – in which each had a theoretically equal or even money chance, the bookmaker could offer one of the contestants at the true even money odds – the equivalent of 50 per cent in betting percentage terms – and the other at, say, 4/5, or 55.56 per cent.

Now, if the bookmaker accepted bets of £10 for each runner he would break even if the even money chance won the event, but would make a £2 profit if the 4/5 chance was successful, as the backer would receive an £8 profit on his stake money. In percentage terms, the bookmaker would be making a book of 50 per cent plus 55.56 per cent, giving him a theoretical profit margin of 5.56 per cent in a hypothetical ideal world. The downside of this system is that there is nothing to prevent the two punters who, in our first example, staked £10 each on the two different runners, both deciding to back the same one. In that case the bookie would be left in a highly undesirable situation, whereby one result would mean all the bets he had taken were winning ones, the other would mean they were all losers.

This is where fixed-odds betting differs from pool betting where the operator is not worried on which selections the bets are placed, because the amount paid out, divided amongst how ever many winning bets there are, is only the amount taken in, less expenses and profit margin. It is impossible for the operator to lose money.

Back to the bookie, who tries to guard against this situation, by amending his odds in an effort to encourage people to back the unfancied runner. Let's say the punters had plunged on the 4/5 chance, ignoring the even money shot. The bookie might decide to make the 4/5 chance less attractive by shortening those odds to 4/7, enticing people to back the other runner by lengthening the odds from even money to 11/8. He would then be betting to a percentage of 63.64 per cent (4/7) plus 42.11 per cent (11/8), which equals 105.75 per cent, still just over 5 per cent in his favour, but enabling him to encourage the punters in the direction which suits him, i.e. towards the outsider.

By maintaining this theoretical profit percentage – known as the over-round – the odds can be adjusted no matter how many runners or teams contest an event, to ensure that, in the previously mentioned ideal world, the bookie's potential liability on the ultimate winner would never exceed the total stake money collected in. If the over-round becomes an under-round, this desirable situation – at least, as far as the bookie is concerned – is jeopardised.

Now, you will never find a bookie offering odds against about both runners in a two-horse race, e.g. 11/10 and 5/4, because, if you calculate the percentages you will find that they add up to 47.62 per cent plus 44.44 per cent which equals 92.06 per cent. So, for the outlay of £92.06 punters could back both runners to win a return of £100. That way lies disaster and bankruptcy for the bookmaker.

Similarly, in a football match with three possible outcomes – home win, away win, draw – the bookmaker will generally bet to a percentage of around 112. But it is possible that, when a number of bookmakers are betting on the same event but have different opinions, a punter could win whatever the result. In a football match, for example, one bookie could make Liverpool a 6/4 chance to beat Manchester United which he makes 11/8 favourite, with the draw at 9/4. However, another bookie disagrees violently, and makes Liverpool 2/7, with United at 7/1 and the draw at 7/2. It is now possible, in theory at least, to back Liverpool at 6/4, the draw at 7/2 and Manchester United at 7/1 – a total percentage of 40 per cent + 22.22 per cent + 12.5 per cent, or 74.72 per cent. Both bookmakers are safe within their own percentages, but by backing all three results at the longest odds available, the punter can, in effect, make a book of his own, in which he cannot lose.

Do not believe this is a frequent occurrence!

Of course, in Cup competitions or divisional championships of 20 or more runners in the real, as opposed to the ideal, world, perhaps six or eight teams will be seriously backed, half a dozen more will be nibbled at in the betting market, and the rest will be virtually ignored, regardless of how long their odds are. So, in effect, the bookmaker could lose heavily if any of the first six or eight in the betting should win, break about even if any of the next six market leaders were to oblige, and clean up in the event of one of the outsiders springing a shock result. Although the total percentage profit margin of a betting book is not always a guide to individual value, it can enable you to check how fair a particular set of odds for a match or tournament is in general terms.

PERCENTAGE TABLE

	ODDS ON %	ODDS AGAINST %
Even money	50	50
6/4	60	40
2/1	66.66	33.33
5/2	71.42	28.57
3/1	75	25
4/1	80	20
5/1	83.33	16.66
7/1	87.5	12.5
10/1	90.91	9.09
20/1	95.24	4.76
25/1	96.15	3.84
33/1	97.06	2.94

FOOTBALL BETTING EXPRESSIONS

Abandoned match If a match is abandoned short of its allotted 90 minutes, for whatever reason, the normal ruling is that for betting purposes, the match is void.

Accumulator A bet of four or more selections in which the total returns from each successive selection are re-invested on the next.

Ante-post betting Ante-post prices are those offered on major events prior to the day of the event, e.g. for a team to win the FA Cup before the first round is played.

Away A football bet selection requiring the team which is playing away from home to win. Should be indicated on a football coupon by means of the number 2.

Correct score Football bet requiring punters to predict the score of a match after 90 minutes play. Any subsequent addition to a score, in extra-time or in a penalty shoot-out, replay or second leg, does not count.

Double A bet involving two selections in which the total return from the first selection is invested on to the second selection automatically. If either selection loses, the entire bet is lost.

Double result A special bet in which punters must forecast the outcome of a match at both half- and full-time.

Draw A match which ends level at the end of 90 minutes' play. Should be indicated when filling in an individual-odds coupon by means of the letter X.

Each way A term referring to win and place, e.g. a client placing £1 each way on a selection in the FA Cup requires £1 to win the Cup and £1 to reach the final, total stake £2.

Extra-time Extra-time is that time played in certain Cup matches which have finished all-square after 90 minutes play. For the purposes of individual-odds match betting, extra-time does not count. The score which is taken for settling all bets other than those marked 'to win outright' is that which pertains after 90 minutes.

Favourite The shortest-priced participant in an event.

First goalscorer Betting on the player who scores first during 90 minutes' play. In the event of dispute, most bookmakers pay out according to a poll of national newspapers.

Fixed odds The original name for the form of betting in which fixed prices were offered on football matches or groups of matches ending in certain results, e.g. 20/1 three draws.

Green Seal service A free arbitration service for punters and bookmakers operated by the *Sporting Life* newspaper. All reputable bookmakers will agree to be bound by their ruling.

Handicap list Special list available on football coupons in which the compilers select a number of matches which appear to be probable home wins. They handicap these home teams by awarding the away team a goal or more start and then offering prices on the outcome.

Home A football bet selection requiring the team which is playing at home to win. Should be indicated when filling in an individual-odds coupon by means of the number 1.

Individual odds The form of betting in which each match on a list of the major matches on the day in question is individually priced. Although these odds are guaranteed once the punter places his bet, they are subject to fluctuation in price at any time up to kick-off.

Internationals Matches between countries on which singles are accepted.

Last goalscorer Bet offering opportunity of gambling on player to score the last goal of 90 minutes' play. Popular choices are goalkeepers known for charging into opposition penalty boxes in the final minute or two.

Long shot An outsider in a betting list.

Odds against A betting price where the odds are greater than even money.

Odds-on A price where the odds are less than even money.

Patent Consists of seven bets involving three football teams in different matches or events – a single on each team plus three doubles and a treble.

Permutation Permutations can increase chances of winning by insuring against a number of losing selections. For example, seven selections can be covered in a permutation of five, six and seven-folds. In this case, even two losing selections would guarantee a winning five timer.

Postponed match Treated as void for betting purposes.

Single A bet – home, draw or away – on just one game.

To win outright Where a football match may be subject to extra-time or a penalty shoot-out or replay, you can opt to bet 'to win outright' which means that the punter takes one or other of the two teams to win regardless of when the outcome is decided.

Treble A bet involving three selections in which the total returns are invested on each successive selection.

Yankee A bet consisting of 11 component parts involving four selections in different events or matches – six doubles, four trebles and an accumulator.

CHAPTER EIGHT

You Win Some – You Lose Some – (Well Almost!)

Fifty-seven-year-old coach company owner Jim Wright from Teignmouth won so much money from Ladbrokes that they were forced to exceed their own limits to pay him out in full. Jim's £1,000 each-way treble was placed on the 1992–93 season. He picked Newcastle to win division one at 8/1; Stoke to win division two at 6/1 and Cardiff City – owned by his brother Rick – to win the third at 9/1. They all obliged and that comparatively modest initial stake snowballed to a record-breaking £654,375, busting the bookies' £500,000 limit and prompting Jim to declare: 'I'm determined not to invest the money wisely.'

Tom Davis and Phil Korny teamed up for a £1 accumulator bet in October 1987, and hours later found themselves world record holders. Former postman Tom and publican Phil, from Clitheroe, picked out 14 matches. Thirteen of them were played on Saturday, 24 October and the pair had them all correct. The 14th was the Scottish Skol Cup final to be played on the Sunday. They'd tipped a draw, but with five minutes to go Rangers were a goal down – then they equalised. Tom and Phil thought they may have won about £5,000 so a happy Tom went down to the local William Hill on Monday to collect. He was told they had won a then best-ever payout of £97,726.99p. One hopes they spent some of it on a ready reckoner, after Tom's comment: 'Our previous largest win was £261 and I thought we'd beaten that this time, but I wasn't sure by how much.'

Their record now belongs to a gentleman called Graham Jenkins from Bournemouth – and I can't make up my mind whether this man is the King of Punters, as he was dubbed by the *Sporting Life,* or the Clown Prince.

Consider the evidence. This man went into his local betting shop, a branch of Ladbrokes, on Saturday, 25 January 1997. The 56-year-old had been betting on fixed-odds coupons for 20 years and decided to invest £10 on a 15 team accumulator. Not for him the hard slog of looking through the form and ticking off what he reckoned to be the best bets of the day.

'It took me only about 30 seconds to fill in the coupon,' he said later, 'and I don't know anything about form.' In fact, he doesn't seem to have known much about anything connected with this bet, as we will see. Fourteen of the 15 games he selected were due to be played on that Saturday afternoon. One of them was postponed. Fourteen winners to go.

The games all kicked off at 3 p.m. One of them, Torquay at home to Mansfield, was abandoned during the first half without a goal having been scored, Graham had gone for a home win, so thought that was his bet down the Swanee. Despite his 20 years' experience, he clearly didn't bother to check the rules which applied to his wagers. Ladbrokes, who had previously operated a regulation which meant that abandoned matches were settled according to the scoreline at that time, had recently amended their rule and now voided abandoned games, thus meaning that Graham's bet was unaffected. Thirteen to go. Incredibly, all 12 of his Saturday afternoon selections which remained went the way he had predicted – eight home wins, four aways.

His bet had produced a return thus far of £117,000 – all of which was now riding on the outcome of a match on Monday evening between Airdrie and Raith, in the Tennents Cup. Graham's selection was an away win for Raith which, if it came up, would boost his kitty to £292,882.98p, at odds of 11/5. What would you do? What *should* you do?

If you are ever faced with this situation you should feel obliged to beg, steal or borrow as much cash as you can find and shovel large amounts of it on the two other potential results which you have not covered with your original bet.

For example, you know that if Raith win you collect over £290,000. Now then, Airdrie are quoted at 6/4 to win at home, the draw is a 6/4 chance. The match is a Cup game. Singles are accepted. By placing, let's say, £100,000 plus tax on both the home win and the draw you would then be guaranteed a profit of £32,000 if either of those results came up and a profit of £74,000 if the game turned out to be an away win.

Okay, I know it would be virtually impossible to get hold of two hundred grand at short notice (and equally difficult to bet it all on one match) but you see the principle. This method does cut down the potential winnings enormously, but – and this is a mega but – it totally eliminates any danger that your bet will become just another loser on the pile balanced on the betting shop counter. Let's face it, if, when you walked into the betting shop to place your £10 bet, the manager positively *guaranteed* you minimum winnings of £32,000 there would be a queue of would-be punters from the shop door to Bournemouth Pier!

Bookmakers themselves don't like to promote the idea of 'hedging' bets in this manner – after all the odds are still in their favour if the punter just lets the stake money ride.

However, Graham Jenkins considered none of this – in fact, he didn't even put himself out to discover the result of the Monday evening game, or check what was happening on Teletext. If he had done so he might well have suffered a heart-attack as Raith went a goal down in the first half, only for Airdrie to self-destruct as they had a player sent off before crashing to a 1-4 defeat. Graham Jenkins knew nothing of this drama. He went to bed early because he had to be up early to begin work at Warren's Taxis the next morning.

'It was only when I bought a paper on my way to work that I saw Raith had won,' he said later. Answering questions about why he hadn't considered hedging the wager, he came up with what must be the betting quote of the century: 'What's the point? If it wins, it wins; if it loses, it loses.'

Well, you can't argue with his logic. But there was a very good point to be made and many people would have made it to him had Raith failed to win, even though Graham would clearly believe to this day that he had merely lost his £10 stake money and the 90p paid-on deductions.

There's more, though – at this point, easily shocked punters should avert their gaze. Graham could have won himself an additional £55,000, just by taking a short stroll down the road to the nearest branch of William Hill where, had he been remotely interested in finding out, he could have discovered that they were offering longer odds about no fewer than eight of his successful selections, which would have bumped his winnings up to an awesome £348,792 plus a bit of loose change.

It wouldn't have worried a character like Graham, though. And there are hundreds of thousands, if not millions, just like him, who honestly couldn't give a damn that they are handing their bookmakers a living on a plate by not checking the rules, not comparing odds and not taking advantage of the system where it favours their best interests. Long may that continue, say I – at least for as long as I earn my living working for a bookmaker.

Graham Jenkins found himself an ally from an unexpected source when the *Sporting Life* sports betting tipster Bruce Millington took me to task in his column for issuing a press release pointing out how much extra Mr Jenkins' family fortunes could have been had he bothered to check out the better odds available.

> What was the message? [asked Millington, clearly not thinking straight.] It couldn't have been that Hill's football prices are universally better than Ladbrokes'. They aren't. And Sharpe surely isn't saying that punters who want a quick and easy chance to get rich without risking the family silver should spend hours with a ready reckoner sussing out which of the five main coupons offers the maximum payout potential before striking their bets. It all seems rather petty.

I was flabbergasted at this from a man who devotes hundreds, sometimes thousands, of words each week to explaining to readers just why they should avail themselves of odds of 10/11 from one bookie instead of 5/6 from another all in the cause of getting better betting value. Here he was excusing a punter who, for the sake of a couple of minutes with a calculator – not hours with a ready reckoner – had cost himself £55,000 on the bet of a lifetime, by accepting an astonishing 5,000 points under the odds. If Millington regards that as 'petty' then I have to say he is doing his job under false pretences.

Don't just take my word for it. Listen to 'Statistician' who in *Betting Systems that Win* remarked:

> It is a good idea to shop around. Different bookmakers will often rate the odds about some matches differently, and if you have access to several coupons you should make your entry with the firm offering the best prices about your particular fancies.

I was comforted to find another ally, albeit it from 45 years ago, in betting expert E. Lennox Figgis, who wrote three books on the subject between 1951 and 1976. In his *Focus on Gambling*, from the earlier date, he dealt with the imaginary situation in which a pools punter who believed that he had hit the jackpot, only to discover that he had made the wrong entry, was apprised of his ghastly error. Putting himself in the character of the disappointed gambler, Figgis said: 'Anyone who risks his hard-earned money on something which he doesn't understand, is not only a gambler, but an idiot,' adding, 'and a more unfortunate combination of characteristics it would be impossible to imagine in a human being.' I rest my case.

Other notable fixed-odds winners include Harrow, Middlesex, driving instructor, Nimai Datta who, in March 1992, revved up for a payout of £119,723.69p from William Hill, courtesy of a successful £10, 14 match accumulator. It was ironic that Hill's were his victims, considering the name of his wife – Coral.

A Brighton man who found a pound coin in the street back in October 1994, decided his luck must be in so he went straight into a nearby William Hill betting shop in Burgess Hill and put the £1 on a football bet. He named 14 would-be winning football results, all of which obliged, winning him £15,514.64p for what he told staff in the shop was his first-ever bet. The anonymous businessman, in his mid-40s, joked as he collected his cheque, 'I'm only sorry I told the wife, otherwise I'd have sent her a postcard from Rio.'

In March 1991, another Coral client – 'a 19-year-old canny Scotsman in England looking for employment' – placed a 10p, 15 match accumulator in their branch in Chippenham, Wiltshire. Fourteen of his selections won on the Saturday and he was waiting on Arsenal to beat Liverpool at Anfield. The game was goalless at half-time until Paul Merson's winner early in the second half won the match for the Gunners and £163,071.07 for the triumphant exiled Scot, who presumably changed his mind about looking for work for a while.

Sensational though those winning odds were, I have since discovered that 15 winners in a football accumulator do not a record make. In October 1971, a William Hill client from Leicester found *seventeen* football winners for a £1 accumulator which paid £7,227, while in May 1991 exiled Scot Jackie Wileman of Harlesden in Greater London also collected £79,777.33p for a £5, 15 game accumulator which was rounded off with a 4–1 victory for Falkirk over Ayr.

These noteworthy wagers are all remarkable enough of their type, but I must doff my cap in undying admiration to the unnamed Lincoln punter who, in November 1992, staked just £1.50p on four matches each producing a 3–2 scoreline. He was right every time and was enriched to the tune of £110,249.90p – now that's what I call tipping.

Talking of correct-score wagers, one of the most memorable correct scores involving the England side must be their 4–1 walloping of Holland during Euro '96. Wonderful though that result was for the mood of the nation, it was also unexpected, to say the least, to the point where I believe that there was only one punter in the whole of the land brave enough to stick a £50 bet on it happening. At odds of 100/1 businessman Ernie Witcomb of Paddington, London, collected £5,000.

Arthur Pownall, a Disley, Cheshire, company director, set himself a six-year target to win £20,000 on fixed-odds football betting. On Saturday, 4 December 1962, almost six years to the day after he had set the target, he achieved it. He correctly forecast seven draws on William Hill's list, and at 20,000/1 to a stake of £1 that gave him his desired win. Mr Pownall said at the time of what was then a life-changing win, 'Frankly, I didn't visualise it this way. I thought I had a system for winning £20,000 in six years, but this win came out of the blue.'

Remarkably, for a man with a mission he had left something to chance, relying on his secretary to fill in and send off his coupon – let's hope he gave her a generous reward, not just redundancy.

You might think that having done the difficult part by backing a winner or two, punters would at least be bothered to relieve their bookmaker of the burden of looking after their winnings. But they don't always.

I mean, you or I might take the trouble to check our selections if we had placed a 12 match accumulator bet. If all 12 of our selections had come up as predicted, you or I might make an immediate bee-line for the betting shop where we had placed our bet in order to ascertain that they had not gone out of business and were good for the £1,378.50p of readies that we calculated were rightfully ours. Not Mr Yun Yang of North Harrow in Middlesex, who in October 1995, placed such a bet for a £1 stake, and then did absolutely nothing.

Despite enlisting the help of the local paper, the *Harrow Observer*, staff at the William Hill branch where the bet was placed had all but given up hope of locating the customer, when *ten* weeks later Mr Yun Yang finally arrived for his cash, apparently 'unaware that his bet was a winner and very excited to find he had over £1,300 to collect just before Christmas,' said shop manager Maurice O'Neill.

But how can anyone overlook a win like that? Not all bookmakers are so obliging, either – some will only guarantee to pay out claims received within a couple of months, although the majority of companies will honour a valid betting slip whenever it is presented, provided they can be 100 per cent sure of its bona fides.

For example, in November 1995 a Crystal Palace fan, Mr I.J. Dunnell of Beddington in Surrey, wrote to William Hill asking for his winnings from a bet placed way back in the 1990–91 football season on his club finishing in the first three of the then first division. He sent the bookmakers a plaintive letter: 'I have only just found the ticket, having hidden it in such a safe place that I'd forgotten it by the end of the season.

'I realise that your records will only go back so far, but as Palace are unlikely to finish in the top three of the Premier League again in my lifetime, would it still be possible to collect on this ticket?'

Fortunately for Mr Dunnell, Hill's took his word for it and shelled out the £15.75 due on the wager.

Even more bizarre was the case of East London man, W. Bennett, who finally claimed for a bet on Aston Villa and Newcastle from three years earlier, claiming that he had been 'under terrible stress' following the disappearance of his teenaged son, Billy, from the holiday island of Tenerife in 1985, since when he had not been seen.

'I have just got round to sorting myself out and I'm hoping that you can pay me what I was due,' he wrote, somewhat oddly as the boy had been missing for over ten years although the bet had been placed just three years previously. However, Hill's were able to confirm that the £19.80 bet had won returns of £204, which was duly paid over with the compliments of customer relations manager John Quinn. I don't, though, recommend suddenly discovering that you've come across a betting slip in the loft for Wanderers to beat the Royal Engineers 1–0 with Betts scoring the goal in the 1872 FA Cup final, as I think you might have more chance of getting a payout from the *Antiques Roadshow* than from the bookie who laid the bet.

A big winner in early 1989 gave me my first personal experience of Gazza. Spurs fan Mike Coulson, a painter and decorator, was working in London's Hatton Garden in early 1989 when he and his partner decided to go for a drink. *En route* to the pub, Mike's mate said he wanted to pop into the betting shop for an individual-odds bet. Mike had never had a bet before in his life, but his pal insisted that he should have a go, so he laid out a whole quid on two 50p, 14 match accumulators. He deliberately left out his side, Spurs, as he didn't want to jinx them.

So unusual was it for Mike to have placed a bet that he made a point of telling his wife Elaine how naughty he had been. Mike didn't bother to check his selections until the next day when he discovered that all 14 on one line had won.

'I checked it time and again, and realised that we had won about £3,500,' said Mike. Wrong. He'd won £89,738.96p.

Mike had included a Sheffield Wednesday versus Liverpool game as a draw and Liverpool had come back from two down with John Aldridge scoring the equaliser. However Mike, the ungrateful wretch, turned down my offer to get Aldridge to present him with his cheque. He wanted to meet the Spurs players, so off we went to their North London training ground where Paul Walsh and Terry Fenwick did the honours and where, as I wrote at the time, 'I was astonished at the ability of Paul "Fat Gazza" Gascoigne, who managed to put away the best part of an entire bottle of HP sauce over his after-training dinner.'

After receiving his cheque Mike vowed that not only was this his first bet, but also his last. I've often wondered whether he stuck to that vow.

Two squash champions teamed up for a football bet which won them a substantial payout on a unique event. Former Scottish champion Mark Maclean, and Welsh champion Adrian Davies staked a £10 accumulator between them with Coral's on all six Scottish premier division matches ending in a draw in mid-January 1994 – and for the first time since the division was established in 1975, all six finished all-square.

'I had a gut feeling that the matches had "draws" written all over them,' said Maclean, who failed to persuade Davies to double the suggested stakes, which would have won them twice the £10,800 they actually collected.

Two massive bets paid off 33-year-old Paul Tolley's mortgage in May 1996. Record company sales rep Paul from Dudley, West Midlands, faced years trying to pay off the £50,000 he owed the building society so he persuaded his wife Jacky to let him gamble the mortgage away. He laid out £300 on a double bet, coupling Brazil to win the 1994 World Cup with Birmingham winning the 1994–95 second division title. That returned him £27,000 with which he paid off over half the mortgage before staking a further £600 on South Africa to win the Rugby World Cup, which they did at 4/1, going on to 7/1 chance Preston to win the 1995–96 third division title, which they also did, producing a return on the bet of £24,000 – enough to pay off the rest of the mortgage.

There has never been a bigger football bet loser than 24-year-old out of work woodcutter Brain McGregor from Hexham. How much did he lose? Well, the small matter of £3,826,470,000,000,000 – yes,

£3,826.47 billion – which he had 'won' for a 50p stake from Ladbrokes by successfully predicting the outcome of every one of the 61 games on their soccer coupon on Boxing Day, 1992.

Ladbrokes begged to differ. They believed it was somewhat unlikely that he had actually managed this staggering feat – at least, in any way likely to persuade them to hand over the readies; or, indeed, anything at all. Just to be on the safe side, they rather thought they had better consult the police as to what they felt they should be doing.

It transpired that the results had been entered when the scores were already known. As a result, Brian McGregor appeared before Hexham magistrates in March 1993. Who, instead of recommending that he should receive the monster payout – which was actually 17 times the total income that the Government expected to raise in 1992–93 – felt that they should award him 12 months probation and request that he pay £20 costs.

'He had no idea about the amount of money involved and did not know security at Ladbrokes was so tight. He could not have received that amount of money which is 10 to 12 times the amount currently in circulation in the UK,' said Andy Travis, mitigating for McGregor.

A Ladbrokes spokesman was more to the point: 'He didn't stand a hope in hell of being paid that kind of money.'

A bookmaker who hadn't done his football homework was a loser to a clued-up football punter in season 1995–96. In April 1996, with Torquay nine points adrift at the foot of Divison Three, a customer visited a branch of Joe Jennings and asked for odds that Torquay would *not* be relegated. He was offered 33/1 and staked £42, giving himself potential winnings of £1,428.

Punter and bookmaker were happy with the bet – until the bookmaker realised that Torquay could only go down if the team due to replace them – whoever won the Vauxhall Conference – had facilities acceptable to the Football League to enable them to replace Torquay. Stevenage were running away with the Conference, but unfortunately did not have facilities thought suitable by the Football League. Therefore they couldn't go up. Therefore, Torquay couldn't go down. The punter had done his homework and fully deserved his win – after all no one forced Jennings to offer odds.

They didn't quite see it that way, though, and a spokesman commented, 'It's a small time coup and we'll pay out. But there's a principle here. The lack of integrity is what disturbs us.

'The punter had information that we didn't have before placing the bet.'

The words 'losers' and 'bad' spring to mind – not necessarily in that order!

When flamboyant (and later to be jailed) businessman Owen Oyston bought his way into Blackpool Football Club, he decided to produce a major incentive for the players to do well by staking a huge bet on them to win the third division, and announcing that he'd give them and the manager a cool quarter of a million if they managed it. I received a phone call asking me if my company would lay Mr Oyston a bet of £15,000 each way, plus tax, for Blackpool (a) to win the division and (b) to gain promotion. At odds of 20/1 and 4/1 respectively, Mr Oyston stood to land a win of £360,000 clear profit if the Seasiders won the title, thus making it potentially the largest single winning bet on a side landing a divisional championship.

Mr Oyston summoned the press, local dignitaries and anyone else he could drag along to witness the handing over of the stakes to me on the pitch before the home game with Sunderland. His team obviously hadn't read the script – they lost, and went on to finish in mid-table mediocrity. Incidentally, the FA never indicated that they had any objection to this kind of bet in general or this one in particular.

Judge for yourself whether you believe that London punter Lee Thickbroom lived up to his name when he lashed out a substantial £200 on a 1000/1 shot.When Bordeaux lost 2–0 at AC Milan in the 1995–96 UEFA Cup quarter-final first leg, Coral's quoted them at 1000/1 to win the final. Lee reckoned they should only have been 75/1 so stepped in with his two hundred quid. Bordeaux won the second leg 3–0 to go through, and made it into the final where they were a biggest priced 5/2 to beat Bayern Munich. Bordeaux lost and Lee's bet of a lifetime went down, although he was shrewd enough to have laid his bet off and ensured himself a winning outcome regardless of the result, but the point here is that his bet represented a value for money, over the odds flutter. If all punters accepted such odds over a period of time, punters would gain the upper hand in the eternal battle with the old enemy.

If only – fortunately for us bookies, we know that scenario is hugely unlikely; and if it did happen, and we went out of business, well, who would take your bets then?

CHAPTER NINE

How Football Finally Out-Bet the Grand National

In 1994, the World Cup officially eclipsed the Grand National as the biggest betting event of all time, according to British bookmakers.

I was quoted at the time by many newspapers as saying, 'The Grand National has always been the world's biggest betting event. But William Hill have taken £15 million on the World Cup, compared with £13.8 million on Grand National Day 1994. I estimate that £60 million has been gambled industry-wide on the World Cup.' Estimates from other British bookmaking sources confirmed this assertion, with post-event statistics even suggesting it may have erred on the side of caution, although it has to be admitted that some of the biggest players during the World Cup had been foreign clients. An Australian client of William Hill (a Melbourne-based businessman) was probably the biggest-staking punter, laying out £482,000 in total on matches, and ending up £100,000 down on his transactions.

This chap fascinated me, not so much for the sheer volume of his business, awe-inspiring although that was – I mean, you are forced to wonder why anyone who can afford to bet like that would feel the need to do it – but for the staking plan he utilised. Staking 17 bets in the space of ten days, totalling £482,000, giving an average stake per transaction of £28,350, he still found time to stake one £500 wager. Why? Given that average stake of over £28,000, what was the point of a miserable 'monkey' flutter? It was as if you or I, who might normally risk a tenner or a score on a good thing, suddenly bothered to splash out between 25p and 50p on one bet; rather irrelevant, surely. Perhaps he'd just found a few spare notes in the lining of an old jacket; perhaps it was left-over petty cash; perhaps it was the change after sending out for a pizza; perhaps a small bet for his butler. I guess I'll never know, but I'll always wonder.

Another major betting story to come out of the '94 World Cup concerned the William Hill client who won £395,000 when Brazil's triumph rounded off an £8,000 accumulator he had staked, which also included Manchester United and Crystal Palace to win their respective divisions. He had also staked £5,000 at odds of 11/1 that the final would be between Brazil and Italy.

Initially, the man was only willing to be identified as a 'flower importer from Birmingham'. I sent out a press release including that description. Within a couple of hours our man was back on the phone: 'Okay, you *can* use my full name – not that I've much choice in the matter. I've just found out that there are only two flower importers in Birmingham, and I've already had the other one on the phone telling me he's fed up being pestered by the press asking about his World Cup winnings!'

The 'outing' of Adrian Fitzpatrick did his business a great favour, though. He appeared all over the media, including *News at Ten*, and was able to give his floral future a real boost. He was still in demand from the national media during 1996, when the *Daily Star* roped him in as a guest tipster for the Euro '96 tournament – but he wasn't much 'blooming' good that time around.

Holborn clerk Harold Anand, a 56-year-old North London punter, was probably the calmest person watching the World Cup final, knowing that he stood to win £124,000 if Italy won it and a mere £106,000 if Brazil came out on top. Okay, I don't suppose he was that calm when Baggio blasted his penalty wide of the goal to cost him £18,000! He had ended up in this happy position by staking two £400 accumulator bets as long ago as the previous August which gave him £17,700 running on to Italy at 6/1 and the same amount on to Brazil at 5/1.

Those punters seemed to have clairvoyant powers, but one Malaysian client of William Hill had no need of a clairvoyant to tip him losers, he was quite capable of finding them himself. He went down in betting history when he twice gambled the largest single amount ever staked on a match with a British bookmaker during the course of the 1994 World Cup tournament. He laid out a staggering £121,000 on Mexico to beat Bulgaria and the same amount on Brazil to beat Italy in 90 minutes play. Both selections were losers.

He should have consulted the Hong Kong restaurant owner who turned up in Dorset where he placed and landed the biggest single winning soccer bet ever when his returns for a £115,000 stake on Brazil to beat Sweden at odds of 4/7 were £165,000 – not a bad take-away, particularly in view of the fact that he had previously won £126,362 after placing £74,000 on Brazil to beat Holland.

An Essex woman raised a few eyebrows with a total turnover of £99,500 on the World Cup, including a slightly eccentric plunge on the Romania versus Sweden quarter-final, betting £29,000 on Romania to win in 90 minutes' play – and £24,000 on Sweden to win in 90 minutes' play. The game ended 1–1 and she lost the lot. She reappeared in 1997, staking £150,000 on Labour to win the General Election, teamed with Rangers and Manchester United winning their respective Premierships, and collecting £175,000.

A mystery gambler from Lancashire waited for over a fortnight before collecting the £45,000 he made from a £1,000 double on Mexico and Nigeria winning their World Cup groups in a Southport betting shop. No-one could understand why he had failed to call in for his cash until it was explained that he had gone to the States to watch the tournament, and had got so excited when Nigeria scored the goal which clinched his win that he was nearly thrown out of his hotel. Before claiming his hard-earned readies, the punter sent his bookie a postcard: 'Greetings from Las Vegas, the gambling capital of the world, though Southport runs it a close second – don't worry, I haven't forgotten about my little footy bet. I'll be in to collect after I've closed Caesar's Palace down.' By the time he did arrive for his winnings the local media was in a frenzy trying to identify him, but he was cute enough to retain his anonymity.

The World Cup seemed to tempt all kinds of people who had seldom if ever previously risked cash on the outcome of a sporting event. One of the oddest examples was Cornishman Gerald McSorley who went so far as staking £50 on talismanic Republic of Ireland manager Jack Charlton being knighted as a result of his exploits with that country. He received odds of 33/1.

Essex lorry driver Tony Tredwell, who said that he hated football, had no Irish connections and had never had a bet before, was so caught up in the World Cup hysteria that he lashed out an amazing £400 at odds of 200/1 that Big Jack's lads would win the World Cup final by 3–0, regardless of who they might meet.

As well as the noteworthy individual punters who appeared on the scene, a number of matches attracted phenomenal betting turnover, and they weren't always the ones which might have been expected to do so.

William Hill, who reckon to have around a quarter of the industry betting turnover, reported that a £500,000 gamble went badly wrong as Cameroon took on Russia. A rumour began to do the rounds of the gambling community that Russia weren't 'off' – in other words, that they wouldn't be trying. Russia were virtually out of the tournament, anyway, went the story, whereas Cameroon could still make an impression if they won – the Russians would be lying down and accepting defeat.

Money poured in from all over the globe, and it was all for Cameroon to win. Their odds plunged from odds-against to odds-on, as Hills struggled to attract more than the odd fiver or tenner for a Russian win. I personally saw bets coming in from Australia, Hong Kong, Malaysia, Italy, Germany, Holland, USA and, of course, Britain. One man even staked an unprecedented £10,000 on a correct score of 3–0 to Cameroon.

We braced ourselves for the payout of all time – until the game got underway in San Francisco in front of 74,914 fans, at which point it became obvious that one person who certainly hadn't bet on a Cameroon victory was the Russian striker, Oleg Salenko (once wanted by Spurs, but they could not get him a work permit). He proceeded to score no less than five times as Russia annihilated Cameroon 6–1. We hadn't taken a rouble for Salenko to top the World Cup scoring charts prior to this feat which catapulted him to 5/4 favourite to end up as the leading marksman – and we took barely a rouble for him after the game.

Vodka was much in evidence after that game as we celebrated a total payout of just £6,000 to punters who'd backed Russia. This game saw the biggest gamble of all, but the game between Colombia and USA, and the Romania–Switzerland match weren't far behind. These, too, produced results to the liking of the bookies, enriching the coffers of William Hill alone by some half a million pounds, as one punter lost £67,500 on the two matches.

The gambling patterns on these three matches in particular did give rise to speculation that attempted match rigging may be taking place, at least within the betting fraternity. No evidence to support such a theory was ever forthcoming, to my knowledge, and I prefer to think that a more likely explanation for such a plunge on comparatively low-profile games was that they were deemed to offer excellent betting value by certain high-rolling punters or syndicates who therefore staked hefty amounts on the games.

This kind of money being placed cannot help but be noticed by others on the periphery of the gambling circuit who would then draw their own conclusions and spread their own gossip whilst rushing to make sure that they didn't miss out on what by this time was being talked up as a betting coup. In actual fact it was nothing more than a bandwagon out of control, which ultimately suffered a jarring crash, as a direct result of which there were some nasty financial casualties, some of which may have proved fatal.

Although the 1994 event was chock-full of mega punters, Britain's first £1 million punter turned up during the 1990 tournament, when he ended an extraordinary two-week spree with a net profit of just £18,000.

The punter, believed to be a foreign gentleman based in London, was almost £500,000 down to William Hill at one stage, before winning £230,000 on England's third-place play-off against Italy. He invested £70,000 on Italy winning that game, and a further £20,000 on the 2–1 correct scoreline. He followed this up by collecting a further £28,000 when his £60,000 on West Germany to win the final and £20,000 on the 1–0 scoreline also proved successful as he clawed back his earlier losses.

His big losing bets had included £100,000 on West Germany to beat England in 90 minutes' play and £60,000 on Italy to beat Argentina.

In total he turned over £1,028,000, and then disappeared whence he'd come, never to be heard of again.

Euro '96 made a respectable attempt to outdo the '94 World Cup in the betting stakes, and may well have achieved it had England won that dreaded penalty shoot-out against the Germans and reached the final. It wasn't to be, though, and estimates at the time suggested that the total betting turnover on the event had fallen just short of £60 million, which still left it as the biggest betting event to be staged on British soil.

With the Derby being run on the same day that Euro '96 got underway, Ladbrokes racing PR man Mike Dillon was quoted as saying: 'Derby turnover was well down. Punters are now more interested in football betting.' That opinion was echoed by the *Racing Post*'s sports editor, Derek McGovern, who added, 'There is now little doubt that betting on sport in general and football in particular is a serious threat to racing for top-dog status in betting turnover.'

An English involvement in the Final would have added at least a couple of million to the turnover and you could argue that in terms of average turnover per game the tournament did outstrip the '94 World Cup, which had more matches.

Opinions differ as to what was the biggest betting game of the tournament, with Ladbrokes somewhat surprisingly nominating the opening game, England v Switzerland, while William Hill's biggest turnover game was England v Scotland. The money staked – getting on for a million with Hill's alone – was predominantly on England, with bets of £60,000, £50,000, £42,000, £30,000 and £10,000 being plunged on them at odds of 6/5, while Scotland, quoted at 7/2, attracted a largest stake of just £500.

That same Euro '96 was the backdrop to one of the most remarkable feats of multi-sport betting I've come across when a Folkestone gambler won £201,069 from a £122 nine-event accumulator which ended successfully when Germany won Euro '96. That win rounded off a bet which had opened with a rugby league selection – St Helens for the Silk Cut Cup. Next up were two horse-racing winners – Mark Of Esteem in the 2,000 Guineas and Bosra Sham in the 1,000 Guineas. The rest of the selections were all football as Manchester United's Premiership triumph, Sunderland's division one title, Preston's division three championship, Rangers' Scottish premier win and Dunfermline's victory in the Scottish first division all edged the bet to its winning conclusion.

The 1998 World Cup must be an odds-on chance to set yet more football betting turnover records and it cannot be long before the £100 million betting barrier is broken by a World Cup or European Championship tournament. In fact, the potentially mind-boggling betting bonanza likely to take place in France in 1998 prompted Pat Flanagan, a Ladbrokes executive, to predict: 'A million pound bet on the finals of the World Cup would not be out of the question.' It won't be me placing it!

It was the 1966 World Cup which elevated readily and legally available football betting on a major tournament to previously unheard of heights.

Excitement and anticipation was already growing in the betting world months before the event got underway when London credit bookmakers Rosspoint advertised World Cup odds in the *Sporting Life* on 1 April 1966. They weren't taking any chances when they quoted England as 5/1 second favourites behind 9/4 market leaders Brazil, with West Germany at surprisingly attractive odds of 25/1 eighth favourites. England were also offered at 2/1 to make the final. Ten days later, Rosspoint had eased England to 6/1 while the Germans had come in to 22/1.

Previewing the forthcoming arrival in the country of the world's greatest footballing nations, *Sporting Life* writer Graham Taylor (no relation to the future England manager) lambasted the pools companies:

> Surely with the resources of the vast pools empire it would be possible for at least one firm to issue an advanced special Cup coupon.
>
> Unlike the pools, many bookmakers have shown considerably more enterprise. Any layer will quote you a price about outright winners and many are to issue special lists for individual games.

By 9 July with the tournament only two days away, England were being supported by patriotic punters. 'Anything over 4/1 is quickly snapped up,' said the *Life*, quoting one bookmaker as saying: 'A home triumph could cost us dear.'

Meanwhile West Germany had also been supported down to 9/1. England faced Uruguay on the opening day of the competition, 11 July. Ladbrokes reported a £1,000 bet from a London wholesaler and cut England to 7/2 second favourites while William Hill's prices as the World Cup began were: 2/1 Brazil; 4/1 England; 7/1 Italy; 9/1 Argentina; 10 W. Germany; 11 Russia; 22 Hungary, Portugal; 25 Spain; 33 France; 40 Uruguay; 66 Bulgaria, Chile; 100 N. Korea; 150 Switzerland; 200 Mexico.

Following a 0–0 draw, England were lengthened to 6/1. The Germans hit Switzerland for five, and their odds were cut, also to 6/1. Favourites Brazil got off to a losing start, going down 2–1 to Hungary. They went out to 6/1 while England and Germany headed the lists at 5/1.

England now beat Mexico. The *Life*'s Graham Taylor said, 'All the bookies seem to agree – England have a very good chance indeed. At 5/1 they are still value.'

Italy crashed out while Brazil looked set for an early trip home, but Portugal began in impressive style and became 3/1 favourites by 20 July, ahead of England at 4/1, Germany 9/2, Hungary 5/1, Argentina 7/1 and Russia 9/1.

Now England defeated France 2–0 and were cut by Hill's from 4/1 to 7/2 second favourites.

As England prepared to meet Argentina in the quarter-final, William Hill made them 4/6 to win in 90 minutes' play with the draw and Argentina both 11/4 chances. Portugal were 11/4 tournament favourites with England 7/2; Hungary 4/1; Germany 5/1; Argentina and Russia both 10/1; Uruguay 20/1; North Korea 150/1.

In a bad-tempered match England beat Argentina 1–0 and

Ladbrokes made what looked like being a costly mistake by quoting them at 3/1. Said their MD, Cyril Stein: 'Immediately our prices were announced on TV there was a rush for England and they were backed to lose us £6,000.'

One Hill's client, though, fancied Russia and staked £2,000 on them at 7/2, although they were fourth favourites at that price while England were 5/2 with Portugal at the same odds and Germany 11/4 in a desperately close-looking book. Ladbrokes had the Portuguese as clear favourites at 9/4.

England were now offered at even money to defeat the mighty Eusebio and his Portuguese colleagues in their semi-final. The Germans were 5/4 to beat Russia.

William Hill announced that so far they had taken £103,000 on the competition – a 'staggering' amount compared with the £120,000 in that year's ante-post book on the Derby.

West Germany saw off the Russians 2–1 in 90 minutes' play and immediately became 6/5 favourites with Portugal at 2/1 and England 9/4.

As the England v Portugal game kicked off, Margolis & Ridley were advertising 11/8 England, 6/4 Portugal, 11/4 the draw. A thrilling game resulted in a 2–1 win for England and Hill's made them 8/13 favourites to lift the trophy with Germany 11/8.

London's Margolis & Ridley quoted 4/5 England in 90 minutes' play with the Germans 15/8 and the draw 11/4. There was no shortage of takers wanting to punt on England who went into the final 8/11 to win without extra-time, with Germany at 9/4 and the ultimate outcome of a 90 minutes' draw, 3/1. England were 1/2 to win outright with Germany 7/4. Of course, England won 4–2 after extra-time, and William Hill said: 'Of course we lost – it cost us £8,000. But business was tremendous, reaching nearly £150,000.'

Ladbrokes were asked by Graham Taylor of the *Life*: 'Were you delighted?' An anonymous spokesman responded: 'Delighted? Please don't put it as strongly as that, after all, they cost us dearly – £11,000 in fact. Perhaps you had better just say that as an Englishman I am delighted but as a Ladbroke employee I have known better days.'

Oddly, Coral's claimed to have profited from the final, although losing on bets to win the Cup outright.

CHAPTER TEN

On Betting Grounds

It is common-place these days to be able to place a bet when one arrives at a football ground. The majority of Premiership clubs boast betting shop facilities, as does Wembley Stadium.

The first club to invite a bookmaker on to the premises was Luton Town. At the beginning of the 1987–88 season, local company Worldsport became the first bookmaker to operate inside a Football League ground. The club secured a racecourse betting licence from the local council and Worldsport set up two shops as well as providing a courier service for Kenilworth Road's two dozen-plus executive boxes.

The company's shops opened for business from 11 a.m. on match-day mornings and Worldsport director Steve Short commented at the time: 'We commenced negotiations last year with Luton. As we are a local firm we believed we would prove suitable. As Luton exercise a tight control over their supporters with their membership policy we envisaged no crowd problems.'

Punters were charged 5 per cent deductions from their wagers – less than from a High Street betting shop – and were given football betting coupons as they entered the ground through the turnstiles.

Worldsport took bets on the matches at the ground as well as other sporting events and horse racing. However, as the club's fortunes on the pitch took a turn for the worse so, presumably, did the betting turnover and the club no longer boasts betting facilities.

As grounds of lower league teams, even non-league, have betting shops within walking distance, it is not unusual to see odds chalked up about the local match. I have seen odds being offered in the bar of a non-league side prior to the game.

Other grounds have forged links with betting by, for example, staging greyhound racing at the ground. Perhaps the earliest example of such a link came in 1909 when hard-up Scottish side Cowdenbeath staged whippet racing at their ground to help raise funds.

In October 1927, the FA Council appointed a committee of 11 members to investigate greyhound racing's links with football. They decided that although it would be too great an interference to prohibit the use of grounds for dog racing, clubs should nevertheless be warned that they would be held responsible for preventing betting on their grounds at football matches.

The Football League declared in 1932 that 'dog racing is a menace to our game', for reasons best known to itself, presumably not unrelated to the association between greyhound racing and the betting business. They prohibited clubs from having anything to do with the recently established sport. The FA Council were also of the opinion at this time that 'it is undesirable that clubs should be financed or controlled by proprietors of greyhound racing'.

This attitude seemed to overlook the fact that Wembley Stadium had hosted dog racing since December 1927, before the sport had even celebrated its first anniversary.

Clubs already committed to staging racing were permitted to continue their relationship. Watford, for example, had begun staging greyhound racing in 1928, receiving an annual rent of £1,500. In 1930, the club was hauled over the coals for the heinous crime of allowing the dog track lights to be switched on during a murky afternoon fixture – floodlit matches were prohibited in those days and were only finally permitted in the mid '50s.

In 1969, Watford dispensed with the dogs when their financial fortunes were looking bright. By 1975, events had taken a turn for the worse, and the greyhounds returned until 1979.

Bristol Rovers moved their terraces to allow room for a dog track, which was first used in July 1932 at their Eastville ground. In 1940, the ground was actually sold to the greyhound company for just £12,000 and when Rovers left Eastville in 1986 it was one of the busiest dog tracks in the land with a four-meeting a week schedule.

Chelsea threw out speedway to accommodate greyhounds in 1932, and in 1935 they covered one of their terraces, not for the benefit of their fans but to protect the bookies who bet at the dog meetings. Dog racing continued at Stamford Bridge until August 1968.

In 1946, Bolton Wanderers proposed a resolution at the Football

League's Annual Meeting, to the effect that no grounds used by Football League clubs could also be used for greyhound racing – presumably the earlier, similar declaration had lapsed into disuse. Those grounds already in such use could carry on.

Special dispensation was granted to Queens Park Rangers in 1962–63 to permit them to play at White City, where greyhound racing was regularly staged.

In spring 1997, Brighton FC, in severe financial straits, announced that they were considering a move to Hove Greyhound Stadium, which never materialised.

Wimbledon, homeless for several years, have also been rumoured to be moving into the Wimbledon Greyhound Stadium on a number of occasions.

During 1997 it emerged that there were plans underway to build a complex at Swindon Town FC which would include within it a casino. Swindon PR manager, Jason Harris, confirmed that the scheme, involving the club in an agreement with Grosvenor Casinos Ltd, was being actively pursued.

'This will be a unique development,' he said, 'the first time a football club and casino operator have worked jointly anywhere in Europe.'

Swindon Town director Rikki Hunt commented: 'We believe that this announcement fits in very well with Swindon Town Football Club's vision and mission.' Claiming 100 jobs would be created, Hunt added: 'We are the first football club in Europe to have a Casino actually at the ground.' Also the first to have another betting link via the addition to the board of former champion jockey, Willie Carson.

Ladbrokes now provide the betting facilities at a great many professional grounds, including most Premiership sides. One of the few major clubs not to have a betting shop facility at their ground were Manchester United, whose secretary K.R. Merrett, told me: 'We do not have betting facilities at the ground. However, we do have our own matchday lottery involving a half-time cashdash.'

In September, 1997, though, Ladbrokes opened for business in Old Trafford, which meant they had facilities at every Premiership ground except Bolton while in Scotland they had recently opened for business at Rangers.

William Hill provide the regular betting kiosks at Wembley Stadium, even at one time carrying out transactions in the currency of countries visiting for internationals. This has since been discontinued for administrative reasons.

CHAPTER ELEVEN

Celebeties

The great and the good of football have been known to get involved in the odd wagering activity. Take former England skipper David Platt who revealed the reason why he named French star Michel Platini as his idol. It was not entirely because of his legendary skills but because racehorse-owning Platt 'put £7 on him at 9/1 to score the first goal in the 1985 European Cup Final'. So there you have the price of hero worship – £63.

It should be music to your ears to learn the story of the soccer-inspired bet between famous brothers Andrew Lloyd Webber and Julian, both of whom supported Leyton Orient.

Julian remained a fanatical supporter while Andrew's loyalty began to wane. So, one season, when Orient needed a point to avoid relegation with one match to play, Andrew bet Julian they wouldn't get it, and each staked writing a piece of music on the outcome of the wager. Orient won the point, Julian won the music, which turned into the hit album *Variations* which turned to gold. Appropriately enough, Julian presented the gold disc for the record to the Orient chairman of the time in the centre circle just before the start of a home match, which they lost.

A large number of big names in football have enjoyed an association with horse racing and betting, not least amongst them former England internationals Francis Lee and Mick Channon, both of whom went on to become respected and successful trainers. At one stage, Channon took on another big name, Mick Quinn, as an assistant, and also half-

169

humorously suggested that when Kevin Keegan quit as Newcastle manager he may be the next one to turn up on his doorstep looking for a job in racing.

Lee, who also dabbled in producing toilet paper and became Manchester City chairman, tells the story of how he and a colleague bought a horse between them.

'As a youngster I had always fancied owning a racehorse, but I wouldn't have one until I could afford it. Then, when I was at Derby, Rod Thomas and I bought one for £13 each! One day we had an accumulator bet for £26 and they all won. We picked up two and a half grand. So we bought this horse, Clydebank.

'I remember the first time we really fancied it. He was running at Chepstow, but it was a Saturday and we were playing Wolves at home, so we couldn't go. We needed to win to go top of the League.

'That morning the assistant manager, Des Anderson, came in and told me and Rod, "I've got some very bad news." We thought, bloody hell, the horse has broken a leg, but instead he told us that the match had been abandoned. We said, "What a shame," but really it was all we could do to stop laughing.

'We raced down to Chepstow and watched the horse scoot in at 8/1. I remember thinking "Christ, this is easy."'

Channon recalled ruining his training programme when he and Kevin Keegan became joint owner of Man On The Run.

'After finally persuading Kevin to come into partnership, I got him to come along to the races. Our horse came last, so we got legless on champagne.'

England keeper Peter Shilton has been known to dabble in the betting market; indeed I recall him once ringing my office to discuss matters equine on a day when he was due to take part in an important match abroad. One of his horses, Between The Sticks, came up trumps at 33/1 first time out at Newmarket in April 1989, only for Shilton to claim that he had been caught in traffic and arrived at the course too late to back the horse.

Wales boss Bobby Gould revealed in March 1989 that when he was Wimbledon manager he had an unusual clause written into his contract – permission to attend the Cheltenham races on Gold Cup day. He proved the wisdom of insisting on that clause when he went to the festival meeting at the course and cleaned up by backing 66/1 shot, Observer Corps.

Cheltenham also featured on the agenda when the then Shadow Minister for Sport Dennis Howell, now Lord Howell, surprised colleagues with the vehemence of a 1985 speech about soccer hooligans which he made in the House of Commons. The reason for the aggression shown by Howell was later explained when he told friends that he had been called in at short notice to make the speech, and had to cancel a day at Cheltenham races as a consequence. He had no time to back the three horses he'd picked out, all of which, inevitably, won.

A row over a £200 bet resulted in football legend George Best being bound over in the sum of £100 to keep the peace for 12 months and ordered to pay £50 compensation to builder Paul Davis in May 1991. Best had organised a pub sweepstake on the outcome of the American Superbowl. Said Davis, 'I asked him for my £200 winnings from the Superbowl sweepstake and he lunged at me, ripping my shirt and punching my neck. He was drunk when he came into the bar.'

Best retorted, 'I never hit him. He punched *me* in the chest. Mr Davis was slightly inebriated at the time, to put it mildly.'

Having once claimed gambling wins of £26,000 in a casino and £12,000 on a yankee on the horses, George Best told an interviewer in 1993, 'These days if I lose a fiver on a horse I want to go into the toilet and throw up.' I know how he feels.

Meanwhile, boss Dave Bassett wound up his Sheffield United team by betting them £500 that they would *lose* to Oldham in February 1993. They won 2–0 and a 'delighted' Bassett handed over the readies.

Unorthodox keeper Bruce Grobbelaar confirmed to me that he once walked the length of Wembley Stadium on his hands in order to win a bet.

Almost as unlikely was the £80 bet won by soccer hard-man Dave MacKay of Spurs and Scotland in the '60s, when he ate a bouquet of flowers.

Former Chelsea star, defender Ron 'Chopper' Harris, made a fortune by selling a golf club in 1990 and invested much of it in a string of top-quality greyhounds, which won him a series of top prizes. One of them, Dempsey Duke, retired to stud at £400 a time after winning Harris £41,000 in prize money and an unsubstantiated amount in bets. Harris revealed that he'd become interested in dogs as an apprentice on the groundstaff at Chelsea when 'they had dog trials there and I used to have sixpenny bets'.

Former Celtic, Manchester United and Scotland midfield player Lou Macari found himself in the midst of a furore over a £6,500 bet on the team he managed being beaten. Macari was boss of second division Swindon Town when the bet was struck on his team to be beaten away in an FA Cup tie at Newcastle in January 1988. Newcastle were 8/13 favourites and won the match 5–0, providing a £4,000 profit on the £6,500 stake.

There was no suggestion at all that the match had been fixed, but following a hearing in February 1990, Macari – by then manager of West Ham – and Brian Hillier, the Swindon chairman, were found guilty by the Football Association of breaching their rule regarding betting on matches. Macari was fined £1,000 and censured, while Hillier was suspended from taking an active role in the game for six months. Swindon were fined £7,500.

The rule breached was Rule 26 (a) (iv) which stated that members shall be found guilty of misconduct if they are found guilty of 'betting on any football match other than on authorised and registered Football Pools'.

The incident returned to haunt Macari when he later became manager of West Ham. They were trailing 6–0 to Oldham when the opposition fans launched into a new song with the refrain, 'Has Macari got a bet?'

I thought it might be interesting to hear Lou Macari's opinion about whether those involved in football should be able to bet on the game, so I dropped him a line, beginning by saying that I fully expected the letter to go straight into the wastepaper bin. Some time later I received a phone call.

'It's Lou Macari. The letter's not in the bin – yet!'

He had rung to explain that he did not believe it would be in his best interests to make any direct comments on football betting, following his run-in with the authorities. However, he did make the point very strongly that he believed he had been unfairly treated for what was a minimal direct involvement with the Swindon bet which, he vowed, had only ever been placed as a direct commercial transaction to defray the accommodation and travel expenses of a small club visiting a larger one in a game they were widely expected to lose.

He was asked to act as a go-between to take out what was regarded as a form of insurance and believes that certain individuals subsequently 'stitched me up'. He hinted that he may yet consider taking legal action to redeem what he regards as a tarnished reputation.

Lou told me that at the time he had drawn the football authorities' attention to other public examples of a chairman, manager and player who had placed wagers on games, but that the FA would not accept his defence and finally found him guilty of 'knowingly allowing or permitting it to happen'.

Although he clearly has a strong enough character to have overcome the slur, it obviously still rankles with him, particularly as he says, 'I've hardly ever had a football bet in my life. I don't like it and I think it is bad value. I prefer horse racing.' He also appreciates the irony of football's major involvement with and profits from betting these days.

Some time before he became Newcastle manager, Kenny Dalglish was enjoying the other love of his life, golf, taking on TV commentator Richard Keys and offering to bet him a fiver that he could beat him on the par five hole. Keys accepted the wager. Dalglish prepared to tee off, checking the line to the green, only to tell Keys that he would let him play first. Keys duly drove off and Dalglish congratulated him on his shot, adding cryptically, 'Your second will be even longer.' Keys wondered just what Dalglish meant. He soon found out as he teed up his ball and drove off – in the opposite direction.

Former QPR maverick star Stan Bowles loved a bet. In fact, he told a tale of joining Gamblers' Anonymous to try to beat the bug – but ended up betting on how long he would stay with the therapy group.

In his autobiography, *Stan the Man*, Stan declares that he was friendly with the players of the Manchester-based 'Quality Street Gang' who first invented the 'slow count'. This is a betting shop scam which plagues the industry to this day and involves large bets being placed and counted out very slowly as a horse or dog race gets underway. If the selection backed starts well the count continues and the money is handed over, if it gets away slowly or falls the money is quickly gathered up and the punter scarpers.

Bowles says that while he was at Nottingham Forest, he would go racing with Peter Shilton and Martin O'Neill ('quite a big gambler'). Bowles says he once won £8,000 at Southwell, and lost £4,000 when his selection was beaten in a Newbury photo-finish. He and Kenny Burns also took £2,000 from Peter Shilton, who had bet that Arsenal would win a match which was drawn.

Bowles didn't get on with Brian Clough and, one presumes, Frank Allcock would go along with that. It was reported in the *Guardian* that Allcock, a director of Nottingham Forest, had announced his resignation in February 1986, after Clough had alleged in the programme that Allcock and a former director, Derek Davis, were offering odds of 7/1 against Forest winning at Manchester United in a league match. Ironically, Forest did win, 3–2, and Allcock commented: 'The article made me look ridiculous. There was merely a conversation in which I offered a bet to a friend.'

Incidentally, the Clough fan for whom I laid a bet of £5 at 1000/1 about him becoming Prime Minister has still not given up hopes of collecting.

Former England goalkeeper Gordon Banks has betting in his blood – his grandfather and uncle were full-time bookmakers, and his father was a part-time layer.

'Even when I was at school, I always had a little bet on the Derby and Grand National,' confessed the man who made that immortal save against Pelé. However, Banks clearly failed to inherit too much of the family's betting nous as he regards the time when he 'backed four horses each way in the Grand National and three of them finished in the frame' as his finest punting hour. Any bookie will tell you that someone who bets like that is to be welcomed with open arms – after all, if you back four horses you are immediately throwing away three of your bets as there can only be one winner.

Mind you, perhaps the Banks bookies weren't over successful at their trade for he told the *Sporting Life Weekender*: 'I think the bookmakers could be a bit more generous with their odds. They seem to be very tight these days and, when there is a horse with an obvious chance, they are much more reluctant than they used to be to give anything away.' Well, Gordon, if your Dad, Uncle and Grandad were keen to give anything away when they were bookmakers then I'm not surprised you had to make a living in goal.

Many football-loving punters decide their bets these days on the basis of the soccer allegiances of their favourite jockeys, trainers or owners. I know of one particular Spurs fan who missed out when Frankie Dettori rode those seven winners at Ascot in September 1996, because Dettori is a mad keen Arsenal fan! Many Gunners followers have made a killing by backing Frankie's rides, even though the Italian-born jockey also confesses to a fondness for Juventus.

Walter Swinburn, on the other hand, is a fanatical Manchester United fan, and that paid off in a big way for the Old Trafford side in May 1994 when they visited Chester races and were told to invest their win bonuses for clinching the Premiership title on Walter's mount, Cicerao, which duly obliged at 2/1. After cleaning up, Bryan Robson, then a United star, later Middlesbrough boss, commented: 'Coming racing is a relaxation – in football it is high tension.' Robson is also a keen owner. His Taylormade Boy enjoyed a few successes.

Other notable soccer fans amongst the racing cognoscenti include TV's Julian Wilson, a Swindon fan; betting pundit John McCririck who follows Newcastle; trainer Doug Marks is a Forest supporter while trainer Peter Chapple-Hyam splits his loyalties between Portsmouth and West Brom. Owner, racing writer and keen punter Sir Clement Freud is a Plymouth Argyle man, while owner Andrew Carruthers admits to supporting Alloa Athletic; fellow owners opt for Charlton (Mrs Heather Alwen), Derby (Robert Ellis) and Millwall (Malcolm Spencer).

Yet another link between racing, punters and football is the naming of racehorses. Current and recent horses appearing at a track near you have included Craven Cottage, Dennis Wise, Wilkins, Little Gunner, Kenilworth and Mellors as well as the more obscure Now Young Man (Brian Clough's catch-phrase) and Essayeffsee – named in honour of Stirling Albion FC, no less.

Tony Alper, 49-year-old chairman of non-league side Farnborough Town, registered five-year-old gelding Express Routing in the club's name in early 1997 and specially selected royal blue and yellow colours to match the club's kit.

Manchester City and Sunderland striker Niall Quinn found himself 'completely wrapped up in racing' once he became an owner of the very useful Cois Na Tine, which he later sold for £250,000, explaining: 'I would have had to win about five league championships and three European Cups to earn the same money. It was put to me that by refusing the offer it would have been like putting on forty or fifty thousand pounds to win, every time it ran, should it fail in the future.'

Veteran trainer Reg Hollinshead numbered Stoke City chairman Gordon Taylor amongst his owners. Taylor invited Hollinshead to witness the historic occasion when Stoke City signed the legendary (Sir) Stanley Matthews. Recalled Reg: 'Stanley had a clause inserted into his contract which said the chairman should provide him with a winner a week while he was at the club.' I *assume* he was joking!

In February 1997, the *Daily Mirror* revealed that husky-voiced TV celebrity Mariella Frostrup had won the pools. This was news to Mariella as well as to *Mirror* readers. The cheque sent to Mariella by Littlewoods had misrouted and ended up with someone who had handed it on to *Mirror* showbiz writer, Matthew Wright.

'But don't pop the champagne just yet, Mariella,' wrote Wright, 'because I'm afraid you're not a millionaire. Your Littlewoods jackpot amounts to just . . . £1.45p.'

Flamboyant former Manchester City boss Malcolm Allison is unashamed to admit to a penchant for the occasional flutter.

'I have had a few nice touches in my time. I was in Deauville with some footballing mates and we really fancied a horse of Paddy Prendergast's called Linacre. It was in a four and a half furlong sprint, a distance not raced this side of the Channel, and I remember getting quite excited when looking at the *pari-mutuel* boards and seeing him open up at 33/1. He was a very fast horse and I knew Prendergast hadn't sent him down there to run down the field. Needless to say he won, but I was more than a little disappointed to see him returned at 8/1. But it was still a nice bet.' I wonder if Malcolm has twigged yet that it was almost certainly the weight of his own money – and that of his chums – which forced the odds from 33/1 down to 8/1, such is the delight of a *pari-mutuel* system.

Allison gave the *Sporting Life Weekender* a clue about the size of a typical Big Mal wager when they asked him for advice about betting to pass on to readers: 'Take a set amount, for example, £200 and write it off. Count it as part of the expense of the day, and if you have it off, then well and good.'

Former Ipswich and Scotland star Alan Brazil insists that his international career was brought to an end prematurely by Scottish boss Jock Stein, after Brazil refused to share a bet with him. Brazil was in the Scotland squad to play England at Wembley in 1983. The game coincided with the Derby. Brazil, a keen punter, had had a sizeable bet on favourite Teenoso some while previously at highly attractive odds of 33/1. Brazil told his team-mates about the bet and word got back to Stein.

'Big Jock loved to punt and wanted a piece of the action,' Brazil told *Daily Record* readers in December 1996. 'The lads kept winding me up that I had to give him part of the bet. This went on right up to the off at Epsom. Big Jock told me it was my last chance, but I told him I'd struck the bet and, win or lose, I was sticking by it.

'I got one of those dark looks from Jock. He was obviously raging. All he said before he left the room was, "Son, have you ever played at Wembley?"'

Teenoso stormed to victory. Brazil was left out of the Scottish team and never did get to play for his country at Wembley.

'I sat on the bench and John Wark kept looking at me and laughing his head off,' recalled Brazil.

Angus Loughran is one of the country's shrewdest punters, and he particularly enjoys a flutter on the beautiful game. You will know him better as Statto, the pyjama-clad anorak from TV's *Fantasy Football* programme. Angus travels the world in his role as a pundit, commentator and author. He pens a regular sports betting advice column in the *Guardian* and he rings me once a week from some bizarre location around the globe to check on the latest betting moves.

I hope I'm not giving away too much by revealing that it was Angus who tipped my company off that perhaps the 7/1 odds we were quoting about a particular Premiership manager no longer being with his club by the end of the season were a little on the generous side. We took the hint and, with supporting evidence beginning to appear from other directions, cut the odds. Days later, and *before* the season had even begun, that manager was on his way. An industry colleague of mine, Paul Austin, once PR for Ladbrokes, also recalls a time when a tip from

Statto was worth hearing – even if the time of its arrival was less than welcome.

'Angus makes money because, if something moves in the world of sport, very few people know before the bookies. Angus is one of them. During the 1994 World Cup he rang me at four in the morning to tell me that Maradona had failed a drugs test. "You might want to change your odds on Argentina," he said. I won't tell you what I said to him.'

Angus also once used his enviable all-round knowledge of soccer to win a bet which saved him from a beating-up. Surrounded by thug-like Ajax fans in an Amsterdam bar, who made it clear that their preferred entertainment for that evening would be to give him a good kicking, Angus endeavoured to delay that particular pleasure by wagering them the cost of a round of drinks that he knew more about Ajax than they did. Presumably lost for words at his impertinence the Dutch 'bovver boys' agreed to the contest. Angus correctly answered nine of the ten questions put to him – the skinheads managed just three out of ten. Impressed, they spared him his life, and got the beers in.

Two of the finest sportswriters in the business are Ian Wooldridge of the *Daily Mail*, and Hugh McIlvanney of the *Sunday Times*, both judges for the William Hill Sports Book of the Year Award. Wooldridge told me of the day when McIlvanney was enjoying the hospitality of the owner of a box at the races one afternoon when he remembered that he wanted to place a bet on a game involving Liverpool in Europe that very day. McIlvanney got on the phone to his credit bookmaker and was heard asking for a price about Liverpool. He was next heard spluttering: 'What d'ye mean I can't have a bet. My account isn't in the red, I *insist* on having a bet.' The telephonist apparently refused once again whereupon the writer demanded in no uncertain terms to be put through to the department supervisor.

A minute or so later a much quieter McIlvanney put the phone down without another word and sat down. Wooldridge asked him what had happened: 'Well, the supervisor told me that I could have the bet if I really insisted, but felt she should point out that the game was played earlier this afternoon – and Liverpool lost.'

Labour MP and Sports Minister Tony Banks came up with a dream system – literally – for football betting in early 1997.

'I know this sounds stupid, but they [results of Chelsea's FA Cup matches] come to me in a dream while I'm asleep [best way to dream!]. I hear voices,' he told the *Guardian*. The voices advised him that Chelsea would beat Liverpool in round four by 4–2. He put on £5 at odds of 66/1. Chelsea won 4–2. The voices told him that round five against Leicester would produce a 2–2 draw.

'I never bet against Chelsea,' he said, failing to place a wager. Chelsea drew 2–2 at Leicester.

Word of his apparent paranormal powers got out before the replay against Leicester and Banks declared: 'I hope something will happen because there's a lot of people standing by waiting to bet on my forecast.'

In the event, of course, Chelsea won the replay 1–0 courtesy of a hotly disputed extra-time penalty which even Mr Banks could not have dreamed up. When Chelsea reached the Final I was able to put Mr Banks's nocturnal predictions to the test. By now the Minister for Sport in the new Labour government, I offered Mr Banks a free £1,000 bet on the outcome of the Final to place on behalf of the charity Scope. He opted for Chelsea to beat Middlesbrough 3–2, with the first goal being scored by Zola. The odds about this happening were 75/1. Di Matteo opened the scoring in under a minute and Chelsea won 2–0.

In September 1997 Mr Banks caused controversy by apparently suggesting in an interview that he thought England were unlikely to win the World Cup. In a bid to counter criticism he visited a William Hill betting shop in London to place a bet on England. Thinking he would announce that he would donate his profits to some worthy cause I laid him odds of 20/1 although they were actually 12/1. Imagine my surprise when he staked £50 and said he hoped his £1,000 winnings would cover the cost of his trip to see England in the Final in Paris!

Norwich City and Irish international Keith O'Neill told the *Sporting Life Weekender* about his first-ever bet: 'It was on a match between Ireland and England at Wembley. I was still very young and, of course, my Dad and I backed Ireland to win. It shows you how mad keen I was that I bet we would win 6–0. Sadly, for both of us, the match ended in a draw.' O'Neill also confessed: 'Most of my bets are placed after I get a tip for a horse. There are always plenty of those flying about when footballers get together.'

In May 1996 well-travelled striker Steve Claridge, by then with Leicester, confessed to the *News of the World* that he had lost a quarter of a million pounds by betting.

'It started when I was at Luton Town. I did £35,000 in two months and pretty well lived in a betting shop.'

He claimed to have won £3,500 'after betting £400' on his then club, Birmingham, 'to win the Second Division title in May '95'.

The legendary George Best needed to be a grand loser in May 1997 for that was precisely what he had become after handing over £1,000 to his wife. It was in settlement for a bet he had struck 12 months previously that he would stay off the drink for a calendar year. His attempt to stay dry had lasted a mere two months. On the anniversary of the bet, 22 May 1997, Best vowed: 'There'll be no daft bets about not drinking this year – I can't afford to throw my cash away.'

As Roberto di Matteo was setting a new twentieth century record by scoring the fastest FA Cup final goal in 42 seconds in 1997, the widow of the former record holder was cashing in with a winning bet on the Chelsea man. Laura Milburn, wife of the legendary Newcastle striker Jackie, who had held the record for 42 years, had selected di Matteo in a 50p-a-go first goalscorer sweepstake as she recovered from an operation in hospital. The grandmother of six collected £7 for her 50p stake and commented: 'It was a cracking goal to beat Jack, and ironic that I picked him out.'

When exciting young Leicester City striker Emile Heskey was called into England's squad for the vital World Cup qualifier against Moldova in September 1997, his father, Tyrone, had mixed feelings. Several years earlier his wife, Albertine, had persuaded him not to accept the 1000/1 odds he had been offered for a £20 stake that Emile would represent England at all levels. The 19-year-old would have a full set of honours when he made his senior debut, having already achieved Youth, Under-18 and Under-21 level. 'If only I'd placed that bet I'd have been laughing all the way to the bank,' said Tyrone. 'I told his mum when he was 14 he'd be the best in the country. £20,000 is a small price to pay for Emile proving me right.'

Another angle to these kinds of bets emerged in June 1997 when former Spurs star and German international Jurgen Klinsmann was reportedly shocked to discover that Bayern Munich team-mate Lothan Matthaus had bet 10,000 marks (almost £4000) that Jurgen would fail to score 15 goals during the season just ended.

Matthaus lost the bet, struck with Bayern's business manager Uli Hoeness, when Klinsmann hit exactly 15 goals and commented: 'There are much better ways of spending so much money than making bets against a team-mate. I just can't take Matthaus seriously now.'

Matthaus himself said, 'It was the first bet I was glad to lose because I knew that if Klinsmann scored 15 goals we would be champions.' There may well be those who will wonder what might have happened had Klinsmann been on 14 with seconds of the last game remaining with Matthaus in a position to pass to him to set him up for a goal scoring chance!

CHAPTER TWELVE

Gambling Gossip

SOCCER BETTING QUOTES...

'My hunch is that legal betting on soccer in Europe has to be one of the factors behind the many riots that mar matches there.'

And my hunch is that *Sports Illustrated*'s William F. Reed was spot on – you see it all the time, don't you, betting slips being hurled into the air as the thugs wade in to punch seven kinds of ordure out of each other!?

Another typically open-minded American comment about betting on sport came from National Football (American football, that is) League Vice-President Jay Moyer in 1993 who, apparently, was not being ironic or sarcastic when he declared: 'It's like a cancer. If states say citizens can legally bet on sports, you risk turning fans into gamblers. And if that happens we'll diminish the significance of sports.' Can you believe this guy?

Someone else I often find it difficult to take seriously is *Independent On Sunday* writer Peter Corrigan, who won't, I'm sure, be upset to know that – after all, he rarely has anything other than a bad word to say for the betting industry. In May 1995, he gave his readers this priceless gem: 'If you took gambling away from football it would not make a jot of difference to the game or its mass appeal.'

Considering the hundreds of millions of pounds gambled on the game with British bookmakers alone, not to mention on the pools, you'd surely have to conclude that betting is most certainly contributing to the mass appeal of the game – witness the regular reporting of the odds as they relate to various aspects of the game, by all sections of the media.

As to whether it makes a jot of difference to the game itself, well, I rather think this is a total red herring. Why should it make any difference to the game, any more than attractive kit or players visiting sick youngsters in hospital makes any difference to the game itself. What cannot be denied, however, is that gambling certainly gives an awful lot of people an extra reason for watching and enjoying the game, whether Mr Corrigan approves of it or not.

Do football folk know about betting? They might like to crack on that they do but sometimes you wonder, like the time in November 1995 when Steve Coppell told readers of the *Racing Post* that his side, Crystal Palace, were a good bet at 8/1 to win at Middlesbrough because: 'In any two-horse race you've got to sit up and take notice of those kind of odds.' Particularly when there are three runners in the two-horse race – Steve overlooked the draw.

Not to be outdone, at about the same time the *Sporting Life* carried some pearls of wisdom about betting from another former footballer, Alan Hudson, who was pontificating about the case of a punter who had staked the not inconsiderable sum of £10,000 on Newcastle to win the Coca-Cola Cup at odds of 9/2. Mr Hudson was outraged that, having accepted this bet in full, the bookmaker concerned had trimmed the Geordies' odds from 9/2 to 7/2 as would seem entirely reasonable given that he had just added to his potential liabilities by £45,000.

'Does this mean that this man has inside information?' stormed Hudson, producing no evidence at all to suggest that anyone had ever alleged or believed such a thing. 'How can bookmakers do such things? It doesn't wash with me about balancing books. You should only adjust your betting odds after each round or perhaps after each draw is made.'

Fine, so in the somewhat unlikely event that 'Onest 'Udson Bookies ever open for business we can obviously expect to see them maintain their odds for any given team no matter how much cash they take for them, and no matter whether the first and second favourites or other fancied sides have just been knocked out of the competition?

All I can say is, think twice about ever betting with 'Onest 'Udson Bookies, because if they were to operate to those sort of rules they wouldn't survive in business from the third round of the FA Cup until Cup Final day. All this from the man who followed up that column with one slagging off the allegedly ill-prepared and unqualified people who dare to try to coach youngsters to play football.

'If you wanted your kid to pass his English exam, you wouldn't send him to a footballer,' he declared. No, Mr Hudson, certainly not – and no more would I send him to an ex-footballer to learn how to become a bookmaker.

Another wayward star who peaked in the '70s was the subject of one of the most famous remarks ever made about football and betting by the former manager of Crewe Alexandra, Ernie Tagg, who said of Stan Bowles: 'If he could pass a betting shop as well as he could pass a ball, he wouldn't have had a problem.'

With so much travelling involved in their lives, I suppose it is inevitable that many players will become devoted to gambling in card schools to kill the time. A quote from England and Manchester United legend Nobby Stiles reveals just how important the gambling games can become. He recalls being on a trip to Italy when he and his team-mates were taken to see the world-famous leaning Tower of Pisa:

'When we finally arrived we were playing cards on the coach. Somebody said, "Oh, look, the Tower." A perfunctory glance over our shoulders and we were back to the nine-card brag, without ever getting out of our seats.'

In his book *The Soccer Tribe*, Dr Desmond Morris describes how one manager attempted to turn the players' love of a flutter to good effect on the pitch. An unnamed club in close proximity to a greyhound track is said to have purchased a dog to run in the name of a players' syndicate. On one occasion it ran whilst a game was going on, carrying, no doubt, large amounts of club money. The team were a goal down when word came through that the greyhound had just won at odds of 3/1 thus giving the squad a nice bonus. Word was sent out to the players via a tic-tac message, and within minutes the scoreline was turned on its head as the delighted players were given new heart and scored two quick goals.

Paul Merson, the Arsenal and England star, who confessed a number of personal problems – gambling amongst them – told the *News of the World* in October 1990: 'I've blown £100,000 in betting shops. And it wasn't only the gee-gees. I'd bet on anything – football, snooker, dogs, cricket, even bowls.' Perhaps the surprising thing is not how much he lost, but what he was betting on. Bowls? He doesn't strike me as a master of the crown green world!

'My granddad was a corner-end bookie. There were no betting shops in those days, so if you wanted to bet you went to the bookie at the end of the street. My grandparents had a bowl full of silver. The money would go in there and he'd pay out the bets with it.

'When I was about seven my mother said, "Never take anything out of there," and I said, "I never have, mother, and I never will." Well, I never did after that, but it was a lie because I had taken sixpence out once before.'

Scandalous confession from Jack Charlton.

'All I can say is, I tried to bring the match to a conclusion. I hope he wins again – maybe as big an amount.'

Referee Marcello Cardona abandoned an Italian second division match in the 89th minute during 1996, to the great distress of an Italian punter who would have collected the small matter of 12 billion lire – £4.8 milion – on the pools, had the game ended in a draw – which it was at the time.

'And a buzz is what Grobbelaar got. Along with the other players and the match officials. For a swarm of killer bees took part in a pitch invasion that nobody could possibly have bet on.'

Comment from *Daily Express* journalist Jeremy Martin, reporting on a bizarre incident during a 1997 World Cup qualifier between Zimbabwe, for whom Bruce Grobbelaar – at that time facing trial on match-rigging allegations – was in goal, and Ghana. The game was interrupted when large numbers of bees dive-bombed the pitch.

'For the overwhelming majority the football pools are a purely mechanical activity implying no personal skill or initiative whatsoever, where, in pursuit of a major once-and-for-all windfall, they are willing to sacrifice fully their entire customary stake.'

Otto Newman, Principal Lecturer in Sociology at the Polytechnic of the South Bank, London, in his 1972 book, *Gambling: Hazard and Reward*. He was reflecting on the implication of survey evidence that 94 per cent of bettors on football pools invested all, or the major part, of their stakes on the treble chance – the most difficult section to win. This backs up the opinion of most serious students of gambling that the football content of the pools is to a large extent incidental to the majority of those who enter them. An inherent fault in any suggestion that the pools can be won by form students is that, if that were the case, so many people would win that the returns would be hardly worth having. If form was that important and predictable, the ideal system would be to follow the predictions of the Pools Panel.

You might believe we suffer from the nanny state syndrome these days with do-gooders endeavouring to control our every action, but I can assure you it was much worse in the past.

Consider, for example, this comment by one Lord Kindersley, the head of the National Savings Movement, to the 1951 Royal Commission: 'The principal competitors with, and enemies of, the Savings Movement are the Football Pools and the Dog Tracks. And I say without hesitation that they are the enemies of the people as well.'

I have no hesitation in siding with the opinion of Alex Rubner, author of 1966's *The Economics of Gambling*. He writes that 'the real enemies of "saving" are holidays abroad, the acquisition of a car, central heating, smoking, drinking and other forms of non-essential consumption.' Thank God, it's entirely up to *me* whether to salt away my excess dosh for the proverbial 24 hours of precipitation, or to blow a few quid on the correct score of the FA Cup Final.

In their Annual Report, 1965, bookies Joe Coral declared that they provided fixed-odds betting opportunities for 'the more realistic punter . . . adherents of what are commonly known as the bread and butter pools, who prefer to make a steady and regular profit rather than for those who indulge in the dream fantasy of a many millions-to-one win.'

Discussing pools and fixed odds in 1954, W.R. Williams, a Calvinistic Methodist and MP for Droylsden, said in the House of Commons: 'My second prejudice is that I do not like Littlewoods, Vernons and the other big pools promoters because, in my opinion, whilst there is little to be said for the bookie, he does take a certain risk. These other people have not taken one single risk since they put the first coupons out and found mugs willing to fill them up every week.' Praise indeed – grudging, but nevertheless praise!

Another man of religion, Monseigneur C. Cowderoy, was rather more well disposed towards the pools when giving evidence to the 1951 Royal Commission: 'I am going to submit that the Pool is the best of all forms of gambling because there is not the temptation to plunge. The man who wants to make a bit of money by betting on horses or dogs, because of the restricted odds, has got to plunge a big stake in order to get back a big sum of money, whereas with the Pool you know that if you fill up your Penny Point Pool you might get £48,000 and you have not got to increase your stake at all; consequently there is very little excess in the Pools.'

But they can't resist telling us what's best for us, can they? And if they, as paragons of higher moral virtues than we common folk possess, have never enjoyed a flutter themselves then how the hell (sorry!) can they appreciate the appeal of gambling?

'Shouldn't Lottery and Pools ads carry a message that says something like "Oi. You. Sucker. You stand a one in 14 million chance of getting rich by doing this. Just face up to it. It's not going to be you"?'

Creative partner Robert Campbell of advertising agency Rainey, Kelly,

Campbell, Roalfe bemoaning the fact that financial service ads have to carry disclaimers such as 'the value of your investment can go up as well as down' and wondering why similar rules don't apply to pools ads. He also told *Guardian* readers in January 1997, 'If I were advertising the pools, I'd consider running ads saying "Did you know your chances of winning pack-up-work money on the pools are greater than your chances of winning pack-up-work money on the lottery?"' A novel approach, but I can't see it being taken on board, somehow.

In January 1997, there was something of a furore when snooker's John Spencer allegedly advised certain players to bet on their opponents in big matches so that in the event of them being knocked out and deprived of their prize money, they would have some financial compensation to soften the blow. I was a little surprised when Tom Kelly, a man I respect greatly and who does a fantastic job rebutting much ill-conceived criticism of bookmakers in his role as the mouthpiece for the Betting Office Licensees Association, issued a statement in response to these allegations.

'Whilst not wishing to comment on any specific allegation, governing bodies should prohibit sportsmen from betting on games or matches in which they are participating. The integrity of the activities on which betting takes place must be beyond reproach, and this must be totally apparent to the public.'

In theory I would go along with most of that, but the specific allegations referred to had not involved the slightest suggestion that any game had been deliberately lost in order to profit from a bet and it seemed to me that Tom's statement could be used against footballers backing themselves to score the first goal of a game, or even owners backing their own runners in a horse race – neither of which suggestions would get my support.

Now, this is really something, revealing as it does the attitudes of 50 years ago. That world – did it ever really exist? – has now well and truly ceased to operate. Could you make a case for the end of civilisation as we know it because of one person's complaint that a football team's defeat had cost him a winning bet?

E. Benson Perkins, Chairman of the Churches Committee on Gambling did just that in 1950. Writing in *Gambling in English Life* he said:

> It sounds an exaggeration to say that the spirit of sportsmanship
> has been affected by gambling. We like to think that the genuine

sporting spirit is one of the admirable traits of our English character. There is no doubt, however, that gambling has undermined that great quality.

John Macadam, writing in the *Daily Express* in 1947 spoke of a conversation he had with a young fellow in the train, who inquired how the 'Spurs' had got on. When he was told that they were beaten, his only comment was: 'Blimey, that's done me ten results'. John Macadam comments: 'Soccer is still essentially a game . . . how long, in these circumstances, can it remain so?'. It is impossible to tie together permanently the spirit of sportsmanship and the hope and intention, if possible, of securing financial gain by guessing the results.

The publisher's blurb for *Fever Pitch* by Nick Hornby describes it as 'The best football book ever written' and who am I to argue with that – after all, it did win the William Hill Sports Book of the Year Award. However, there is one glaring flaw in this superb tome – the almost total absence of reference to betting in connection with Mr Hornby's beloved Arsenal. In fact, the sole line devoted to betting which I can detect within its pages occurs on page 230 where Hornby is debating just what other feeling in man's experience can match clinching the first division (as it was then) championship with a last minute, last game of the season, victory over Liverpool away from home.

'And what else is there that can possibly provide the suddenness?' he asks. 'A huge pools win, maybe, but the gaining of large sums of money affects a different part of the psyche altogether, and has none of the communal ecstasy of football.'

And that's it – the entire Hornby dissertation on betting.

As well as articulating his concerns about the social fabric of his day and the years to come, author George Orwell, whose *Animal Farm* and *1984* have become classics, was clearly a man who looked benevolently upon gamblers, once saying: 'During the between-war years the football pools did more than any other one thing to make life bearable for the unemployed.'

Not quite as tolerant was the Bishop of Durham who, when the pools were beginning to make an impact in the '20s, wrote a stern letter to *The Times*, protesting:

'Much as I admire and love the game, I would sooner football died out than it should become the tool of the gambling fraternity.'

In his younger days as an independent MP, the late Sir Alan Herbert was one of those who tried to get the pools prohibited.

However, he experienced a remarkable conversion on his own particular road to Damascus, and by 1953 he had written a book called *Pools Pilot*, in which he outlined his reasons for now being an enthusiastic poolite:

> At first, brothers, your conscience may trouble you . . . you probably think that it is a nobler thing to bet on horses. But you can never win so much on these dumb animals as you may win on your intelligent fellow men. You may also flatter yourself that, in backing horses, you are supporting 'British Bloodstock'. Up to a point it is true – it depends where you bet. But what about the art or science of football, that highly skilful and wholesome sport? The FA, before the last Royal Commission, testified that if anything, the pools had increased the public interest – and the attendance. Tell Conscience that.

One who was never likely to be converted to the pools was our previously mentioned friend, anti-gambling crusader E. Benson Perkins who, in 1950, was still following the Canute school of thought by suggesting: 'Football pools ought never to have been allowed and might have been stopped at the beginning if our statesmen had had insight and courage.' And, just to emphasise the point, he went on to suggest that 'dog racing should have been brought under such a system of control that it would have continued only as sport, but not as a betting medium.'

Mr Benson Perkins would undoubtedly have regarded Major Seton Churchill as a kindred spirit, lapping up the sentiments expressed in his 1894 tome, *Betting and Gambling*, a flavour of which can be gleaned from this rant about football and betting:

> How often at great football contests, when huge crowds are drawn together, instead of a lot of fine manly young fellows engaging vigorously in the game, we find them looking on while teams of professional players are engaged in playing for high stakes. A large proportion of the spectators have money on, and the interest they exhibit is not love of the game, but an eager desire to see that side win which they happen to have backed . . . Surely something can be done to rescue our national recreations from the cursed gambling mania. If it were only a matter of a few shillings passing from pocket to pocket upon the result of a match, it would not be worthwhile to make much protest. The evil has spread far beyond that, and in the north of England especially, we find that the true sporting instinct and love of play is being prostituted in

most alarming degree to the vile purposes of the gambler.

Young men are unconsciously led away in this matter, and become the dupes of a body of professional gamblers who seek to make them associate sport with betting and gambling.

Anyone who has carefully studied the subject, must see that true sport and manliness are being seriously damaged by this spirit of gambling. In the days of the Romans, the principal reason why the authorities endeavoured to stop games in which pecuniary gain was at stake, was that they were found to have a distinct tendency to make young men effeminate and unmanly.

There's no level-headed retort to such a tirade.

'There are a lot of myths about the pools – and one of them is that people go out and buy pink Rolls-Royces.'

Another, Mike Birkett of Littlewoods, is that anyone, anywhere actually believes that they do.

'A lot of pools winners end up less happy than they were before they won the money. Most are working class. Most give up their jobs and move house, and this is where the problems start. They ignore the benefits of work; although the job may seem badly paid, unskilled and boring, there are advantages.

'They lose friends, lose a sense of achievement and companionship. And if you take these things away from people they tend to become bewildered. When Pools winners move away they become isolated and lose what they eventually recognise as the real assets of their community.'

Perceptive insight from psychologist Dr Adrian Furnham of University College, London – or was he just being patronising?

Nicholas Fishwick, a social historian, looked closely at the early links between football and gambling in a book devoted to the period between 1910 and 1950. One of his observations was: 'By simultaneously strengthening football's popular appeal and linking it with what some saw as a social and moral disease, betting threatened to establish football as the people's game but subvert it as the national game.'

'The man who bets on horses is foolish, but the one who bets on football coupons is an absolute fool.'

An anonymous (naturally) bookmaker quoted by a *Glasgow Herald* correspondent in a piece about football betting, in March 1914.

In 1993, Manchester-based bookmaker Fred Done declared: 'I would like to see a return to the old fixed odds for football, which proved extremely popular.' Interestingly, this is a viewpoint which I have since heard from a number of other different sources within the bookmaking industry and just wonder whether anyone will be bold enough to re-launch such a style of betting.

'What anyone who has any interest or love of football depends upon is that the game is decided in a fashion that cannot be corrupted.'

High moral principles indeed from *The Times*' Rob Hughes who was discussing the no-verdict outcome of the first Grobbelaar match-rigging trial. I suppose it depends on your definition of the word 'corrupted'.

Tommy Tynan, a striker who played for many clubs including Liverpool, Lincoln and Plymouth, between 1972 and 1992, also played many games of cards and spent many an hour in the betting shop, but finally concluded: 'For all its popularity among footballers, players make very poor gamblers.' Just like jockeys traditionally make lousy tipsters.

'If anyone at the start of this season had said that Chesterfield would reach the FA Cup semi-finals, you would have said they had stumbled on the mother and father of betting syndicates.'

Ken Dyer of the *London Evening Standard* putting Chesterfield's 1997 FA Cup run into perspective.

Sir Clement Freud came up with a brilliant ploy, one which I must admit to have taken advantage of myself on one or two occasions: 'The only sensible football bet,' he opined in the *Sporting Life*, 'is to shovel money at never-mind-what-odds on the team you hope will lose. That way you either achieve joy or become rich.'

CHAPTER THIRTEEN

X Files

To the best of my knowledge the pools companies don't claim a Royal Warrant, but it emerged in October 1993 that they might be able to boast of royal patronage. Author Andrew Morton, who caused a storm of controversy with his book, *Diana: Her True Story,* revealed to the *Daily Star* that the Duke of Edinburgh is a keen, regular pools punter. The story included a comment from a 'royal insider' that 'the thought of Prince Philip checking his pools in front of the telly on a Saturday night will come as quite a shock to most people. They'll wonder if he puts a cross for no publicity.' One wonders whether he picks out his selections by form, or perhaps he chooses numbers at random – how many diamonds there are in the Queen's tiara, or the number of times the Corgis go walkies each day.

Doris Binfield of Nottingham scooped £500,000 when she bought a 45p bingo set and threw the numbered balls down on to her kitchen floor, marking off the numbers that came up.

Neighbours Ron Phillips and Beatty Phillips, 85 and 58 respectively, also stayed ahead of the game in June 1992 when they used dominoes to pick the numbers which won the Gwent pair £159,189.

Stuck for a way of picking his numbers, Sussex man David Rushen enlisted the assistance of his pet stick insect, which obliged by tipping enough draws to land him a £19.20p win in November 1993 after 49-year-old David lined her cage with 58 squares, and let nature do the rest.

Fred Campbell figured lightning might just strike twice so he filled in all the numbers which had come up as draws the previous week. He won over half a million.

Eric Birks had a great system of using people's ages. The trouble was, he couldn't remember how old his wife was. Forty-three, he thought and put down that number, duly collecting £138,000. She was 42.

Forty-six-year-old bus fitter, Mick Walters was dubbed 'The Most Honest Man In Britain' by the media when he split his £554,363 win with former boss, Tom Neal.

Some years before, the two had decided to enter both pools and Spot the Ball coupons each week and agreed they would split whatever they won. Before Mick's win they had not seen each other for over five years, but that didn't stop him calling his old friend and splitting the winnings.

When Vernons sent 47-year-old Birmingham painter and decorator Albert Horton a first-dividend cheque of £766.05p in June 1992 he splashed out nearly half his winnings on a big night out for friends and relatives. Five days later Vernons were back in touch, explaining that they had sent the winnings to the wrong Albert Horton and that they had cancelled the cheque.

Four workmates formed a syndicate in 1990, apparently agreeing that they would make a joint entry. All winnings would be split between them and, should any of them hit a million-pound jackpot via solo entries, they would give the other three £25, 000 each. The agreement was sealed with a handshake. But when one of the syndicate, who all worked at Pall Europe Engineering in Portsmouth, won over £1,800,000, his memory of what had been agreed was different.

Paul Pitt, 28, refused to hand over anything other than a round of drinks to Martin Foulds, Andrew Sullivan and Graham Ware. So the four ended up in court in September 1995 after the trio sued for breach of contract – and won. Judge Mrs Jane Bonvin ruled that 'on a clear balance of probability there was not only discussion about sharing any winnings but that it was made clear between them that the winner would pay over to the other three £25,000 in the event of winning more than £1 million.'

Mr Pitt had to pay over £25,000 to each of the other three, along with £14,000 in interest and up to £80,000 in legal fees.

Eighty-one-year-old Matt Clark was blasé about accepting a £750,000 cheque from Vernons in August 1993 – but he had had a practice run in 1969 when the Cleveleys, Lancs man won £778,426 from them.

In February 1980, brewery worker Dave Preston of Burton-on-

Trent scooped the first-dividend jackpot on *both* Littlewoods and Vernons in the same week, winning £953,874.10. Five years earlier he had won £10,000 and one week later he won again – 90p.

Pantelis 'Lucky' Menicou of Brighton failed to live up to his nickname in May 1990. Despite winning £216,000, he cost himself an extra £1,250,000 by deciding to knock one selection off his coupon to reduce the entry cost.

In March 1984, three separate first-dividend winners with Littlewoods were called Gamble, Luck and Riches.

In October 1993 the press were all ears when they heard that Sandi Gall and Barbara Dixon had won £518,553 from Littlewoods – but the pair with the famous names were unknown members of a Hartlepool syndicate.

Sheffield Wednesday acquired a new mascot in 1985 when pools jackpot winner George Daws, a great fan of the club, bought a two-year-old colt, which he named Weloveyouwednesday.

Former top soccer referee, Lester Shapter, then 53, won £30,000 on the pools in September 1993.

'It's only the second time I've won,' said the man who once sent George Best off. 'Last time it was fifteen shillings [75p].'

The pools companies aren't too keen on winners who become losers, and they still have nightmares whenever the story of Viv 'spend, spend, spend' Nicholson, who won £153,000 in 1961 and blew the lot in not much more than four years, is brought up as a cautionary tale of the evils of a big win. But although Viv is now a humble shop assistant in Wakefield, or was last time we met, she has few regrets.

Other yarns guaranteed to reduce the pools companies to apoplexy include the woman who bought her son a Harley Davidson on which he killed himself, and the woman who moved to Spain, signed over her villa to her new German lover to avoid tax, and was promptly evicted by him.

'If people think winning the pools causes misery they won't do them,' Littlewoods' winners liaison man, Ged Kermode, told *The Times* in 1994, adding, 'Winners wasting their money is bad publicity as far as we're concerned.'

I shouldn't think Ged would be too keen on this next tale, either. Pools collector, Cameron Baxter, 27, was jailed for two and a half years in September 1995, when he pocketed the £5 stake he had collected from five Scottish Power workers instead of passing it on to Littlewoods. The five would have had the only winning line of the week, and would have won £2.3 million.

Three friends who had filled in the same numbers on their coupons for 16 years missed out on a jackpot win of £600,000 when their collector failed to pick up their coupon, because he was at a funeral. Bill Smith, Lenny Lowther and. Frank Higgins were left fuming after their usual collector missed out on his round and arranged for someone else to collect the coupons in January 1994. His stand-in failed to show. The unlucky trio pleaded with Vernons to check their records to prove that they always used the same numbers, but they were out of luck, and vowed to switch to Littlewoods.

Using the same set of numbers regularly paid off in January 1994 for aircraft fitter Robert Slater of Bournemouth. On 1 January he won £5 and despite missing out on 8 January he persevered with the same numbers and won £15.75 on 15 January. Then on 22 January that set of numbers landed him £16.35. But on 29 January he really hit the big time when those lucky numbers won him £566,530.10p from Littlewoods. Robert's numbers were 3, 11, 16, 18, 25, 29, 35, 37, 45 and 47, but he confessed that he had 'no idea' how he originally came to choose them.

A Brighton postman called Payne believed he'd discovered a first-class scheme to con his way to a massive pools win. The 26-year-old franked an envelope four days before the matches were due to be played and then filled in the results later on, sealing the envelope down and sending it off.

He was exposed when his winnings were totalled up at £1.7 million and Littlewoods' officials became suspicious.

Payne admitted fraud and, in March 1991, was sentenced to 100 hours of community service.

But a quick-thinking pools punter was well within the rules when he won himself £50,000 and made the pools companies rethink their regulations, when he spotted a loophole in the system in February 1970. London dentist Sydney Lewis realised that with 30 games postponed because of adverse weather, and the Pools Panel of experts not called into action – they only operated at that time when 31 games were off – he was in a great position to make a full cover entry for the remaining matches, and be able to guarantee himself first-dividend payouts. By notifying a pools agent in time to place his bet, having previously supplied him with a blank cheque, just a couple of hours before kick-off time, he was able to outwit the rules and be confident that hundreds of thousands of entries would already be in from punters who were unaware of how many games would be called off. With just 24 matches remaining on the Vernons coupon, which he had chosen for his coup, Mr Lewis required an outlay of £1,600 to cover every possible combination of eight results. The dentist cleaned up with nine first dividends and a host of smaller wins, totalling £50,000. In a way, Mr Lewis had done the pools companies a favour – the major firms immediately got together to close the loophole.

David Gray, allegedly single-handedly, forced a Spot the Ball-type competition out of business when he devised a supposedly infallible way of winning. The 30-year-old Glaswegian won £173,000 when he discovered that by using a magnifying glass he could detect which parts of the pictures used for the game had been doctored by computer in order to remove the ball. To make sure he covered all the options, Gray had to stake £900 – but it was well worth it, as he hit the jackpot in October 1990. The next week organisers of the Skilball competition had taken it off the market. They denied it was because of David's success, saying: 'It has been a success but market research showed that many people found the entry procedure too complicated.'

In January 1995, the Labour Party announced that it had done a deal with Littlewoods, under the terms of which 12.5 per cent of Party members' stake money would be donated to Party funds.

In the 1936–37 edition of the Vernons *Handbook*, issued to customers of the company, readers were invited to enjoy the Vernon alphabet. Having lain dormant and unappreciated for 60 years, I believe the time is right to restore this forgotten poetic masterpiece to public prominence:

A is for Aintree where Vernons reside –
Spacious the building – an object of pride:
Lovely to look at both inside and out
One of the finest – of that there's no doubt.

B for the brains which have studied and schemed
Long of this home they have fancied and dreamed
Now it stands firm as a symbol of fame
Solid and trustful as Vernons own name.

C is for clients – we treat them as friends.
Gladly we offer our best dividends;
Service our motto – and fairness our creed,
For your past favours we're grateful indeed.

D is for dividends – still going up!
Drink, through our coupons, from fortune's gold cup;
Study the figures – read what winners say –
Look out for success – it's coming your way!

E is for efficiency – this is our aim,
Keep the tradition of Vernon's good name;
Quick and concise is our organisation
Aided by comfort and co-operation.

F is for football – the sport that is king,
Joy to the millions each season it brings.
Add to its pleasure – by trying your skill –
Forecast correctly – your bank book you'll fill.

G is for growth – which our business has shown,
Based on integrity – just that alone.
Valued your patronage – studied your needs
Success has sprung from fidelity's seeds.

H is for home which is dear to our hearts
Standing for union and all it imparts;
Make your home brighter – get comfort and ease,
Stick close to Vernons for profits that please.

I is for interests – we're studying yours,
Giving you chances on various scores;
Keeping in touch with you gives us delight,
Past records show that our policy's right.

J is for joy which a big prize can bring,
Poverty flies like a bird on the wing;
Each week big sums go to winners in scores,
Keep right on trying – the next maybe yours.

K is for keenness, a virtue to prize,
Fortune awaits eager minds and keen eyes;
Study the game and your forecast record,
One of our 'bumpers' may be your reward.

L is for luck which we can't do without,
Plays a big part in our lives without doubt;
May you be one who can joyfully say –
'When I found Vernons was my lucky day.'

M is for money – we make it go round,
Stupendous prizes our clients have found;

Have you a scheme you would like to see through?
Vernons big cheques make your day dreams come true.

N is for news from the world's varied maze,
Newspapers bring it each day to our gaze;
Some of it's 'jannock' and some of it's bluff,
But Vernon's big prizes are real 'front page' stuff.

O's opportunity – stood at your door,
Six first class pools – can we offer you more?
Fortune may bless any coupon you send,
Your big success may be just round the bend.

P is for pools – and first view our selection,
Our 'Nothing Barred' gives you choice of each section;
'Five Starred Results' – 'Penny Pool' and 'Three Draws',
These and the rest bring our clients' applause.

Q is for questions – have these three a chance?
Are these 12 winners? Will home teams advance?
Chance plays a part and so doubts must prevail,
But one thing is certain – that Vernon's won't fail.

R is for records – you'll find in this book,
When there's an argument – just have a look;
Speaking of records – just look at ours too,
Clearly they'll show you what Vernons can do.

S is for security – year in, year out,
No broken promises – no shade of doubt;
Service and safety are good business ways,
Vernons have proved that Stability pays.

T is for travel – to new sights and sounds,
Customs and climates change all the world round.
Do you aspire to new realms and conditions?
Let Vernons help to fulfil your ambitions.

U is for unseating depression and care,
Coupon and pencil – a nice easy chair;
Worries forgotten – your weariness goes
Content – and maybe a fortune – who knows?

V is for Vernons, well known and respected,
King of all Pools – by the clients selected;
Straightforward rules – fair and square allocations.
Introduce them to your friends and relations.

W is for winners – just read what they say,
'Thank you for paying in such a prompt way.'
'Starting a business to run on my own,'
'Since I met Vernons, big profits I've shown.'

X for the unknown, and also a sign
Multiplication of figures in a line,
Here's an example it's easy to see,
Your stake X Vernons give more £.s.d.

Y is for youth – with its quest for romance,
Challenging customs and playing with chance.
Happy are they with their daydreams of gold,
But Vernons gives pleasure to both young and old.

Z is for zeal which we will renew
All our endeavours to satisfy you;
Value to your business and study your ends,
Live to the slogan 'Our Clients – our friends.'

They don't make 'em like that anymore – thank goodness!

A January 1938 Copes Pools coupon, subject of an article in the December 1996 edition of *The Football Collector* magazine, featured an unusual pool, called the novelty nine. Eighteen teams were randomly selected and paired off, and for a stake of three old pence, the punter had to forecast which of the two teams would score most goals on the day in question.

A.P. Herbert, the MP who in 1938 introduced a Bill which would have abolished the pools, but later wrote a book in praise of them, recommended one of the barmier draw-picking systems: 'Think of some appropriate message, take the first letter of each word and select your matches accordingly for the home teams which are printed first. For example, God Save The Queen, Long May She Reign might come out as Gillingham, Stoke, Tottenham, Queens Park Rangers, Leeds, Mansfield, Southampton, Bristol Rovers.'

A bizarre anomaly was thrown up on 17 January 1982 when, courtesy of the Pools Panel, Rangers were involved in two separate fixtures. They turned out on the park at Ibrox where they defeated Dundee United 2–0, but they were also adjudged by the Pools Panel to have been playing away at St Mirren at the same time where, perhaps even more peculiarly and illogically, they were deemed to have participated in a score draw.

Perhaps the most pointless outing of the Pools Panel came on 18 February 1989, when they sat in splendour at the Waldorf Astoria Hotel, London, to debate the result of a single game, the vital Beazer Homes League clash between Gosport and Ashford.

In 1964, author Roger Longrigg made a startling and perceptive observation which few before, or since, seem to have cottoned on to. In his book *The Artless Gambler*, he drew attention to the fact that big pools winners had one thing in common: 'One quality, as many people have noticed, they share. They are all ugly. The explanation, if any, must be spiritual; it is fate's recompense for a great, fleshy nose, pig eyes, gap teeth, bad breath.'

Here's a real 'not many people know that' kind of trivial titbit. Remember actor Arnold Ridley, Private Godfrey in *Dad's Army*? Well, back in 1947 he wrote the script for a film called *Easy Money*, which extolled the virtues of winning the pools, whilst also warning against the temptations of cheating to win. The film was described by none other than the niece of Lord Kitchener, Madge Kitchener of the British Board of Film Censors, as 'a healthy deterrent to would-be cheaters'.

CHAPTER FOURTEEN

Foreign Flutters

A Yugoslav soccer player named Vlado Kasalo was arrested as he prepared to fly home from Germany during 1991. He was accused of deliberately scoring own goals against his team, Nuremburg, to assist a Mafia-led betting racket. Kasalo was sacked from his club after netting the own goals in matches against Karlsruhe and Stuttgart.

In 1995 the Canadian Ontario Lottery Corporation allowed gamblers to help themselves to winnings of £365,000 after they continued to take bets on four English soccer matches which they believed to have evening kick-off times. The matches had actually been played during the afternoon and the results were already known to astute punters. As bets were still being accepted, punters were able to stake their wagers, already knowing the outcome. Incredibly, the Corporation paid the punters out, with their spokesman Don Pister, commenting ruefully: 'We have to assume everyone was playing in good faith. The mistake was ours.'

Colombian star player Escobar was shot dead after returning from the 1994 World Cup to his home country, amidst allegations that the Colombian team had been involved in match rigging for betting syndicates linked to drugs barons. Escobar had scored an own goal during Colombia's defeat by the USA thus, according to some reports, effectively signing his own death warrant.

In January 1990 gunmen shot dead a Colombian referee, Alvaro

Ortega, who had been in charge of an important match. A caller to the media later claimed that Ortega's death was ordered by Mafia members who had lost money on the outcome of the game between Independiente Medellin and America. Two days later another referee was kidnapped, but later released.

The Colombian Government ordered clubs to declare themselves free of influence from drugs cartels and betting syndicates.

An anti-corruption group calling itself Cleansers of Colombian Soccer then claimed responsibility for the murders of six people alleged to be members of a betting syndicate including the Presidents of two clubs.

Thirty players, amongst them Paolo Rossi, reputedly the highest-earning footballer in the game, were banned in Italy for their part in widespread match rigging, allegedly on behalf of an illegal betting ring, which involved the fixing of *Serie A* matches.

The scandal was eventually brought to light when two members of the illegal betting syndicate complained to the authorities that they had lost over £1 million after players had taken cash to fix games but then not done it, meaning that bets became losers. Rossi's 1980 ban was lifted in time for him to lead his country to their 1982 World Cup triumph.

Perugia defender Mauro Dello Martira was banned for three years in January 1982 for being involved in a betting syndicate.

Napoli general secretary Iallo Allodi resigned in 1986 when allegations that he was involved in a betting scandal came to light.

The last thing Ajax might have expected when they visited Scotland for a European Cup game in October 1996 was to be given a hero's farewell as they flew out of Glasgow having won the match by the only goal of the game. But for some reason that Ajax victory provided William Hill with their biggest-ever payout on a match played in Scotland – and it was the Rangers fans who collected when they lost.

Hill's had made Ajax 11/10 favourites to win the game against a Rangers side which had endured a nightmare in its previous matches in the competition that season. The money just poured on and Hill's finally found themselves at kick-off time with a potential payout of over £600,000 if Ajax won and just £6,000 if Rangers won. Ajax's victory resulted in payouts of £7,350 in one Glasgow betting shop, £6,300 in another, £6,720 in a West Lothian shop and literally hundreds of smaller payouts at scores of shops throughout the country.

Rangers fans turned up at the airport to see Ajax off and they sang and waved their betting slips in the air, according to newspaper reports.

Betting was said to be at the root of a major incident in Hungarian football in 1983 when 260 players and 14 referees were suspended and 75 people convicted of conspiring to fix matches in the country's lower leagues.

One man, Tibor Molnar, allegedly the mastermind behind the scheme to land pools wins, was said to have made £130,000.

Football in the Far East seems to have had more than its fair share of betting scandals. A tournament in Singapore in 1987 saw several Canadian internationals being accused of accepting £60,000 to influence the outcome of games against the home side, with the cash being supplied by a local gambling syndicate.

In 1995, almost one hundred Malaysian premier league players were kicked out for match rigging – 22 of them were even banished to remote areas of the country. Teams admitted taking money to throw games, including top state side, Sabah. If any good emerged from this débâcle it was that the authorities appeared to be making genuine efforts to clean up the game.

However, in June 1997, when England were competing in the World Youth Championships in Kuala Lumpur, *Sunday Telegraph* correspondent, Steve Curry, sounded a warning about the advisability of choosing a venue linked with corrupt practices for such a prestigious tournament. 'For those in this country whose life revolves around multi-million pound illegal betting syndicates it presented a lucrative opportunity to further perpetrate their sinister trade.'

FIFA spokesman, Keith Cooper retorted: 'If you decide to take the championships away from a country then you are giving in to the syndicates. The Malaysian FA and the police have gone a long way towards cleaning it up.'

Curry reported that two illegal betting operations had been raided during the course of the tournament – one of them actually operating out of one of the stadiums hosting matches. Don't forget, though, that in England a perfectly legal betting facility is available for matches at Wembley Stadium, and it does not, presumably, follow automatically that illegal bookmakers are indulging in any suspect practices relating to the matches themselves.

Meanwhile, football betting has been flourishing in Hong Kong to such an extent that the gambling boats which now sail regularly out of the harbour there in to international waters to enable passengers to punt all night, happily accept massive soccer wagers. Bets of a million Hong Kong dollars – about £80,000 – are reportedly commonplace: 'A number of our regular customers love to bet on English football' said retired policeman Lawrence Yip, who has an interest in one of the betting boats. Much of the football business transacted in Hong Kong finds its way to bookmakers based elsewhere, who have agents in the former British controlled Territory. One, C. M. Leung, was quoted by the *Racing Post* in August 1997: 'There are a lot of people genuinely interested in betting on the Premier League because they know the games cannot be fixed. That's the bottom line in Hong Kong where they believe – although there is no real evidence – that racing is simply bent.'

In April 1996, a ban on Dutch international referee, Dick Jol, imposed by the Dutch FA after he was accused of placing wagers on games in which he was officiating, was lifted.

William Hill operate an International Division catering for clients based all over the world. In February 1997, the company boasted customers from 34 different countries: Australia, Austria, Belgium, Britain, Brunei, Canada, Czech Republic, Denmark, Finland, France, Germany, Hong Kong, Hungary, Indonesia, Israel, Italy, Japan, Kuwait, Malaysia, Malta, Netherlands, New Zealand, Saudi Arabia, Seychelles, Singapore, Slovakia, South Africa, Spain, State of Bahrain, Sweden, Switzerland, Thailand, UAE, USA. Even Mike Quigley, who runs the business, declared himself 'surprised' at the total.

In September 1992, William Hill had first introduced a new service enabling Germans and Italians to bet on a whole range of sporting events, including major football matches and tournaments. Hill's recruited German- and Italian-speaking staff for the service and set up a freephone, freefax and freepost deposit betting system allowing the Germans and Italians to place a 'bank' of betting money with the company and then bet on any event to take their fancy.

At the time, punters in Germany and Italy were limited to a small range of legally permitted wagers available from domestic outlets. The new system proved attractive, particularly in Italy where questions were asked in their equivalent of the House of Commons about whether the introduction of such a facility was legal or desirable.

In order to permit their existing telephone credit clients to bet when abroad, Hill's set up an international freephone credit betting service which in 1997 allowed customers to ring their soccer bets in to the company's HQ from 15 different countries, free of charge.

In 1992, respected English bookmaker Victor Chandler opened up five betting shops in Cyprus. Punters could not bet on English racing but enthusiastic football fans flocked to bet on English, German, Italian, Spanish and Dutch matches. Widening their clientele, Chandler employed Italian-speaking telephonists to accommodate Italian clients who were punting on *Serie A* games. The company also took out adverts in Spanish newspapers, offering credit and deposit accounts.

Allegations of match rigging during a World Cup qualifying match between Cyprus and Bulgaria in December 1996 caused a furore when they became public in January 1997. The Cyprus FA called for an investigation into bookmakers' records to discover how much was gambled on their side being defeated. The Cypriot media alleged that some of the home players had wagered large sums on their side losing, and had advised others to do likewise. Bulgaria won 1–3.

British bookmaker Victor Chandler, who manages a number of shops on the island, reported no unusual betting patterns for the 14 December match, according to the *Racing Post*, which quoted them as saying: 'We never saw anything on the game. Soccer betting is big business in Cyprus, so perhaps Cypriot bookies saw the money.'

The *Post* said it had learned that 'several surprisingly large' bets of £1,000 or more were requested but rejected on the island.

Betting in Cyprus is predominantly on football and Cyprus FA Chairman Marios Lefkaritis declared: 'What concerns us is that the integrity of football is at stake. We are trying to collect as much information as possible from betting shops to see what kind of amounts were at stake.'

Football authorities on the island allegedly believed that up to £40,000 in bets (over five times the normal amount gambled) was staked on a Bulgarian victory.

Although the neutral might imagine that Bulgaria would be 'nailed on' to beat Cyprus, the Cypriots had beaten Israel 2–0 in their previous qualifier, while Israel had beaten Bulgaria 2–1. Cyprus were unbeaten in their last six home games.

Cyprus FA vice-chairman Costas Koutsokoumnis was reported by the *Independent* as saying: 'I can only say the performance of some players was not as it normally is in other games.'

Shortly after the allegations were made public, Cyprus team coach Andreas Michaelides walked out. The *European* newspaper reported that 'it is understood that on the morning of the Bulgaria game Michaelides was the first to contact the [Cypriot] Federation about rumours that heavy bets were being placed on Cyprus to lose.' The paper also said that the game in Cyprus is rife with match-fixing rumours in the domestic championships. The Cyprus FA was reportedly pushing for a national ban on all betting involving local teams and the national side.

'We need this measure if we are to dispel such rumours,' said Marios Lefkaritis.

Two international players were charged with conspiring to rig games during the 1994–95 Cypriot league championship, but the case was dismissed.

Foreign fans who came over to watch Euro '96 in England may not have wished to bet their bottom dollars on the outcome of matches, but thanks to William Hill they were able to gamble their guilders, flutter their francs, punt their pesetas and lay their lire.

For Hill's were accepting bets in their 1,600 branches throughout England, Scotland and Wales in sterling, deutschmarks, guilders, pesetas, French and Swiss francs, escudos, kroner, koruna, Italian and Turkish lire. Difficulties in obtaining accurate exchange rates prevented them from accommodating fans of Bulgaria, Croatia, Romania and Russia.

The experiment proved a great success and led to a humorous moment when a punter went into a William Hill betting shop and asked to bet 'forty million' on Italy to beat Germany at odds of 13/8. Panic-stricken staff at first thought the man was talking about pounds, but it transpired he meant lire. It translated into a still respectable wager of £16,000 – which was a loser.

Rumours – believed to this day by usually reliable bookmaking sources – have abounded that Maradona deliberately scuppered his team Napoli's efforts to win the 1987–88 *Serie A* championship, because the underworld Camorra organisation did not wish to lose millions of lire to those who had backed the club to retain the title. Napoli's 3–2 defeat by AC Milan in the last but one game of the season cost them the championship.

Maradona's biographer, Jimmy Burns, poured scorn on the allegations in his 1996 book, *Hand of God,* declaring: 'Not even those who lost believed that.' Burns refuted other similar stories about possibly rigged games by commenting that the Camorra, who tightly control Italy's black market pools according to the author, 'appear to have accepted from the outset that Maradona's presence on the pitch was so prominent and his performance so idiosyncratic that any fix would have been immediately identifiable.'

CHAPTER FIFTEEN

Odd Boot Betting Banter

In his book *The Black 'n' White Alphabet*, which is a complete who's who of Newcastle United, author Paul Joannou recorded the tale of Charlie Watts, a goalkeeper and trainer for the club. He apparently cut his own throat after losing a bet to clear £3,000 of debts in 1924.

Going back even further into the mists of time, Jack Hillman, goalkeeper and skipper of Burnley in the 1899-1900 season at the end of which they were relegated to division two, was a larger than life character at 6ft and 16 stone. He once won a bet by keeping goal using just one hand during a charity match, which his side won 1–0. The amount of his winnings is not recorded.

Decorator Steve Vincent never dreamed he'd be backing an 80/1 winner when he awoke from his slumbers in November 1988, having 'seen' West Ham hand Liverpool a victory of 4–1 in the Littlewoods Cup. To his surprise the two teams were actually playing that week and the 28-year-old risked £4 on the shock outcome of his dream. He placed his bet in a Beckenham bookies and collected £291.60 after tax for his troubles.

'Perhaps I'm a witch,' said Steven.

A similar dream scenario enriched Cirencester punter Richard Inkpen who couldn't resist staking a £1 win double after dreaming that Swindon would win the Fourth Division championship and West Tip would win the 1986 Grand National. His £936.90 winnings prompted bookie Mike Gannon to express his earnest hope that Mr Inkpen would become a victim of insomnia.

Butcher Roy Hannam, a winger with his local soccer side, bet the opposition centre-half, Don Withers, half a week's wages on the result of their match. Don's team won and Roy paid up – 47 years later. The bet of 2s 6d (12½p) was struck in 1939 and Roy finally handed over the cash in November 1986 when he was 69. He paid with an old-fashioned half crown, no longer legal tender. Don was delighted: 'I'll frame it.'

There was an element of delay involved when Gilbert Claughton of Cambridge paid William Hill 7½p for a football bet in October 1980. Nothing strange about that, you might think, except that he originally struck the bet on 8 November 1958, 22 years earlier.

'The reason for the delay was that the bill got lodged inside an old football annual and I forgot all about it until an advert for Hill's in the *Daily Mirror* all those years later jogged my memory.'

Reading postman Trevor Child staked £1 at odds of 500,000/1 that Mr Blobby would be appointed England soccer manager in succession to Graham Taylor. Asked what he intended to do with his winnings he commented: 'Buy a balloon and float away.' He must have been devastated when the appointment of Terry Venables shattered his dream.

Restaurant owner Francesco Sorrentino and butcher John Hartwell were at odds over who would get further in the 1986 World Cup, Italy or England. So they struck a £1,000 bet. John was to pay for that amount of free food for Francesco's customers if Italy got further, and Francesco was to pay up by buying a grand's worth of bangers from John if England triumphed. England did the business for John, so Francesco paid up, but it was local pensioners in the pair's home town of Bedford who benefited as Francesco donated the sausages to them.

The win was sweet revenge for John, who had lost the last bet the pair made in 1982 when Italy won the World Cup. On that occasion John had to pay up by kissing Francesco's shoes.

I received a letter from a would-be client in spring 1992, consisting of a list of entirely unlayable bets, for example, members of the Royal Family to become involved in sexual scandals (surely not!); well-known people to die in bomb blasts or at the hands of assassins; earthquakes to claim the lives of thousands; and famines to hit a large proportion of the earth. At the end of this tasteful list my correspondent added that he would like to double up all the bets he had mentioned – with Derby County to win the FA Cup.

Well, of course, I wrote back immediately, explaining that such a wager would be out of the question as I felt it would be tantamount to taking money under false pretences – after all, how could Derby win the FA Cup?

In the mid '80s a group of friends were in a pub in Ipswich prior to a local Sunday League match, discussing the financial plight of their team, Sorrel FC. Player's wife, Jan Sherwood suddenly offered to bet any takers that she would be prepared to do a streak during the match, with the proceeds of her winning bets to go to club funds.

There were plenty of people willing to bet her at even money. Shortly after half-time, the couple of hundred spectators, the referee and linesmen were all stunned as Jan peeled off and raced across the pitch – to the absolute consternation of her 28-year-old husband, Dave, who was playing in the game at the time.

The slogan 'It's so easy to be a winner' devised by the Cardiff-based *Western Mail* newspaper to promote their Spot the Ball competition, looked like a real own goal in January 1993 when they printed the entry coupon with the ball still firmly in place in the photograph. One thousand copies of the paper had come off the presses before the error was spotted and the mistake corrected.

Staff at a betting shop in Denny, Stirling, Scotland, were surprised to receive a picture postcard from Spain in 1982, which featured the message: 'Thanking your organisation for the financial aid in the last football fixed-odds season. Travelling through Spain watching World Cup soccer – f***ing great. A. Client'!

A couple of years ago I was surprised to receive a letter asking for odds that 'the next Pope will be a Newcastle supporter.' Well, I knew that Pope John Paul had played football as a younger man in Poland, but could only imagine that my correspondent was predicting that Kevin Keegan – their manager at the time – or Les Ferdinand would leave the game to become Pontiff.

Upon carrying out a little research, via a Catholic newspaper, I soon discovered that a certain Cardinal Basil Hume is, in fact, a Newcastle fan. The punter was duly offered the 100/1 about Cardinal Hume assuming the highest office in his Church.

Have you heard the one about the bookie who tried to bribe players to *win* matches? It happened in 1919 when East Dulwich bookie Henry Thatcher approached two Millwall players, Douglas Thomson and Richard Griffiths, offering them a total of £4 each if they managed to beat Brentford in their forthcoming game. Thatcher told the two that he had £50 riding on a Millwall victory at odds of 5/4, but they refused to take his inducement and reported the approach to the club.

A further meeting was arranged to which Thatcher requested the Lions keeper and skipper should be invited. He offered £15 each for a victory over the Bees.

When the police decided to bring the case to Bow Street court,

Thatcher was given a three-month sentence. You cannot help but wonder how he could have been accused of doing anything worse than offering the players the equivalent of a win bonus. Thatcher appealed against his sentence, which was reduced to a £50 fine with £100 costs, after which he is reported as having reflected ruefully: 'I did not realise I was doing anything seriously wrong.'

One of the oddest bets I ever accepted was from a couple who said they hated football so much that they had deliberately timed their wedding to coincide with the kick-off of the 1992 FA Cup Final. They wanted to place a bet that it would pour with rain in London at the time, soaking the crowd at Wembley Stadium. Bride Tracy Owen-Williams and her fiancé Paul Faulkner staked £20 at odds of 20/1 about the scenario, to be confirmed by the Minister conducting the wedding ceremony at the Welsh Congregational Chapel in Southwark Bridge Road. As the pair took their vows and Liverpool lined up against Sunderland, the heavens opened and it poured. The couple won £400 to defray their honeymoon costs.

In January 1991, Newcastle fan Peter Evans bet £10 at odds of 1000/1 for Newcastle to reach the FA Cup Final and his wife Linda to give birth on the same day, 18 May. Neither 'happy event' transpired.

If Cornishman Phil Barber's September 1994 bet had come off, I'd have been convinced he was in league with, if not the Devil, at least some kind of higher power. Not content with wanting to back Andy Cole to score a hat-trick for England against Romania, he also wanted to name the precise minutes in which each goal would go in – 12th, 33rd and in injury time at the end of the first half! He was offered, and accepted, odds of 5000/1 for his £10 stake, but never looked like winning.

John McKenna, President of the Football League from 1910, was so rabidly anti-gambling that he once accused his barber of betting on football when he saw coupons hanging up in his shop. The barber pleaded innocence and managed to convince McKenna that the coupons were old ones, used to clean his blades.

One of the few bets you can have where you are actually on a winner at the time you place it, and something has to happen to prevent you being paid out, is to bet on a football match ending up as a 0-0 draw. But many soccer punters like to speculate on who will score the first goal of a game and it has become one of the most popular side-bets on big matches.

However, it brings with it its own problems as there is no official adjudicator as to who has scored a goal. As long as he is satisfied the goal has been scored legally, the referee is not obliged to note who put the ball in the back of the net.

For obvious reasons players are not always keen to admit to deflecting the ball in for an own goal while strikers can be relied upon to claim a goal even if the nearest the ball came to any part of their body was as they picked it up out of the net to jog back to the centre spot.

How about relying on TV to decide who scored? Fair enough, but not every game is on the box and, as we all know, an incident can look different depending from which angle you watch it. Newspapers, then? Again, a good idea but as a journalist of over 20 years' standing who has covered thousands of matches over those decades, I can tell you that football writers are not always the most perceptive or conscientious of observers. Many's the time in a press box I have heard the cry, 'Who scored that, then?' to which the reply is often, 'Dunno, let's give it to the boy Spiggins.'

So, with bookmakers doing such a roaring trade on first scorer bets they obviously needed to come up with an acceptable system of making a decision in the event of a dispute.

Back in the late '70s when Arsenal played Manchester United in the FA Cup Final, Brian Talbot and Alan Sunderland appeared to strike the ball at exactly the same moment for the Gunners' first goal of a 3–2 victory. Observers, fans, players and officials were genuinely baffled and although the history books now credit Talbot with the goal bookmakers decided that it was impossible to split them and paid out on both at full odds, even though they could have declared a 'dead-heat' and halved punters' stakes.

Not wishing to be forced to be so generous again the bookmakers have now come up with their own ways of deciding who scored the first goal.

For example, at the time of writing, William Hill pay out on a majority verdict of national newspapers; Stanley bookies use a panel of five papers – *Mirror*, *Mail*, *Sun*, *Express* and *Telegraph*; Ladbrokes use what they describe as the 'common-sense approach' – in other words they make a unilateral decision of their own; Coral's abide by the decision of the *Sporting Life* and Super Soccer stand by the verdict of the TV station covering a game.

Generally these different methods will still come up with the same outcome, but just occasionally it is a recipe for confusion, as in February 1997 when one game produced several conflicting versions of the first goal scorer. Bradford were at home to Sheffield Wednesday in the FA Cup in a Sky-televised game. The first goal appeared to be hit netwards by Wednesday's Ritchie Humphreys, only to be deflected in by Bradford's Nicky Mohan. Coral and Ladbrokes both ruled that Humphreys had scored. Hills, Super Soccer and Stanley tagged it an own goal.

The confusion did not end there. While Stanley quote odds for an own goal, Hill's and others exclude own goals in their betting and will pay out on the next goal as the first in the case of own goal(s). So, with Wednesday winning 0–1, different bookies ended up paying out on three different 'winners': Coral and Ladbrokes on 7/1 shot Humphreys; Stanley on 25/1 shot own goal and Hill's on 8/1 chance no goalscorer. Confused? You should be.

Mention of bookmakers who don't recognise own goals calls to mind a little tip for punters: if you fancy a game to end 0–0 then place your bet with a bookie who offers odds for 'no goalscorer' because that way you'll win either if the game is a goalless draw or if there is a disputed goal, or goals ruled as own goals.

East Anglian bookmakers Krullind launched a football fixed-odds coupon for the 1985-86 season, offering odds about 25 matches each week in the eight divisions of the Suffolk and Ipswich League. This is almost certainly, with due respect to the 112 teams who participate, the lowest level at which any organised betting has ever been operated.

Bert Hatcher, a partner in the business, came up with the idea. He was a local footballer and figured that the scheme would attract punters into the company's three shops. He arranged for the local newspaper, the *Ipswich Football Star* to carry results from all the League's games on the evening of the day on which they were played.

Punters were even allowed to combine the results of their local Division Six match with selections from the first division if they wanted.

During the 1994 World Cup a punter from Dingwall in Scotland bet £10 that live TV transmission of matches would fail on 16 July because of a comet colliding with the satellite linkup. It didn't happen.

The *Today* newspaper reported a truly bizarre bet on 14 February 1994 when Des Kelly's exclusive story revealed:

> Sam Hammam honoured his unique wager when he kissed Dean Holdsworth's backside at the weekend. Wimbledon owner Hammam puckered up after the striker scored in the 4–2 win over Newcastle.
>
> Last year Hammam gave Holdsworth a bronze bust for reaching the 20 goal mark. The stakes were literally lowered this season, but he proved as good as his word when the centre-forward hit his 15th of the season.

Soccer fan Jimmy Orr can't wait for the World Cup Final in the year 2006. In a vivid dream he saw his son Stephen cracking in a goal for England during the match – and if the dream comes true he will win £250,000 from William Hill.

Decorator Jimmy, from Wimbledon, placed a £25 bet on his son, then ten years old, after waking up from the dream in which 'I saw him scorching past two defenders and shooting into the roof of the net.' The odd thing about Jimmy's dream is the fact that he saw Stephen playing for England even though he, Jimmy, is a Scot!

A bet which took the punter an incredible *nine* hours to write out was believed to be the world's longest long shot – over 11 feet long, to be more precise. The William Hill punter, who turned up in area manager Ron Barnes's Sparkhill betting shop in Birmingham in November 1993, had no less than 974 correct-score accumulators on the 1994 World Cup. Having spent three hours a day for three days writing out the bet, the client must have been somewhat miffed when his banker selection, Sweden to win 3–2, failed to materialise – thus immediately scuppering the entire wager.

The man who read the Saturday afternoon football results on BBC TV's *Grandstand* for 37 years was ruffled just once during his lengthy career – and that was when Len Martin suddenly realised that he was reading out a result which meant that he had won the pools himself. On 23 October 1971, he gave the result of the Scottish League Cup Final: Celtic 1, Partick Thistle 4.

'I'll repeat that one,' he said, after the slightest of pauses, and then continued with the rest of the results. His lapse was excusable as that scoreline completed his own line of eight draws, which won him £500.

It was almost enough to pay the tax demand which arrived on the same day as his winning cheque.

What has to be the unique occurrence of a streaker being given a man-of-the-match award, took place because of a wager. Twenty-nine-year-old scaffolder Mike Browning, was watching a Cup Final in Sussex between Heath Pilgrims and Wivelsfield Green in April 1997 when he stripped off and dashed across the pitch during the game, which ended 1–1. Said Browning, 'I did the streak for a bet and it was a bonus to be named man of the match.'

Middlesbrough fan Shaun Keogh thought he'd got the real inside track on a certain winner when clairvoyant Madame Zaza told him that she 'saw' the 1995–96 premiership title trophy being handed over at the Riverside Stadium. Shaun rushed out and backed Boro for the title and was baffled at the inaccuracy of Madame Zaza's forecast as they never threatened to challenge for honours. All became clear when the

Premiership title trophy was indeed handed over at the Riverside – to visiting Manchester United!

The ultimate stake? An Albanian soccer fan staked his *wife* on Argentina beating Bulgaria in the World Cup in 1994. They didn't, and she was duly handed over to the winner, known only as E.G., after which the pair disappeared. Although this sounds like a 'friend of a friend' type story, it was actually confirmed by a Reuters correspondent interviewed on BBC's Radio 5 Live.

In 1988, a Scottish punter staked £50 at odds of 150/1 with Coral's on Rangers winning the Premier Division for the next nine seasons. They did it and he came in for his winnings at the end of the 1996-97 season. Despite having lost his original slip, Coral's were happy to pay out on a duplicate slip when the handwriting matched. They were surprised that, having pulled off such a far-sighted wager, the man wished to remain anonymous – until he explained that he was a season-ticket holder . . . at Celtic!

CHAPTER SIXTEEN

Recalling Bygone Betting Days

I spoke with Charles Layfield, by then in his mid 80s, at the London headquarters of BOLA, the Betting Office Licensees Association, with which he is still connected despite being deep into his retirement from a lifetime involved in bookmaking. He worked for the family firm in the early days both of greyhound racing and of football betting, rising to become a director of the William Hill Organisation.

Charles recalled his memories of the fledgling football business:

'My introduction to betting on football was 80 years ago when, as a young lad, I folded coupons for my father – not very well, it must be said.

'When the Football Leagues were introduced, Layfield Brothers [his father's and uncle's company] and a few others, started to issue coupons to punters for fixed-odds betting, but it was illegal to enclose postal orders or cash for customers in the UK – from them to us or vice versa.

'To avoid breaking the law, Layfields issued coupons with an envelope addressed to an office in Holland. On Saturday night one or two of the brothers went to the Hook of Holland and on Sunday morning they collected the mail at the sorting office and returned to settle the bets on Monday. Clearly it was worth the effort as it produced a bread basket full of coupons to be checked.

'On one black day when Layfields went to collect, their fellow bookies were asking each other: "You're not going to pay, are you?," as the results were so bad that almost every coupon seemed to be a winner.

'Our answer was "We will see," and we settled all the bets, even though my father had to borrow £25 from an uncle.'

Charles recalled the company placing advertisements in the popular *Titbits* magazine ('it cost us half a crown') and remembered that the postal business had to be moved on from Holland to Geneva when the authorities tried to prevent their business operating from the Dutch mainland.

He believes that his father missed a great opportunity of becoming a millionaire.

'He was one of the first to notice that the pools companies did not always pay out when no one got all the draws correct and reasoned that a dividend system – paying out consolations for near misses – would not cost much and would be an attractive proposition to customers. However, he could not persuade the others to go into the pools business – he would have made millions.'

At one time the Layfield business operated out of the prestigious Number One London address but had to have a presence in Scotland to run the postal service for the football coupons.

Tommy Graham was one of those involved in the innovatory idea which resuscitated fixed-odds betting after it had been virtually killed off by the imposition of swingeing betting duty.

The industry put its most experienced heads together and came up with 'individual-odds betting' which involved the three possible outcomes of each game – home win, away win, draw – being given separate odds, all of which would be subject to fluctuation, thus making them no longer fixed odds.

After test cases established that this form of football betting would be subject only to the same deductions which applied to bets on greyhounds and horses, it was launched in 1975 and has grown spectacularly over the following quarter of a century.

I was around at William Hill as a young whipper-snapper when this re-birth of soccer betting was being plotted and am pleased to say that I learned a great deal from Tommy Graham, then William Hill's football betting odds compiler – a job he carried out virtually single-handed.

Then in his mid 50s Tommy was a methodical, knowledgeable man who knew his stuff and didn't like offering odds on some of the less predictable, more esoteric areas of the game. With my instinct for publicity and desire to make an impression in the company and on the world of bookmaking, I would pester him mercilessly to quote odds on all sorts of different aspects of the football season. I must have driven him mad, but he recognised the impetuosity of youth and humoured me – most of the time.

In October 1974, I interviewed Tommy for the company newspaper, *Showboard*, and he revealed some of his background and opinions. Brought up in Clapham, Tom was also Hill's tennis and golf odds compiler as well as doing athletics prices. Before joining the company, Tom had a half share in a small bookmaking concern betting at the dogs, his first love. Before this he was in the Army for seven years, where his talent for making a book stood him in good stead and assured him of extra rations!

'From the age of about 17 I had ambitions to be a bookmaker, once I realised that the odds were on the bookies' side.'

Tommy rated football the most straightforward of sports to bet on.

'It's the easiest because there are no non-runners. I am not influenced by my own fancies. Pricing must be only on current form, although you must try to anticipate public demand.

'The result of a match is not important. If you can lay all three possible results in a football match and show a profit, this is 100 per cent accurate pricing. Knowledge of current form is the only requirement to price a football match but obviously, as with anything else, one gets better with experience.'

Asked how he viewed the punters, Tommy – always, it must be said, cynical of motives for placing a bet – commented: 'The majority are friendly rivals. A small percentage are thieves.' But he also enjoyed a wager himself – 'If I can see value, I will bet on anything' – and with his background of making a book in a factory, on street corners, in a coffee shop and in the Army before going 'respectable' with William Hill, he was one of the last members of the old guard. Even he was surprised at how vigorous and resilient the bookmaking business became.

'I have thought this was a dying business since tax was introduced, but keep being proved wrong.'

Sadly Tommy passed away in November 1996.

Norwich-based bookmaker Jack Pointer sold his business to Ladbrokes in the early 1980s. In 1962, though, the Jack Pointer company was regularly advertising its football betting odds in the *Sporting Life*.

Jack, now 72, recalled: 'At this period only three bookmakers were offering odds in the *Life* – myself, John Hudson from Hull and Ernie Peters from Manchester. So, for a period, we had the market to ourselves. Yet we never contacted each other before placing our adverts, so our odds were quite different – we adjusted them for any large bets.'

Interestingly, Jack invited punters to bet on 'Doubles and Trebles Only' and his list of odds for matches featured only prices for home and away results with no draw odds offered.

'We did not bet on draws as they were not a popular bet at this time – even today I hate to watch a game which I have backed for a draw.'

He was also quoting odds for international games – Scotland 7/4, England 5/4, for example (Scotland won 2–0), while for 90 minutes' play on that year's FA Cup final it was even money Spurs, 7/4 Burnley – Spurs won 3–1.

The adverts also contained the warning: 'Postal commissions on above games must bear Friday post-mark'.

Now in his 80s, Birmingham-based bookmaker and long-standing Aston Villa fan Albert Shepherd told me how his grandfather and father, both named George, had been in at the very beginning of organised football betting.

Albert told me that his grandfather, who worked on the railways, was an agent for a bookmaker. One day the bookmaker failed to arrive to collect the bets so his grandfather decided to take them himself. He set up as a bookie, based at the Monument Lane station, not far from Birmingham New Street.

'At the time it was mainly racing bets and my father, who was then in his 20s, worked with grandfather and began to expand the business. There was a brewery nearby from where they collected more and more bets.

'Football came in when Grandfather was asked to take bets on local games, some of which involved players from the Albion or Villa, who would come down and play as 'ringers' for a pound or so.

'When the Football League was founded Grandfather introduced coupons for his customers, done on a John Bull Printing Press. Then he brought in a local printer and installed a better system in the cellar of his house to print more coupons.

'The coupon featured a nothing-barred list and prices for individual divisions. The most popular section asked punters to find four homes, three draws and three aways.

'Father also invented something called football tickets, which featured 44 teams, each with a number. Punters paid 6d [2½p] a ticket which gave them two numbered teams. A prize of £20 would be paid to the holder of the combination of teams which scored the greatest number of goals. Payment was made on a Monday after the Saturday games.

'When the police told him that the tickets were illegal he found a way round the law by printing a racing tip on each one, so that in theory customers were paying for the tips and not for their bet.'

Albert naturally went into the family businesses, as did his older brother, George. Albert eventually started his own company, Shepherd Brothers, and in the late '50s and early '60s persuaded a number of local bookmakers to come in with him to form BUFFO – Birmingham United Football Fixed Odds.

'We were going really well and expanding,' recalled Albert. 'The most popular list on our coupons was the 12 results – matches which were so difficult to sort out that I remember once there were eight draws on the list. However, when the Government suddenly imposed a tax on fixed-odds betting the business packed up immediately.'

Albert also recalled the days when postal football bets were sent up to Scotland.

'Most companies were reputable, but there were some who were notorious for invariably ruling that large winning bets had arrived late and must therefore be voided!'

Former William Hill employee Bert Arnold was working for the company on the fateful day, 13 October 1962, when the fixed-odds coupons contained no fewer than 26 draws. With the odds about finding draws having been increasing rapidly as a result of cut-throat competition between the major firms, this produced a situation comparable to that experienced more recently by bookies on the famous occasion when Frankie Dettori rode seven winners at Ascot. Bert remembers what it was like at Hill's, who paid out a massive £1,312,810 that day:

'I do remember the 13th of October 1962. I used to go straight to the football office on Saturdays where we would work checking coupons from 6 p.m. to 10 p.m., and then on Sunday all day until 6 p.m. That Sunday we worked until 10 p.m. For the rest of the week we were checking coupons every evening. It was the Thursday before we finished checking. As you can imagine there were thousands of winners, single draws, doubles, trebles, accumulators.

'We used to get thousands of coupons from overseas – Cyprus, and some African places – their favourite bet was single draws at 5/2.

'The football side was a colossal business until Maudling, the Chancellor, imposed an exorbitant tax. It just did not register with him that fixed-odds operators could lose a fortune whereas the pools companies could not lose at all.

'It was a sad day when it all came to an end.'

CHAPTER SEVENTEEN

You Bet I've Gambled On My Career

Carrying out my duties as Media Relations Manager for William Hill, one of the largest bookmaking companies in the world, has ensured that I have acquired a certain public profile thanks to the readiness of the press to quote the wide variety of betting odds with which I supply them on a regular basis and to report comments and opinions I occasionally express about topical matters.

I wasn't aware just how far my infamy had spread until I decided in November 1993 that perhaps the time had come for a change of career. The job of England football manager had become available following the departure of Graham Taylor. I thought my qualifications – four successive titles in the Harrow Challenge League premier division and the Marathon League first division with my team Hatch End – indicated that a future in the higher echelons of soccer beckoned. So off went the job application and c.v.

On 29 November 1993, back came the reply from the Football Association: 'Dear Mr Sharpe, I am in receipt of your recent letter regarding the post of England Manager.' They'd read it. 'Please be assured that the contents have been read and noted. Should we wish to consider your application further, we will contact you again.' How about that, then? Just as I began to swell with pride I noticed the handwritten comment which had been inserted in black fountain pen just after that bit that said 'we will contact you again'. It read, 'But don't bet on it!!' in the same handwriting as the signature, FA Chief Executive, Graham Kelly – the man people like to believe doesn't have a sense of humour.

Perhaps Graham had heard of me following the occasion on which my name first came to the attention of the world of football. That was in 1986 when an outrageous conman was caught in the full glare of the world's media spotlight, but who nevertheless got away with his crime – Maradona. England supporters will never forget that day in June when 'Dirty Diego' punched the ball past England keeper Peter Shilton to give Argentina a 2–1 'victory' in a vital World Cup clash, not only condemning England to elimination, but costing a great many patriotic punters the chance of landing their World Cup wagers.

Punters who had bet on the match to end as a draw were up in arms (sorry) at being deprived of their winnings because of such a blatant piece of cheating. Most soccer fans were also more than a little miffed that England had been knocked out of the World Cup in this manner. Sympathising with both of these views I was struck with a flash of inspiration whilst shaving the next morning – why not refund stake money to all William Hill punters who had bet on the game to end in a draw whilst also, of course, paying out everyone who had backed the official outcome of the game?

It cost over £10,000 in refunded stakes, but caught exactly the outraged mood of the nation and produced millions of pounds worth of invaluable goodwill and publicity – and, I am delighted to say, caused consternation amongst rival bookmakers who sour-facedly rubbished the gesture and claimed it would set all kinds of precedents to take such an action.

Whilst on the subject of Maradona and his Argentinian cohorts, let me tell you about the time during the 1978 World Cup, when the South Americans were the cause of my being accused of perpetrating a gambling con on the British nation by none other than that champion of the consumer, Esther Rantzen. In my defence, I reckon that her attack on me and other bookies was wide of the mark.

The gist of the complaint in the *That's Life* programme of 2 July 1978 was that although Argentina had won the World Cup by beating Holland, according to William Hill they hadn't won the World Cup at all. This confusion was simply caused by the long-standing and still current rule that when a bet is struck on the outcome of a match it refers to 90 minutes' play (or the amount of time the referee deems necessary to allow two equal halves of 45 minutes each to elapse). For betting purposes, extra-time does not count when settling the outcome of a bet on a given game. As Argentina had actually won the World Cup by defeating Holland 3–1 after extra-time, in my opinion the *That's Life* mob decided to have a little fun at our expense.

It would be perfectly possible to introduce betting which took into account the result of a game after 120 minutes. Would Esther have then felt the need to start campaigning on behalf of those people having bets on a game which was decided on a penalty shoot-out or as the result of a 'golden goal' system? Deciding correct scores on the outcome of 90 minutes' play has survived the test of time and proved popular with the great majority of punters. Prospective punters should certainly make it their business to be aware of just what the terms and conditions are *before* they place their bets.

I can't blame Esther's programme for aiming at such an easy target, though. In 1996, Anne Robinson's *Watchdog* programme took similar aim and also fired off a number of blanks in the direction of bookmakers and football betting.

They conducted a survey deliberately designed to entice bookies into enforcing a rule which they could criticise, by placing a number of ambiguous bets in several different betting shops.

The bets were just on 'Bristol to win' – which could have been interpreted as Bristol Rovers, Bristol City, or even Bristol Rugby Club. One bookie paid out on the word of the punter, another divided his stakes between the two Bristols and another voided the bet. *Watchdog* managed to imply that this was disgraceful behaviour when, in fact, it showed an overwhelming desire to rule in favour of the punters' best interests.

With the growth of interest in football betting, there is always a demand for bets on topical matters – as there was when Kevin Keegan surprisingly quit as Newcastle manager in early 1997. We reacted speedily and put together a list of odds for potential successors to Keegan, making Kenny Dalglish our odds-on favourite and including in the list about 30 possible contenders. Obviously, the Newcastle Board had its own shortlist of people to approach with a view to taking on the job. There were probably no more than three or four names on that list, but we had no way of knowing who they were. So, effectively we were betting 'blind' and leaving ourselves wide open to those people in a position to take advantage of their own inside information. Yes, of course, there would be a great many people who would want to have a small speculation on the identity of the new man, but the bigger players would not show their hands until they were pretty sure they had an edge.

And so it proved as, within hours of the book opening, a great many bets began to go on two particular candidates, neither of whom we had rated as likely favourites – Bobby Robson, on whom one of my national newspaper sports editor friends had a £200 bet, and Peter Beardsley. The odds for this pair rapidly shrunk to 2/1 joint favourites from an opening price of 14/1 – so it came as no great surprise to learn that members of the Newcastle hierarchy had flown out to Spain to interview Robson, then boss at Barcelona. In the event, Robson declined the offer from Newcastle, who then turned their attentions to Kenny Dalglish, but we would have 'done our boots' had their first approach reaped rewards.

Earlier in the same season we lost a few quid and got the inside track on another stunning piece of soccer wheeling and dealing.

Every season we put up odds about each Premiership manager no longer being in charge of his team by the end of the season for any reason – the sack, a move to another side, resignation etc. We've been criticised in the past for doing this – once quite vehemently in a newspaper article by a certain Kevin Keegan, who got very hot under the collar when he heard that William Hill were running a book on who would be Liverpool manager at the start of the 1993–94 season, at a time when Graeme Souness was under pressure from fans and the media.

'It's a disgrace,' said Keegan, himself one of the leading contenders. 'You bet on racehorses because they are runners – not on a job that someone has got.' He seemed to think it would add pressure to managers' already taxing jobs. That's as maybe, but surely not as much as a jeering, booing crowd, or a derisory newspaper headline. We're talking about well-paid people in high-profile jobs, who know just what they're taking on when they accept their positions.

I feel no guilt about adding to the stress they may feel. A season or two back, one manager rang me to complain that he was amongst the shortest-priced managers in that season's book. He had no doubt that he would stay in the position and wanted to bet £2,000 that he would survive. I agreed, on condition that the winnings on either side would be donated to charity. The terms were accepted, the bet placed – and he was the first manager that season to lose his job. Did he keep his side of the bargain by donating the money to the worthy cause he nominated? You'd have to ask him.

We had priced up Bruce Rioch at 7/1 no longer to be in charge at Arsenal by the end of the campaign. Several shrewd football punters whispered to us that they would be taking this price and that if we were sensible we would reduce it. Amongst those who made a profit from the bet – not that I am suggesting he had any inside information – was Angus 'Statto' Loughran, of TV's *Fantasy Football* fame, and a man who enjoys the odd flutter.

Of course, Rioch got his marching orders right at the start of the season. The newspapers, who had ignored our pointed warnings in a press release issued a day or two before the axe fell, stating that we had cut the odds about Rioch's demise after apparently informed betting on him, took up the story with a vengeance and speculated about whether any Highbury insiders had cleaned up.

I'm pretty sure I was taken to the cleaners over another high-profile managerial hot seat. I was rather reluctant to offer odds about who would succeed Graeme Souness as boss of Rangers back in April 1991, especially as a number of shrewd punters had already landed substantial bets by backing Souness to take over from Kenny Dalglish at Liverpool. However, such was the interest in Scotland, where William Hill have a great many shops, that we duly opened a book, whereupon it soon became obvious that what we had here was the proverbial 'one horse book'.

No one wanted to back anyone other than Walter Smith, Souness's former right-hand man. His odds plunged from 5/4 to 1/5 in the space of just three hours. I knew we were being taken for a ride – and said so to the *Daily Record*. I was quoted in the 18 April edition as saying: 'We are taking no more bets. Mr Smith is the only person anyone has wanted to back all day. We believe he has either been appointed already or soon will be.'

The next day he was appointed – but not before I'd been woken up in the middle of the night by a phone call from the Night News Editor of the *Sun* in Scotland telling me he was trying to get evidence to back up a story he wanted to run claiming that Rangers' players and insiders had pulled off a massive coup by backing Walter Smith for the manager's job. I told him, sleepily, that we'd taken bets of up to £300, but that I had no idea who'd placed them and no way of ever finding out. I didn't lose too much sleep after he'd put the phone down. After all, that is part of the risk we take every time we open a book – but you won't be surprised to know that we didn't open a book a couple of months later when the Celtic job came up for grabs.

Mind you, inside information has been known to backfire on those in possession of it – witness the incident shortly after the 1991 resignation of Kenny Dalglish. Alan Hansen called the Liverpool players together in the dressing-room to tell them that he had taken over as the new boss. Convincingly, Hansen laid down the law about how he intended to run the show from now on. Completely taken in, several senior players allegedly rushed off to the local bookies to cash in on Hansen's appointment, causing Hansens odds to tumble from 7/2 to 7/4 favourite. Later that same afternoon, Hansen revealed that he had pulled a fast one on his team-mates, and was shocked at their unexpectedly angry reaction as they suddenly realised that they would be losing their stake money.

You'd think that a bookmaker would be safe taking bets on the identity of a new England manager. Surely there could be no leak of information when the highest accolade in the English game comes up for grabs. But I have to suspect that someone, somewhere knew a little more than we did when Terry Venables was handed the job in succession to Graham Taylor. Not that El Tel himself made a profit, he tells us in his autobiography, *Venables*:

> A rank outsider at the start of the race, I did not give myself a cat in hell's chance of taking over his job. If anything, the odds of 25/1 quoted in the papers seemed on the stingy side. If only I had known, I would have had a few quid on myself.

Interesting comment, that. It suggests that Terry Venables would have been quite happy to have profited from privileged information had he been able to do so. Not that he would have been doing anything wrong by having a few quid on himself. When a bookmaker makes a decision to take bets on something of this nature, he has to accept the risks involved and the danger that someone will be able to exploit a little advantage available only to him.

As it happens, there was a somewhat unexpected pattern to the way the betting on the England Boss Stakes panned out.

Journalist and author Mihir Bose gives a fairly detailed breakdown of affairs in his book *False Messiah*, a not particularly flattering examination of Terry Venables and his financial wheelings and dealings. In a chapter entitled 'Of Plots and Conspiracies' Bose refers to Venables' 25/1 place in the pecking order of likely contenders, and quotes me as recalling: 'Venables would have been one of the favourites had we taken away the financial baggage, but with all that, we felt he was out of the running.'

Indeed, we did, but as Bose notes, 'Within a month, all this had changed and Venables had become the firm favourite.'

This was largely due to the role of the FA's 'kingmaker', Jimmy Armfield, charged with the task of sounding out the major players in the game as to who they would like to see as England coach/manager. Armfield's travels garnered an impressive level of support for Venables.

> The longer the race went on, the odds on Venables changed. On 25 November William Hill cut him to 14/1 and the next day to 10/1 . . . The most significant movement came on 14 December when, between 10.27 a.m. and 1.26 p.m., William Hill took nine separate bets of £100 for Terry Venables to become England

manager – in Eltham, Feltham, Richmond (twice), Kingston, Twickenham, Pitfield Street N1 (twice) and City Road. The odds were cut from 7/1 to 6/1, although at this time Keegan was still favourite at 5/2.

The next day the papers were full of reports that Armfield had indeed gone for Venables and by 17 December Venables was down to 4/1. On that day he was made favourite at 5/2 and Sharp [sic] told the press, 'We know all about Mr Venables' well-publicised, non-footballing problems but with so many leading fancies apparently stressing their reluctance to be associated with the job and with the continued support from the punters, we have been left with no option but to promote him as favourite.' He displaced Keegan, who went out to 3/1. By 20 December the book on the England job had been closed. Venables was such a hot favourite that William Hill could not risk taking any more money.

All very true, if anything, under-playing the highly significant betting activity of 14 December – a pattern of bets in a relatively small area of the capital placed in such a way as to suggest that whoever was placing them was trying to get a relatively large amount of money on without drawing attention to what was going on. It is stretching credulity to suggest that every punter who placed bets during that period of three or four hours (and there were many more than nine in all) had all just decided on the spur of the moment to do so.

How 'inspired' the timing of the bets was is also worth considering in the light of the assertions in the Venables book that Jimmy Armfield, having received a very positive response in favour of El Tel, was instructed 'to meet me and open discussions in secret'. Venables then reveals that he and Armfield first met 'a week before Christmas' during which meeting Terry was left in no doubt but that he was right at the front of the race for the job. He got it, of course, even though he was given the title of Coach rather than Manager – and those prescient punters who had backed him were duly paid out.

The fact that Venables was given the job title 'Coach' was to lead to an exhaustive and exhausting exchange of views with one particular punter, a great fan of Brian Clough, who had staked a substantial amount on his hero getting the job of England Manager and who argued that as no 'Manager' had been appointed, all bets should be voided and stakes refunded. I'm not sure what the Venables punters would have said had we tried to utilise a similar escape route to avoid paying!

One man who made no secret of the fact that he was out to make a great deal of money by betting on a proposition which was anything but what it seemed at first glance, turned up in my office a few years back, in the days just before the Premiership was formed. He was quite open about everything, it seemed. He told me his name, and that he'd played a few games at junior level for a pro club before having to give up the game through injury. He was now 38 and he wanted to bet that he would play in a first division game next season.

His wife was about to publish a book on the powers of self-belief, combined with a revolutionary new diet. To support her and help promote the book he had come up with the idea of betting on himself getting into good enough shape to play first division football. Obviously it was virtually impossible, but it would make a good yarn for the papers and would help to sell her book. He'd like to make the bet for enough to give himself potential winnings of well into six figures.

He sat in my office for over an hour discussing the bet. I kept suggesting that perhaps we should make the bet seem more realistic by offering odds for him to play in the Vauxhall Conference, then divisions four, three, two, all the way up to division one.

'No,' he insisted, 'I'm only interested in division one.'

He went off, asking me to contact him with details of the odds I would be prepared to offer. I liaised with the football odds compilers in my company and we were all agreed it was pretty much impossible for him to achieve what he was suggesting, but that if he insisted, odds of at least 10,000/1 might be appropriate – after all, we joked, he might be Kenny Dalglish's brother or chairman of a club, for all we knew. In order to make sure that he wasn't already signed on as a player with some club, we instigated a search or two, but could find no trace of his name.

A day or two later he rang to ask whether we'd decided what odds we would be offering. I told him I was about to drop him a line. I'd decided that 20,000/1 to a maximum stake of £50 would be about right, giving him potential winnings of £1 million.

The next day I arrived at the office and, as I do most days, picked up the *Sun* and turned to the sports pages. There I read the amazing story of how businessman Michael Knighton had just purchased Manchester United. The would-be professional footballer-cum-big-time punter who wanted to boost his wife's book sales was a certain Michael Knighton: the same Michael Knighton who, to mark his arrival at Old Trafford, ran out in front of the fans juggling a ball in full view of the TV cameras; the same Michael Knighton who rang a day or two later to say that he supposed he would not now be getting a letter setting out his requested odds. He wanted to let me know that he would most certainly have insisted on Alex Ferguson selecting him as a sub for an end of season game in order to ensure that the bet was won, and – as I was well aware – my job lost.

Such a possibly disastrous scenario reminded me of the much earlier occasion on which I found my future threatened as a result of football betting. Currently I am a director of Wealdstone Football Club, the first club ever to achieve the non-league 'double' of Vauxhall Conference title (or equivalent) and FA Trophy. They also gave the world Stuart Pearce and Vinnie Jones, both of whom went on to skipper their countries. Those days of glory are some way off now and we ply our trade in the lower reaches of the Isthmian League (we won the division three title in 1996–97) but never give up the belief that a return to the halcyon days is just over the horizon.

Back in the '60s, I was already a Wealdstone supporter, attending the local Harrow County Grammar School – at the same time, it should be said, as Michael Xavier Portillo, whose name still graces the school's honours board to this day, and Clive Anderson, whose name, like mine, does not. At the age of 13 and short of pocket money I hit on a get-rich-quick scheme which basically involved opening a book on the FA Amateur Cup which Wealdstone had never won, and in the outcome of which there was considerable interest amongst my class-mates and chums – not to mention a few masters, as well.

The book attracted a considerable amount of financial investment until I was unexpectedly visited in the playground by the Deputy Headmaster, the rather stern and humourless Mr Cowan who, it was evident, had not come to risk half a crown on the chances of 'Stones' local rivals, Harrow Borough. He confiscated my betting book and called me to his study where he administered a rigorous verbal dressing down, stopping just short of expulsion – this was proof, I like to think, of a grudging admiration of my initiative.

However, my temporary discomfort was to prove to be to my long-term advantage as Wealdstone reached the final and went on to beat Hendon 3–1 to win the Cup, heavily backed by many of my clients. Sadly, though, with the betting book (containing bets in total of over 30 bob) confiscated, I had no way of determining who had backed what as no betting slips had been issued and therefore had no choice but to make void all wagers. I had inadvertently been done a considerable financial favour, even though I had to lie low for some weeks afterwards to avoid physical retribution from disgruntled punters. By the way, guilt has since got the better of me and I am willing to consider paying out to any Harrow County old boy (particularly Portillo and Anderson) who can provide convincing proof that they were amongst those unfortunates whose hoped-for winnings, which would no doubt have been squandered at the tuck shop, never materialised.

A letter I received in November 1990 sparked interest in an unusual form of football betting. It was a similar request to Michael Knighton's, with one notable difference – there was no con involved. Liverpool florist Ray Thomas explained that he was in his early 30s and played for a side in a local Liverpool Saturday afternoon league. He had played a few games for Plymouth Reserves some years back and was sick and tired of the lads he played with in the Liverpool league telling him that he could have made it to the top had he put his mind to it. Now he wanted to give himself one last effort to crack the big time and I was delighted to lay him a £50 bet at odds of 1000/1 that he would play in a First Division match during the next season.

He didn't, despite a local TV station picking up on the story and arranging a trial for him with Everton. The coverage the story garnered suddenly encouraged a flood of correspondence from people wanting to back their children to play top league or international football. This has snowballed to the extent where it is now a quiet week if I don't take half a dozen such bets and I have hundreds of them neatly filed away, waiting to explode, like financial time-bombs, at some stage in the future.

They have become so popular and newsworthy that shortly before Euro '96, the *Sun* arranged for a dozen of the kids whose parents have backed them for international glory to be brought together and photographed with Paul Ince. It made a smashing picture story with the inevitable result that it also produced even more such bet requests in its wake.

The most remarkable outcome of these bets could occur in the World Cup of the year 2018. If the Final that year is between England and Italy I could be preparing to pay out £1 million to two prescient fathers, who both have sons born on 1 October and who both believe said sons will grow up to achieve footballing glory. Steve Caldicott's son Jack came into the world in 1996, exactly two years after the arrival of young Pascal Risi.

Pascal's dad, Packer, was the first to contact me with a betting proposition about his son. Qualified by birth to play for Italy, he wanted to wager that the youngster would take part in the World Cup of 2018 and win the Golden Boot award for top scorer of the tournament, and also score in the final. Fine – 100,000/1 to a tenner was struck. Potential winnings: one million quid – a hefty haul of lire.

Two years later, along came father Steve to back son Jack to score in the self-same final. No problem, twenty quid staked, odds of 50,000/1 laid – another possible million pound pay-day.

Then there was the punter who bet me that Cantona would play for England – young Cantona Lord, that is, whose parents were such fanatical followers of the wayward French maestro that they burdened their boy, born on 3 December 1994, with his name. The boy's grandfather, Albert Brogan, from Newton Heath in Manchester, has staked £10 at odds of 10,000/1 that young Cantona will play for England on or before his 21st birthday.

I would say that the chances are that at least one of these bets will eventually pay off big time – after all, no one thought the bookies would ever have to pay out when they quoted odds about man walking on the moon or the Berlin Wall coming down.

Scottish fans should look out for the name of Alexander Johnston. The Edinburgh lad, nine years old as we went to press, will win £50,000 (£10 at 5000/1) for his dad if he skippers his country at senior international level by the age of 25. Michelle Williams of Nottinghamshire, born in 1979, could land a £20,000 (£20 at 1000/1) win for family friends if she wins an Under-21 or senior England cap.

There is one particular wager which I am expecting to be a winner – and which could even be one before this book hits the streets. Back in February 1991, Liverpool electrician Alex Robb approached me to ask for the odds about a Merseyside youngster captaining England at senior level within ten years. I offered him odds of 200/1, he slapped down £250 and I will have to hand over £50,000 to him if – or rather when – Jamie Redknapp achieves it.

Given the way in which this type of bet, often involving young children, has become so widely accepted and acceptable to the world at large, I wonder whether I was over-reacting by being shocked when I received a letter in January 1997 from Sandie Stephens, the Secretary/Treasurer of Reno Rovers Football Club. She asked whether I would be prepared to offer odds about her team winning the league and Cup double, in the Harrow League third division for Under 10s, 'as we have quite a few people wishing to place a bet on the team'. Under 10s! I could imagine these little lads, not even out of primary school, running round the pitch being harangued by parents for costing them a tenner by not winning a vital game; not an agreeable proposition.

I thought that to accept this request might cause adverse criticism, alleging that we were endeavouring to snare innocent youngsters into gambling – regardless of the fact that it was we who had been approached, rather than the other way round. I also believed that those wishing to place such bets could quite justifiably be accused of deliberately imposing unnecessary pressures on the children involved. And, perhaps betraying the true source of my doubts and the way in which my bookmaking experiences have influenced my character and reactions to other people, the first thing I thought was: 'This team is obviously a certainty to win both trophies, the parents know that and are taking a calculated gamble that I will be naïve enough not to know it.'

I declined to open a book on the team. However, having run this story past a number of acquaintances in the media and some involved in kids' football, I failed to get the outraged reaction I anticipated. Perhaps we've been so successful in associating betting with virtually any situation that the rest of the world has become anaesthetised to the potentially adverse effects on those too young to appreciate the true implications of such an action. Reno Rovers re-considered their original intention of placing a bet.

In 1985 I visited Russia with a group of non-gamblers. They knew nothing about football, either, but couldn't resist visiting the world famous Moscow Dynamo soccer stadium to see a match. I managed to talk them all into betting a few roubles with me at long odds on Moscow Dynamo's opponents, another Moscow side, Torpedo. With my superior soccer knowledge I was well aware that they were no-hopers. The no-hopers won easily. I lost all my holiday roubles and was reduced to dealing on the black market to get them back. Let that be a lesson to you!

As I sit here, slaving away over a hot word processor, Gary Lineker has just told me that Wimbledon, who have knocked Manchester United out of the FA Cup in a replay, have now been made 11/2 second favourites for the competition, with Chelsea the 3/1 favourites. Lineker, who is presenting *Sportsnight* on BBC 1 goes on to run down the odds of every club left in the competition. Extremely interesting, I think, and nice of them to use William Hill odds. I know they are William Hill odds because I have spent an hour distributing them to the media following a busy evening's FA Cup activity. People are keen to know what the betting is, now that the winners for the past two seasons have been eliminated.

But what earthly use is it for Gary Lineker to tell any interested party that Wimbledon are now 11/2? Anyone who might like to take advantage of that information has not been given any indication of where those odds have come from or which company is offering them. Odds without attribution to a bookmaker are virtually useless. You might as well tell a TV viewer that a programme in which he has an interest will be on at 9 p.m. Without knowing which station you might have to search through over 50 channels on your satellite or cable system before you find it.

Announce to shoppers that baked beans are available at 4p per tin or bread at 7p per loaf and just imagine the reaction if you omit the minor detail of where these bargains can be snapped up. Likewise, with odds, if you don't know which bookmaker is offering them, by the time you've phoned round or walked into branches of three different companies, the price may well have disappeared.

It was not only *Sportsnight* who were regularly guilty of this heinous disregard for punters. It has been happening on *Match of the Day* for years. I once went to lunch with *Match of the Day* producer, Vivien Kent – a charming, knowledgeable lady who, when I hesitantly broached this subject, made it quite clear that as far as she was concerned it was just not done to identify individual bookmakers when odds were mentioned. She accepted that it may be of interest but believed that the odds themselves were the newsworthy item and that the name of the bookmaker offering them was purely incidental. She also believed, like many other people involved in radio and TV, that some long-standing instruction from the BBC hierarchy prevented such information being broadcast and that to go against this perceived truth would bring down the wrath of some nameless consumer watchdog quango upon the programme's collective head for inciting people to gamble.

And this from an employee of the organisation which doesn't encourage people to gamble by showing the National Lottery at peak viewing time on a Wednesday and Saturday night. Not much doubt or confusion about where you can buy that product, is there?

If this alleged prohibition on dispensing the source of gambling information is true, then how come I have been able to appear for several years on Radio 5 Live's Eddie Mair midday show at five to two every other Friday afternoon? I am announced as being from William Hill and the current odds for sporting events are discussed and debated. No problem. This has been happening for a number of years now and no objections have been recorded, either from listeners or BBC insiders.

Radio 5 Live presenters like John Inverdale and Sybil Ruscoe are fond of the odd wager – Sybil told me on a recent visit to Broadcasting House that she'd backed Wrexham to knock West Ham out of the Cup. I think that's the difference. Those who understand betting are aware of the importance of knowing where the odds are available and are anxious to pass that vital information on to their viewers and listeners.

John Inverdale presented the drive-time *Nationwide* show on 5 Live on which I have been a frequent guest, chatting about various betting stories, always being fully identified. The programme also features a regular racing slot which reports the latest available odds and their source.

And to dent the validity of the *Match of the Day* argument further, I have just been watching the BBC's TV coverage of snooker's Benson & Hedges Masters Tournament. William Hill have a betting facility at the Wembley Conference Centre, where the tournament takes place, and just before signing off for the evening, highly experienced and respected commentator David Vine, who would surely be aware of any rule against it, told viewers the latest odds for the event, adding that they were supplied by William Hill.

Perhaps Vivien Kent and others could cite the ITC (Independent Television Commission) Programme Code to justify their stance. Section 10.5 of the Code does state:

> No undue prominence may be given in any programme to a commercial product or service. In particular, any reference to such a product or service must be limited to what can clearly be justified by the editorial requirements of the programme itself.

Now if that doesn't apply to the Lottery, as far as I'm concerned it certainly couldn't be held to be contravened by mentioning the source of relevant betting odds. That would certainly not be 'undue prominence' and would definitely be 'justified by the editorial requirements'.

In any case, these are ITC guidelines, which do not apply to the BBC, which has Producers' Guidelines, which say: 'References to trade and brand names should be avoided where possible and made only if they are clearly justified editorially.'

To my mind, the sort of information relating to adjustments in relevant betting odds is plainly 'justified editorially' on a programme which clearly considers the odds themselves of sufficient information to give them out. I can see no criticism which could be levelled at a producer opting to inform his or her audience of an entirely relevant development in the betting market, under the terms of the Producers' Guidelines.

I wonder when *Match of the Day* will finally summon up the courage to complete the service it provides to its viewers.

It is all rather like the bad old days when the BBC would show racing but give no information about the betting taking place on those races.

During 1997 they paid well-deserved and glowing tributes to Peter O'Sullevan, a broadcasting legend whose career could never have taken place but for betting, without which there would be no racing.

It was refreshing, though, to see a broadcaster on terrestrial television (the satellite channels are already showing more awareness of the link between football and betting in their coverage of live football) finally admit that the audience for a big match would be interested in the betting element of the contest. So, well done Channel Five, who had a bookmaker on hand to give out betting details of the England versus Poland World Cup qualifying game which they broadcast live on 31 May 1997.

Newspapers are slightly better than the BBC from a punter's point of view. Many of them now boast regular betting columns which exist purely to highlight the best wagering value available, but the general editorial columns still fall into lazy journo speak, using the term 'bookie' and not attributing the odds they are reporting.

One of the most popular of football betting opportunities is the FA Cup competition, but I fear that its appeal to punters is being diminished courtesy of an increasingly regular phenomenon which seems to be taking hold, with the connivance of the authorities.

A fascinating aspect of the Cup over the years has always been the clashes between the minnows playing at home on their own quirky little pitch with its Yeovil slope or other unfamiliar peculiarity, and the giants, apprehensive at the prospect of defeat or dangerously over-complacent about the likelihood of the part-time players cum butchers, bakers and stock-brokers giving them a bloody nose. Some shrewd observers of the soccer scene, particularly those knowledgeable about the game at its lower levels, have been able to make a financial killing by placing astute wagers on seemingly unpredictable results.

Now the trend seems to be towards switching games from the humble home of the no-hoper to the glamorous lair of the big boys, inevitably, the scope for shock results has lessened.

During the 1996–97 tournament, for example, non-league Hednesford were drawn at home to Middlesbrough, yet opted to play at the Riverside Stadium, where they went down by the odd goal in five.

Brave old Hednesford, chorused the media, how close they ran their mighty opponents, Signor Ravanelli et al. Not me. What a wasted opportunity, I thought. Had they played at home, that narrow defeat may have become a narrow victory. Some decent bets may have been landed at attractive odds by bold punters, and Hednesford's place in FA Cup history assured for all time.

Why should the Hednesfords of this world be permitted to switch their ties. 'Oh, it was on police advice,' we hear so often. But whether that is just a convenient excuse, we can never really know. Yes, of course the cash-strapped little teams are very grateful for the money they bring back with them from the big grounds. But in my opinion they should have to earn the right to play at those grounds by managing a draw at their own place.

The excuse that the supporters of the top teams would run riot if they came down to the little ground doesn't always bear close examination. Stevenage, for example, won the Vauxhall Conference in season 1995–96, but were unable to enter the Football League because of their supposedly inadequate facilities. They spent the entire close season complaining to anyone who would listen that they should have been allowed in, that their facilities were the equal of most clubs already in the second and third divisions, that the only reason they were excluded was because the League deliberately wanted to keep them out. And then, in the FA Cup of 1996–97, Stevenage were drawn at home to Birmingham – what a tricky match that would have been for the football odds compilers to price up, what an attractive heat for the soccer enthusiast.

But we didn't get the chance to bet on Stevenage being able to contain or even defeat a first division side at their own magnificent Broadhall Way ground. Stevenage switched the tie, went to Birmingham, started at 8/1 there, and duly went out, beaten 2–0 in a manner which strongly hinted that at home, on their own patch, and with their own fans roaring them on, a draw would certainly not have proved beyond them.

How could the club maintain the argument that they should be in the Football League when on the other hand they were saying that they weren't capable of staging the kind of game which they might have to play as a straightforward fixture once in the League?

What next? Should Wimbledon have the right to demand that they play away if they get drawn at home to Liverpool, on the grounds that a bigger crowd would turn up at Anfield to see the match? Of course not. So, why are these littl 'uns allowed to get away with it?

The mega clubs are delighted if they don't have to face an arduous trip to a venue at which they could well slip on an unpleasant banana skin. They are perfectly happy to increase the odds in their favour by not having to risk such setbacks. By agreeing to the switches, the FA is helping them to increase the already unhealthy monopoly situation at the top of the game to the detriment of dedicated fans and punters alike.

As I write, the manager of Stevenage is Paul Fairclough. On their way up to the Conference, Stevenage won the Diadora League premier division. William Hill were sponsors of the League's Manager of the Season awards, one of which Paul won. Part of those prizes was a day at the races. Some people are born gamblers. Others are born ultra cautious where money is concerned and there is little doubt in to which category Paul Fairclough falls.

I was hosting the day at the races – Sandown, if I remember correctly – during the course of which Paul asked me whether he could use up the £250 free bet he'd also won as part of his prize. Naturally I told him he could, but was marginally surprised at the staking plan he used to spend the bet. He picked the smallest field of the day – six runners – divided his bet into six, and backed every single horse in the field! Unfortunately for Paul the 33/1 chance was beaten out of sight and the 5/2 favourite won. At least he got something back but you'd have to deduce from that that Paul is a man who looks after his defence before worrying about the attack.

I took another manager to the races once who put his winnings on a non-runner, deliberately so he would get his free bet back as cash. The most successful manager/punter I ever entertained was Gerry Armstrong, who was boss at Newbury at the time. He turned up late having been delayed by a phone call tipping him a horse to be ridden by Michael Roberts. He plunged the whole of his free bet and more besides on the horse and on his advice everyone else in my box that day had a substantial wager which cantered up at 7/1.

Mention of the FA Cup brings to mind a long-running aberration which was only relatively recently cleared up. This was the situation wherby bookmakers were able to accept single bets on the results of Cup matches, but not on league games. In November 1984, I addressed the issue in the *Licensed Bookmaker* magazine:

> There was an entry of just under five hundred teams in the FA Cup. Only 92 teams go to make up our Football League, so some 400 teams outside the League enter the event.
>
> There would seem little interest or income to be accrued by bookmakers offering singles on matches between any two of these non-league teams, none of whom has a ghost of a chance of winning the FA Cup – but bookmakers are perfectly at liberty to offer singles on such a match, or, indeed, on any match at all in the FA Cup.
>
> Let them dare to offer singles on a televised league match between, say, Manchester United and Liverpool and they will feel the wrath of the Football League, who have decreed that

such bets should not be allowed. Why? Well, there is always the possibility of bribery and corruption, isn't there, say the League. In a match which could decide the destination of the league championship? Shown on the box in front of ten million viewers?

Yes, I know funny things happened twenty-odd years ago, but a footballer's wages in those days were a joke – just about what the players in that non-league clash might be earning and the FA are quite happy to allow bookies to take bets on that!

And I know which of the games I'd reckon to be most open to bribery.

Meanwhile, the Football League compound the idiocy by allowing bookmakers to take single correct score bets and half-time and full-time double result bets on individual league matches – so that you can bet that United beat Liverpool 2–0, but not that United win.

Obviously, where there are humans and where there is money there is always a risk of attempted crookery – but bookmakers are big boys now – and after all, if they want to take the risk of betting singles on league matches then it's only they who stand to lose in the event of any bribery scandal, anyway.

So, come on Football League, stop being holier-than-thou and patronising in your attitude to the clubs and their players and also the spectators and punters and telly viewers. Let's face it, these days any would-be coup organisers and plotters would be hard pressed to get a big enough bet on anywhere to make it worthwhile, anyway.

As usual, my words had no impact whatsoever. When the final game of the 1988–89 season between Liverpool and Arsenal was also the League championship decider, I wrote to the League requesting special dispensation to bet on this one vital game. Permission denied.

However, the drip, drip effect obviously paid off, because the League finally relented and allowed singles betting on televised League matches from season 1989–90 and, a year later, for televised League Cup games.

Another controversial aspect of the scene in recent years has been the play-offs. I've always been a fan of this system – I believe it is a further protection against the possibility that some games could be not as fiercely fought as they might otherwise be with the possibility that they will influence promotion and relegation issues. Previously, with the season only two-thirds of the way through, there could often be mid-table games taking place with absolutely nothing at stake – games which had the potential to present all manner of problems for bookmakers.

Abroad, it seems that even games between the side at the top of the table and another at the bottom can be fraught with danger. I recall a game in *Serie A* a few seasons ago in which AC Milan needed a point to win the title and their visitors, Brescia, a point to avoid relegation. There seemed to be an awful lot of interest from people wanting to bet on the game ending in a draw, an option which soon became an odds-on shot – a very rare occurrence. No one would seriously suggest that such a match would be played in anything other than a highly competitive style. I would certainly never wish to suggest that it was a little odd how subdued the celebrations were when AC opened the scoring with a somewhat speculative long shot, nor dare to utter the opinion that Brescia's equaliser owed something to an uncharacteristic lack of concentration on the part of the home defence. I mean, we may be used to reading about corruption scandals in Italian politics, but surely their football has been as pure as the driven snow for years – well, certainly since that rather unpleasant affair involving Mr Rossi some while back, anyway. Hasn't it?

Bookies Eurobet are apparently not convinced, as they took an unusual stance over two games played on 1 June 1997, the final day of the Italian *Serie A* season. AC Milan, who had endured a disappointing season, were at home to Cagliari, struggling to avoid relegation, and mid-table Roma were at home to Udinese, for whom a point was likely to secure a place in European competition for next season. Eurobet refused to allow punters to back Cagliari to win, or on the Roma game being drawn – the implication was clear.

'We think Cagliari will win – they need to win – and that the other game will be a draw, so we are not pricing these up. It is usual in Italy for this to happen,' said their spokesman, Nico Giovando – but not usual in Britain!

Eurobet were prepared to offer Milan at 7/10 with the draw at 5/2, and Roma at evens with Udinese at 10/3, hardly generous odds if they genuinely thought an away win and draw were written in the stars.

In the event, Cagliari duly won by the only goal of the game, while Udinese ran out 0–3 winners. Yet another example of what we've seen so much of in this book – football betting false alarms.

Extra Time

On the afternoon of Saturday, 6 September 1997, the day of the funeral of Diana, Princess of Wales, it was possible to shop at supermarkets or Selfridges; to visit a theme park; buy a National Lottery ticket or a Big Mac. None of these activities attracted allegations of showing disrespect. It was not, though, possible to watch football, play football or place a bet on a football match.

There had been no Premiership matches scheduled anyway, but the football authorities called off all League matches at senior level. Scotland's World Cup qualifier against Belorus was to have taken place that afternoon, but an avalanche of criticism and threats by players not to take part, saw the game switched to Sunday.

Betting shops had received a very hostile press for even considering opening that afternoon. Horseracing and afternoon greyhounds had been postponed, but with Irish racing, evening greyhounds, Sunday football and international tennis, golf and motor racing taking place that weekend there was plenty for punters to bet on should they so wish.

The shops, and all telephone betting services, stayed closed all day. This, though, was a decision which caused me some disquiet – not because of the actual closure – I fully accept that many people found it distasteful that there should be any commercial activity whatsoever that afternoon but because of the implicit suggestion that football and betting should be unacceptable whereas other, equally profit- orientated operations (not excluding the very media which had co- ordinated the campaign to have football and betting shut down) were able to trade without organised disapproval. I suppose that I'll just have to live with the fact that even after 125 years a certain, irrational stigma still attaches to a football flutter – even though, as I hope this book has demonstrated, such an attitude has been proved to be overwhelmingly ill-founded.

Bibliography

The Artless Gambler, Roger Longrigg (Pelham, 1964)

Association Football and English Society 1863-1915, Tony Mason (Harvester Press, 1980)

Better Betting with a Decent Feller, Carl Chinn (Harvester Wheatsheaf, 1991)

Betting and Bookmaking: An Introduction to the Law and Practice, J.T. Chenery (Sweet & Maxwell, 1961)

Betting and Gambling, Major Seton Churchill (J. Nisbet & Co, 1894)

The Betting Man: A Racing Biography of William Hill, Joe Ward Hill (Elcott, 1993)

The Black 'n' White Alphabet, Paul Joannou (Polar Publishing, 1997)

Chance, Skill and Luck: The Psychology of Guessing and Gambling, John Cohen (Pelican, 1960)

The Daily Telegraph Football Chronicle, Norman Barrett (Carlton Books, Ebury Press, 1996)

The Economics of Gambling, Alex Rubner (Macmillan, 1966)

The Encyclopeadia of Association Football, Maurice Golesworthy (Robert Hale, 1965)

English Football and Society 1910–1950, Nicholas Fishwick (Manchester University Press, 1989)

English Life and Leisure, B. Seebohm Rowntree and G.R. Lavers (Longmans, 1951)

Fever Pitch, Nick Hornby (Victor Gollancz, 1992)

Focus on Gambling, E.L. Figgis (Arthur Barker, 1951)

Football Babylon, Russ Williams (Virgin, 1996)

Gamblers Handbook, E.L. Figgis (Hamlyn, 1976)

Gambling, Julian Turner (Fourth Estate, 1995)

Gambling: Hazard and Reward, Otto Newman (The Athlone Press of the University of London, 1972)

Gambling in English Life, E. Benson Perkins (The Epworth Press, 1950)

Gambling Yesterday and Today: A Complete History, J. Philip Jones (David & Charles, 1973)

Hill's Sporting News Annual 1963–64

History of Football, Morris Marple (Secker-Warburg, 1954)

The Itch for Play: Gamblers and Gambling in High Life and Low Life, L.J. Ludovic (Jarrolds, 1962)

The Ladbrokes Story, Richard Kaye (Pelham Books, 1969)

The Law of Gaming, Howard A. Street (Sweet & Maxwell, 1937)

League Football: And the Men Who Made It, Simon Inglis (Collins Willow, 1988)

More Soccer Shorts, Jack Rollin (Guinness, 1991)

The Original Stan The Man, Stanley Bowles (Paper Plane, 1996)

Pools Pilot, A.P. Herbert (Methuen, 1953)

Report of the Royal Commission on Gambling 1978

Soccer in the Dock, Simon Inglis (Collins Willow, 1985)

Soccer Shorts, Jack Rollin (Guinness, 1988)

Sport and the British: A Modern History, Richard Holt (Clarendon Press, Oxford, 1989)

A Strange Kind of Glory, Eamon Dunphy (Heinemann, 1991)

To Win Just Once, Sean Magee and Guy Lewis (Headline, 1997)

Venables, Terry Venables and Neil Hanson (Michael Joseph, 1994)

War Games: The Story of Sport in World War II, Tony McCarthy (Queen Anne Press, 1989)

Appendix

The current rate (since 1996) of betting duty levied on betting shops and credit betting is 6.75 per cent, although the general rate of bookmaker deductions on bets placed by telephone or in the shops is 9p in the £. This duty has varied over the years. In 1966 betting duty was introduced at 2½ per cent. In 1968 it was raised to 5 per cent then to 6 per cent in 1970. In 1974 it was raised again to 7.5 per cent and then to 8 per cent in 1981. It was reduced to 7.75 per cent in 1991.

The rate of deduction for bets placed at a racecourse is different. In 1966 it was 2.5 per cent, rising to 5 per cent in 1968 and 6 per cent in 1970, reducing to 4 per cent in 1972 and being removed entirely in 1987.

Varying rates of deductions may be imposed at football ground betting facilities. Expect to pay less than in a High Street betting shop but more than on a racecourse, as administrative charges are levied by the operating companies, although no betting duty is payable.